D0425574

Paul Simon
The Definitive Biography

Also by Laura Jackson

Bono
The Biography

Queen
The Definitive Biography

Sean Bean
The Biography

Ewan McGregor
A Force to be Reckoned With

Heart of Stone
The Unauthorized Life of Mick Jagger

Mercury
The King of Queen

Daniel Day-Lewis
The Biography

Queen & I
The Brian May Story

Golden Stone
The Untold Life and Mysterious Death of Brian Jones

Paul Simon

The Definitive Biography

Laura Jackson

CITADEL PRESS
Kensington Publishing Corp.
www.kensingtonbooks.com

CITADEL PRESS BOOKS are published by

Kensington Publishing Corp.
850 Third Avenue
New York, NY 10022

First published in 2002 by Judy Piatkus (Publishers) Limited

All Kensington titles, imprints, and distributed lines are available at special quantity discounts for bulk purchases for sales promotions, premiums, fund-raising, educational, or institutional use. Special book excerpts or customized printings can also be created to fit specific needs. For details, write or phone the office of the Kensington special sales manager: Kensington Publishing Corp., 850 Third Avenue, New York, NY 10022, attn: Special Sales Department, phone 1-800-221-2647.

CITADEL PRESS and the Citadel logo are Reg. U.S. Pat. & TM Off.

First printing: June 2003

10 9 8 7 6 5 4 3 2 1

Printed in the United States of America

Cataloging data may be obtained from the Library of Congress.

ISBN 0-8065-2538-X

Dedicated to my husband David
– who is truly one in a million!

Troubadour to the world, you have taken the rhythms of life – as they pulse along, from the bridges of Manhattan to the banks of the Amazon – and given them back to us transformed into poetry.

Your music captures the everyday pain of memory, the pang of a broken heart: yet it has the power to make of this sorrow something more than itself. Rather than collapse into self-pity, there is an indomitable exultation.

'To life!' the philosopher Heraclitus said, 'Into swirling and swirling waters, one cannot step twice.'; the poet Paul Simon has said, 'After changes upon changes we are more or less the same.'

Through changes upon changes, you have found an enduring voice, as clear as it is true, which touches us all. Yale delights in awarding you the degree of Doctor of Music.

Yale University citation

Contents

Acknowledgements

Grateful appreciation to everyone whom I interviewed. My thanks for all contributions to: Dr Robert L. Blocker; Chris de Burgh; Chevy Chase; Bill Fogg; Jack Froggatt; Ed Koch; Joan Mackay; Ralph McTell; Professor Iwan Morgan; Dr Stephen G. Perrin; Noel Redding; Dr Irwin Redlener; Sir Tim Rice; Chris Sherwen; Geoff Speed.

Thanks also to: BBC Archives (Julie Snelling); Elgin Library staff; Mary Garrigan, New York; Kara, New York; David Mitchell, Elgin; Tony Sherwen; Tiffany Braby, the Children's Health Fund, USA; Vicki Wickham.

Special thanks to: David for his sterling help with research and for unstinting help and support. And to Alice Davis and all staff at Piatkus Books, London.

CHAPTER 1

Out of the Shadows

ON 11 SEPTEMBER 2001 the world was changed forever by the carefully coordinated series of acts of barbaric terrorism which took place in the USA. Determined suicide bombers simultaneously hijacked four internal flight passenger planes and promptly piloted them to destruction.

Two of the planes slammed into the twin towers of New York's famous World Trade Center. Another ploughed nose-first into the front of the supposedly impregnable Pentagon intelligence headquarters building in Washington DC. The fourth aircraft came down prematurely in fields near Pittsburgh when heroic passengers tried to overpower the hijackers.

This devastating assault, which left thousands of people dead, was the most audacious terrorist atrocity ever perpetrated. The whole scenario seemed completely unreal. And yet, the watching world was gripped with the paralysing fear that the entire West could be under systematic attack. Particularly so when the American administration named the number one suspects for the outrage as the Islamic militant leader Osama Bin Laden and his Al Qaeda network. Clearly, the repercussions were going to be very far-reaching.

The celebrity world responded by staging a two-hour televised concert called 'America: A Tribute To Heroes'. It was broadcast live in the US ten days after the atrocity and was ultimately shown in 156 countries. The concert was a vehicle for a phone-in appeal mounted to seek public donations in support of the victims and their families. To encourage maximum generosity the telephones were manned by top Hollywood stars.

The concert included performances from Bruce Springsteen, Billy Joel, Bon Jovi, Neil Young, Tom Petty and U2. As befitted the seething whirlpool of emotions, each performer verbalised, through song, their own state of mind. With an air of angry defiance Tom Petty, for instance, doggedly hammered home his chosen sentiment on behalf of a bloodied but unbowed nation with his nakedly mutinous 1989 hit 'I Won't Back Down'.

The concert also accommodated quieter, but no less emotive, expressions of feeling. Indeed, contemporary pop and film stars came and went all evening, everyone eager to play their part in the momentous gathering, until the event was knee-deep in icons. But for many watching, it was a special guest performance towards the end of the night that hit the spot when the legendary singer-songwriter Paul Simon placidly took up position centre stage.

Accompanying himself on acoustic guitar, he cut a lone but immensely recognisable figure as he launched into the classic ballad 'Bridge Over Troubled Water', his clear New York tones cut through with that trademark quaver of hope.

Paul Simon's lyrical brilliance had once articulated the fears, dreams and everyday dilemmas of an entire generation. Now turning in a simple, unhurried, yet shimmering rendition of one of the most famous songs in popular music history, he had a much-needed soothing effect on an audience steeped in sorrow. Never a showy performer, Simon sang in his unique style about the redemptive power of healing. And for the duration of the number, the familiar, much-loved words of 'Bridge Over Troubled Water' somehow managed to assuage the pain for a while and to channel the tumult of emotions raging in people's hearts into the steady, reassuring custody of the veteran star.

This should have come as no surprise. For Paul Simon's stock-in-trade has always been that he seems to see into society's soul. He has long proved that he can pinpoint with unerring accuracy the frailties rampant in human nature and painfully illuminate mankind's propensity to close its eyes to suffering; particularly that which is born of mental isolation.

Four decades ago Paul Simon made an indelible mark on popular music. And among his millions of loyal fans worldwide, there are those who firmly believe that his vintage creative material spanned the mid- to late 1960s, culminating with the masterpiece album *Bridge Over Troubled Water*. Others admire his determination, when going solo in the 1970s, to explore other musical genres. Simon's intuitive feel for pulsating African rhythms, for example, proved in the 1980s and 1990s that he had found a natural habitat in world music, despite the controversy – not to mention the death threats – he attracted along the way.

Undeniably, Paul Simon ranks among popular music's elite. His one-time partnership with singer and childhood friend Art Garfunkel remains legendary; the reasons behind the duo's professional split at the height of their success have never been fully revealed. Nor does interest ever entirely wane in what happened finally to fracture that long-standing friendship.

But what of the man himself? Renowned and rewarded for his songwriting as he is, what is less trumpeted about Paul Simon is his long-time support of a variety of environmental issues and his deep involvement in humanitarian causes. Simon is co-founder of the Children's Health Fund, the biggest provider of free child health-care in the world. Politics, too, are a passion for him. Thirty years ago he greeted television news reports of Republican Richard Nixon's narrowly won re-election as US President with such helpless, gut-wrenching dismay that tears poured down his face. Since then, he has taken part in inaugural celebrations for the Democrat Presidents Jimmy Carter and Bill Clinton.

On a private footing, Simon has not always found dealing

with life, and all its emotional intricacies, easy. Romantic passions have certainly swept him up with delight at times, but occasionally they have also tossed him headlong and bewildered into a tailspin.

Transparently, he is a man driven by a deep devotion to music, to unravelling its intriguing nuances, to understanding its various form of expression. And at times this dedication to his solitary craft has had to be to the exclusion of almost everything else. Small wonder then, that finding sufficient time over the years to give full emotional commitment to the women in his life has not always been possible. The result has been two divorces, and frequent periods of dark depression for the thrice-married star, although he has always remained a doting father to his children.

Perhaps one of the best insights into Simon's ultra-focused approach to his career came early on, when, before the days of his fame, as an intense and sober-minded roving minstrel he hawked nightly gigs around an energised Britain in the throes of the Swinging Sixties. Paul solemnly pronounced to strangers he met on the road, 'If I haven't managed to become a millionaire by the time I am 30, I'll consider myself to be a failure.'

He had given himself a head start, having begun writing songs by the time he was 14 years old. He had chosen a tough, crowded world in which to compete, but by combining intrinsic talent and tireless tenacity with stubborn self-belief, he was almost bound to succeed. And besides, it's not as if show business wasn't already in the family. Paul Frederic Simon was not a down-at-heel, working-class kid from a rough neighbourhood with a giant chip on his shoulder, who was desperate to kick clear of an unfortunate start in life. On the contrary, he grew up in a happy, comfortably middle-class household, supported and nurtured by his loving Jewish parents.

Born on 13 October 1941 in Newark, New Jersey, Paul was the first child of Louis and Belle Simon. Louis Simon was a professional musician, who regularly performed on radio and, more glamorously, on television – 'the family bass man', as Paul later famously referred to his father in the 1969 number 'Baby Driver'. His mother, Belle, was an elementary school teacher before she quit to start a family.

The most striking feature of the dark-haired infant was his remarkably clear, almost luminous, round eyes, which held the first hint of his future single-mindedness and at times afforded him a rather soulful look. Paul's reign as an only child ended four years later when a baby brother, Eddie, was born. By this time the Simon family had left New Jersey and were well ensconced in a new life in 70th Road in Kew Gardens, a pleasant suburb of Forest Hills in Queens, a borough of New York City.

Home was a substantial brick-built house in a tree-lined avenue, situated in a sedate, respectable neighbourhood; a tranquil setting in which to grow up as part of a close-knit family. Approaching his sixth birthday, in autumn 1947, Paul began his education at the nearby P.S. 164 school. A bright boy, obedient and open to influence, he had no difficulty settling in.

Religious instruction, too, was to play a prominent role in his life. Paul's mother appears to have been far stricter than her husband when it came to observing traditional Jewish customs. Simon would later recall that these differing approaches to the various annual rituals sometimes created tension in the home. That said, it was important to both parents to ensure that their sons grew up fully cognisant of their religious heritage. It helped that they lived in a largely Jewish community, its focal point the Jewish centre where, among other things, the local Hebrew school was located. Indeed, such was the insular nature of Paul's religious upbringing that he would later find it an eye-opener that there was more than one religion in the world. He once confessed, 'As a child, I assumed everyone was Jewish.' Still, perhaps taking after his father, Paul never felt the need to be overly absorbed with religion, although he was proud of his heritage.

Louis Simon had a lasting influence on his elder son in several ways. They were very close and his father's involvement in music strongly affected the young boy as he grew up. How could it not? It wasn't everyone's dad who could be seen performing on the relatively new and exciting medium of television. Using the stage name of Lee Sims, Simon senior led a dance band, which toured New York's lucrative ballroom circuit. One particular venue, the Roseland Ballroom, would stand out in Paul's memory because as a youngster he was sometimes permitted to go there with his father.

On these occasions, Paul would hover as near as he dared to the stage, lapping up the pulsating atmosphere and the glitz of performing on stage. But most of all, he absorbed the near-hypnotic rhythms thrashed out by the different bands on the bill. An appreciation of the exotic colour and textures of some South American sounds stayed with him for life. By the time his father's set was over and the gear had been safely stowed away, Paul was usually brimming over with a buzz that had nowhere to go.

Louis Simon enjoyed allowing Paul to share in his world outside the home. And Paul adored the involvement with this part of his parent's life, even at a mundane level. Years later Paul fondly recalled, 'When I was about six, he would bring me to Manny's [a music store] on 48th Street where we bought his bass strings.'

From local gigs, Louis progressed to performing on radio before landing work with some of the resident orchestras that performed on several syndicated top television shows at that time, including *Arthur Godfrey and His Friends*, *The Jackie Gleason Show* and *The Garry Moore Show*.

These programmes were broadcast live from across the water in Manhattan. Back at home in Queens, as a treat, Belle Simon would allow Paul and Eddie to stay up and watch the shows on television. Paul can remember eagerly anticipating those nights when he would spend the entire time, with his intent face thrust too close to the TV set, waiting to pick out his father plucking on his bass when the camera briefly focused on the house band.

Since music was such an integral part of the Simon household, it was inevitable that Paul would be encouraged to learn an instrument. He was steered initially towards the piano, with Louis giving him lessons. But as Paul later put it, despite his dad's immense patience, 'it was a no-go, so he gave up on me'. Instead, his brother, Eddie, became a pianist.

There was plenty of time for Paul to find his own musical direction. Besides, at this point in his life, baseball, not music, was his first love: Paul nurtured and retains an avid passion for the sport. It was a family tradition to support the New York Yankees, one of the city's famous baseball teams. And one of Simon's earliest memories is, as a six-year-old, sitting squashed in a chair along side his father listening to a radio match commentary.

Vividly, too, he recalled his first visit, a year or two later, to the team's imposing stadium in the Bronx. On that first visit, the legendary Joe DiMaggio, one of the sport's greatest centre fielders of all time, was playing for the Yankees and the already electric atmosphere on the crowded spectator benches was building to fever pitch.

DiMaggio walloped the ball and suddenly Paul's world went dark as all the adults around him leapt deliriously to their feet, blotting out the light and leaving him buried amid a forest of legs. Simon said, 'I was a little kid, so I couldn't see a thing. Then my father lifted me up so that I could see that DiMaggio had just hit a home run.'

DiMaggio, nicknamed Joltin' Joe, succeeded Babe Ruth as the New York Yankees' idol. In a total of 13 seasons he hit 361 home runs and had a batting average of 325. Louis Simon tried hard to instil in Paul a grasp of just what a godlike figure Joe DiMaggio was to the older generation. But although Simon would later further immortalise him with a few memorable lines in 'Mrs Robinson', right then it was beyond his comprehension.

What Paul did know, though, was that in addition to being a devoted fan of the game, he also loved playing ball and did so at every opportunity. Every year he tried to make it into the school team. And, to his delight, he secured a place with a team in Queens' softball league for boys. Perhaps the keen-edged competitive spirit that this awakened played its part in the changes that began to take place in him by the early 1950s.

He was still an enthusiastic, inquisitive boy who spent countless laughter-filled hours with his younger brother. They played baseball in the open air whenever possible. If bad weather forced them indoors, they improvised as best they could in the cramped confines of the bedroom they shared; trying their best not to smash up the furniture in the process. Sometimes, as he and Eddie immersed themselves in the game, Paul got so carried away that he would burst into a spontaneous quick-fire commentary on their antics, astutely mimicking the professional commentators, with whose various styles of delivery he was so familiar.

Yet, at the same time, a new, harder-nosed attitude was becoming detectable in his personality. At school he had begun to acquire a reputation – not as a troublemaker, but as something of a burgeoning toughie, who could, if necessary, look after himself. Physically his growth had begun to slow down. But what he lacked in height, he was starting to compensate for in assertive personality. Some teachers at P.S. 164, acknowledging Paul's new confident air, sought to channel it constructively by involving him in extra-curricular activities, which in sixth grade included the school graduation production of *Alice In Wonderland.*

It was summer 1953, Simon was 11 years old and he credits being cast as the fussed and flustered White Rabbit in this amateur musical production as a defining moment in his life. In two very significant ways, it was.

First, Paul pinpoints one split-second during his preparation for his debut acting role as the precise moment when he decided that he could be a singer. With a thoroughness that would become customary, he rehearsed at home for the play by singing along to a children's record of *Alice In Wonderland.* One evening his father, getting ready to go out to a gig, overheard his elder son singing in the privacy of his bedroom. Putting his head round the door, Louis told Paul, who was perched pixie-like on his bed, that he liked the sound of his voice. That simple compliment from his adored dad convinced Paul that he ought to start thinking of himself as a potential singer.

Second, the role of the supercilious Cheshire Cat in *Alice In Wonderland* was played by a schoolboy called Arthur Garfunkel. Born on 5 November 1941 in Forest Hills, Queens, New York, Artie (as he was known then) was the second son of a secretary and a salesman. The Garfunkel family lived in an almost identical house to the Simon family, a mere three blocks away. Yet, surprisingly in this close community, the two boys had never actually met. That's not to say that Paul Simon was a complete stranger to Arthur Garfunkel when they came together for the first time in the school play. The tall, reed-like, extremely quiet-natured pupil had heard of Paul's more robust playground reputation.

For his part, Simon could recall years earlier, having heard Artie sing a Nat King Cole song, 'They Tried To Tell Us, We're Too Young', during a school concert. The astonishingly angelic purity of the blond, curly-haired boy's voice had first hushed the audience into awed silence, then provoked a storm of rafter-rattling applause. It was a heartfelt crowd reaction that Paul Simon, one of the anonymous faces seated in the audience, had registered with a clear admiration that was laced with just a tinge of envy.

Although Arthur Garfunkel's parents had no connection with show business, they possessed melodic singing voices. And his father clearly had enough interest in music to buy his talented boy an early tape-recording machine. Encouraged by his folks from a tender age, Artie discovered that he had a pitch-perfect singing voice, capable of stunning an audience, and father, mother and son even learned how to harmonise their respective tones into a honeyed blend. It was from then on that harmony intrigued the young Garfunkel.

Indeed, his absorption with singing was such that it was not uncommon to find him warbling aloud as he walked alone to school; unusual behaviour that earned him some decidedly odd looks. He was a loner by nature, who felt set apart from his peers. When Artie met up with Paul for the first time, it thrilled him to learn that his unknown near neighbour was also keen on music.

Their fledgling acquaintance had the chance to flourish into friendship over several weeks throughout the early summer of 1953 as they committed themselves to intensive after-school rehearsals for *Alice In Wonderland*. The boys got into the habit of walking home together afterwards and as they chatted, they found that they felt the same way about a number of things.

They talked about the usual adolescent topics, and Artie also liked sport, but music invariably dominated the conversation. Paul recognised that Artie had a natural vocal gift, while acknowledging that he himself would have to work hard to develop as a singer. Not shy of investing the commitment needed to succeed, at home, in the privacy and close confines of the bathroom where the acoustics were best, Simon set about experimenting with throwing his voice off the tiled walls.

It made sense, since Artie was forever flexing his vocal cords, that the pair should try recording their voices together to see what they sounded like. So the first unofficial teaming up of Paul Simon with Arthur Garfunkel happened when as 11-year-olds they would knuckle down at Garfunkel's house at the weekends with the new tape recorder.

Life at this juncture for Paul was satisfyingly full. His rapidly rising interest in music added a new stimulus to an existence already well served by his continuing passion for baseball and, specifically, the fortunes of the New York Yankees.

By now Paul's personal hero was the celebrated switch-hitter, Mickey Mantle. Years later Simon maintained that Mantle represented, 'the promise of youth'. But in a wider sense, the star once gave an insightful analysis as to why – apart from family tradition – his loyalties lay with this particular baseball team, when he told an interviewer, 'I choose not to reveal my neurosis through the Yankees. They gave me a sense of superiority.' In his droll, deadpan manner, Simon also went on to reason that since life had a tendency to throw up enough grief for people, it made little common sense to support a brave but ultimately talentless team.

Right then, when the new school year began in October 1953, Paul ran into some unexpected grief of his own. In a way he was a victim of his scholastic abilities. For excellent exam results at the completion of his sixth grade at P.S. 164 had earned him entry into an academic scheme designed to fast-track particularly bright students, which in turn had resulted in him being enrolled at Parsons Junior High School.

The problem was that to get to the school, the 12-year-old had to walk through a particularly rough part of Queens. The good news was that Artie Garfunkel had also proved his academic worth and was likewise to be sent to Parsons Junior High. The bad news was that although each had the other's company on the half-hour walk to school, neither boy was up to coping with a far tougher class of bully than they had yet encountered in their sheltered lives.

With hindsight, it is easy to suppose that the shared experience of being harried, physically assaulted and basically mugged every day for their dinner money may have fostered a bond of friendship and dependency between Paul and Artie. But that must have been far from their minds when facing the harrowing prospect that the simple act of attending school had become. Paul certainly dreaded it and loathed the two years he attended Parsons Junior High School.

But if this part of his life was miserable, there were soon compensations to be found away from school, as his deepening absorption with music suddenly exploded in 1954. This was the year rock and roll began to spread like a contagion throughout the country. Its early vibrant flames were being fanned by a revolutionarily-minded disc jockey from Cleveland named Alan Freed. Freed's impact began when he took a hot show called 'Rock and Roll Party' to the New York radio station WINS.

For four hours every night, Freed fed a nation of hungry teenagers, who were thoroughly detached from music charts full of squeaky-clean 1940s crooners, a tasty diet of raw, down-and-dirty rock and roll sounds that were almost impossible to hear anywhere else. Tuning in was almost a sin in itself and Paul was quickly hooked. Though he would first find fame in the contemporary folk mould, rock and roll was his first musical love.

1954 swept in a new breed of performer including the Platters, who were to become the decade's most successful black group. Detroit-born Bill Haley, having ditched his hee-haw cowboy image the year before and was now fronting an expanded outfit called Bill Haley and His Comets, burst on to the scene in the summer with '(We're Gonna) Rock Around The Clock'. 'See You Later Alligator' and 'Shake, Rattle and Roll' swiftly followed. The energising beat and liberating, surreptitiously licentious lyrics, designed to entice the younger generation to cut loose from the staid conformity of their parents' lives, fired up Paul Simon.

Another favourite of his and Artie Garfunkel's was the Canadian band, the Crew Cuts, whose rush-released cover version of 'Sh-Boom' in June 1954 would hit the top slot in the US singles chart. Today, some rock experts consider this record to be the very first rock and roll hit. But almost immediately, a dark cloud hung over its success in certain quarters.

Just weeks earlier, the rhythm and blues number had been originally released by the black group, the Chords. But because of the system of segregated radio in America at that time, this first version received a fraction of the blanket airplay given to the Crew Cuts' version and was therefore completely eclipsed. Ethical questions arose as to the danger of exploitation by white artistes of black music. There would be many such instances over the years, and Paul Simon himself strayed into this still-sensitive area decades later with his 1986 *Graceland* album. But with plenty to occupy him musically for now, Paul's attention fastened on two particular performers, each of whom made their own profound impact on him.

One was Johnny Ace. Born John Alexander in 1929 in Memphis, Tennessee, the son of a preacher turned raucous R&B performer, Ace had a successful but short-lived career, which ended in tragedy. Formerly part of a band called the Beale

Streeters, he had gone solo in 1953, and by the following February he had enjoyed his fourth consecutive hit in the American R&B charts with 'Saving My Love For You'.

Sadly, there was no saving the disturbed young man on Christmas Day 1954. After a year of arduous touring Ace had been performing at a dance at the City Auditorium in Houston. Late in the evening Ace, by now drunk, fired a .22 calibre revolver at his girlfriend Olivia Gibbs. He then fired at her terrified friend Mary Carter, but on both occasions, fortunately, the gun failed to go off. Ace promptly aimed the revolver at himself, and at the third squeeze of the trigger, a violent close-quarters explosion ended his life. A subsequent inquest ruled that Johnny Ace had died playing Russian Roulette.

His death hit the headlines and it is probably true to say that this 25-year-old holds the dubious distinction of being rock music's first casualty. For Paul Simon, Johnny Ace took on mythical status. Simon cites Ace as one of his earliest inspirations, and in his 1983 album *Hearts and Bones*, he was to honour his idol as 'The Late Great Johnny Ace'.

For already disapproving parents, Ace's grotesquely messy suicide only served to underscore the dangers they were convinced were implicit in this new music, and it set their hearts and minds even more firmly against its every form. This was particularly so in the case of the main channel for such heat – Elvis Presley, Paul's other great hero.

The most influential solo artiste of the 20th century, Elvis Presley from East Tupelo, Mississippi was a 19-year-old truck driver for the Crown Electric Company in Memphis when, in July 1954, his first uptempo, rocking blues number, 'That's All Right' was released. Presley was a strange hybrid – a white singer with a black blues sound and a unique, outrageously sensual style of delivery. He was to become a recklessly subversive symbol to the older generation and a worldwide phenomenon. The more the establishment freaked out, the more Paul Simon – like millions of his peers – was completely bowled over by this raw firebrand performer.

Newly a teenager on 13 October 1954, Paul's all-consuming passion was now to learn to play the guitar, so he was thrilled to receive a $25 Stadium acoustic guitar for his birthday from his parents. The guitar was a cool instrument and synonymous with the rock and roll image. Simon sank into a world of his own as he began to teach himself to play. To a musician, his guitar can become a part of himself, an extension of his thoughts and a vehicle for expression. Paul cocooned himself in a world in which he preferred to sit in the dark, with his arms wrapped around the instrument through which he could 'talk' out his innermost thoughts and fears.

Right then imagination was his only limit and he later admitted that it was a form of escapism. 'I was able to sit alone and play and dream,' he said. The dedication he showed in overcoming the physical pain barrier of bloodied fingertips, scored by unyielding steel strings, and the frustration inherent in mastering the guitar, surprised some of those around him. Perhaps that pleased Paul, but his absorption with this new music also had a downside.

Louis Simon, like practically every other parent in the land, opposed rock and roll. And his intense dislike, distrust and intolerance of everything that Elvis Presley represented, forced a sudden and serious rift between himself and his elder son for the first time in their lives. Paul was dismayed. His attempts to get his father at least to listen to some of his favourite records or to let him explain why he liked them met with a brick wall. Paul would always love his father, but this development started a strain in their relationship that would take many years to be resolved. In the early 1990s, as a guest on the US show 'Sixty Minutes', Simon candidly talked about his father's complete rejection of a music that meant the world to him.

As a musician himself, it seems odd that Louis Simon should have been so intransigent about trying to appreciate rock and roll's importance to Paul. Belle Simon, whom Paul later described as the first pure nourishing element in his life, had always had the knack of making him feel special. And so while a chasm had opened up between Paul and his father, his mother remained a supportive influence in all aspects of his life.

Simon enjoyed the solitude of playing his guitar in the dark at home, but he was also pleased to have a kindred spirit in his friend, Artie. Garfunkel, too, sat at home glued to his radio and, of course, sang volubly along with the groups. Encouraged by everything they were hearing, Paul and Artie began to spend even more time experimenting with committing their own voices to tape.

Before long these spells developed into intensive practice sessions. Both boys listened over and over again to the hits of the day. Simon began systematically dissecting each song's underlying structure. Garfunkel, already a devotee of harmony, determinedly applied his analytical brain to unravelling the various arrangements and working out precisely what it was that made them tick.

Either at Simon's house or Garfunkel's, now with the facility of two tape-recording machines, they would practise overdubbing their voices. Paying meticulous attention to their task, in the pursuit of a perfect result, they also began to coach themselves in expertly executed fade-ins and -outs, and to achieving split-second timing when they sang. Even their individual pronunciation had to be honed to synchronise exactly.

All this exhaustive endeavour would have seemed a trifle obsessive had it all been solely for their private pleasure. But it wasn't. When they felt they were ready, they looked for outlets at which they could perform. And on occasions they got the chance to entertain at private family parties. It was not until spring 1955 that Paul, with Artie, made his first public appearance when they performed at assembly at Parsons Junior High School, singing the Crew Cuts's hit 'Sh-Boom'.

Paul's tenure at this school was just about drawing to a close, which should have been a reason to be cheerful. The very positive reaction from admiring fellow pupils to the skills of this first Simon and Garfunkel performance ought to have gladdened Paul's heart too. But in fact, as Paul headed towards his fourteenth birthday his hitherto happy mien was gradually fading, leaving him morose and melancholic. Undeniably it is an awkward age when a lot of hormonal and other upheavals occur. But there was an added factor in Paul Simon's case which seems to be responsible for rapidly draining the sunshine from his outlook on life.

He had revelled for a long time now in playing in the softball league – the league for boys under five feet in height. Not unnaturally, Paul had been very self-conscious of his diminutive stature for his age, which was exaggerated when in the company of the willowy Arthur Garfunkel. But in this part of his life – his beloved sport – his failure to grow apace with his age had allowed him to remain in the Queens' softball team.

His team had fought its way successfully through the various stages that season to reach a crucial championship match against one of New York's other teams. Such was the importance of the game that the sporting officials adhered strictly to the rules. And it was at the pre-match examination that there came the earth-shattering news that Paul had grown just enough to nudge him an inch over the regulation height limit. Rules were rules, and he was out of the team.

As cruel blows went, this one went deep with Paul. Either way he felt that he had lost out. Being undersize had kept him playing in a team he adored; growing a fraction lost him that position. Ironically he stopped growing soon afterwards, this time for good. His height stalled at around 5 feet 3 inches, considerably shorter than he would have wished. Simon is said to have stated that his lack of height had a serious psychological effect on his life. Although well aware of his talent and intelligence, he felt that he had an inferior stature.

Outwardly, Paul's whole demeanour changed overnight and he tended to wear a perpetually grave, unsmiling expression. To match that, he also became intensely introspective. But it would be that very introspection that was to unleash in him his greatest talent: songwriting. Few artistes would develop such a sharply observed take on life and human nature as Paul Simon did.

Musically, for anyone who was depressed or troubled by life in the 1960s – Paul Simon was your man.

It is surely no coincidence that Simon embarked on what would turn out to be a distinguished career as a lyricist just as this sudden personality change began to permeate his life. Simon would find fame as a solo songwriter, but initially he wrote songs in conjunction with Artie Garfunkel. Having closely studied the lyrics of the songs currently played on the radio, both boys had objectively come to the conclusion that they could do better themselves.

Paul tackled songwriting with the same dogged dedication he had shown in mastering the guitar, and both he and Artie dreamed of breaking into this field. It was a fertile time when anything seemed possible. Even so they were determined to leave nothing to chance. Garfunkel kept a remarkably close watch on which style of performer and which style of song were likely to perform well in the charts. He set about his study with great precision, to the point of keeping clear-cut accurate charts that followed the varied fortunes of particular acts.

At home, Paul practised on guitar almost frenetically and at the same time pushed his mental processes to the limit. He was 14 years old, in defiance of his father a devoted fan of Elvis Presley, and believed that he adored the rock rebel too much to try to emulate him. But Paul knew that he yearned to make it in the music world in some way.

It would have been too much to hope for that his singular song-writing genius would become apparent with his first effort. But nevertheless it is impressive that it was in 1955 that Paul Simon, along with Arthur Garfunkel, co-wrote his first song called 'The Girl For Me' which was, as the title suggests, a teenage love song. It was not an effort to be proud of only in the privacy of his own room. There was to be nothing half-hearted or unprofessional about what he, with Garfunkel, would do with this first song. So for a fee of $4 Paul Simon and Arthur Garfunkel officially registered their song-writing copyright of

'The Girl For Me' at the US Library of Congress.

That done, the next mission was to try to get the song published. This meant taking on the New York City music-business empire. So, after school and at weekends, a pair of well-groomed, soberly dressed teenage schoolboys, one tightly clutching a guitar case, began taking the F train for the start of their journey from Queens to Broadway in Manhattan.

It was cap-in-hand time, and both were old enough to be aware that they were minnows trying to enter potentially shark-infested waters. It would take an abundance of resilience, guts and aggression to succeed. Like Simon, Garfunkel had the first two qualities, but Artie later readily admitted that he relied upon Paul's steely-eyed relentless thrust to propel them along. Paul Simon was young and he knew it would take time. But he was sure of one thing: he was not about to let either of them down.

CHAPTER 2

Local Limelight

THE FAMOUS BRILL BUILDING at 1619 Broadway in Manhattan was the place to go for an aspiring songwriter, aching to plant his foot on the first rung on the ladder of success. The distinctive facade of the Art Deco structure struck awe deep into the hearts of both Paul Simon and Artie Garfunkel as, in early 1956, they first stood outside it, pausing briefly to savour the moment and summon up the courage to enter.

What they found inside was a maze of mainly cabin-sized offices, each belonging to different music managers, producers, record company executives and music publishing firms. It was basically a factory, dedicated to churning out chart hits. And its most assiduous occupants were a small army of anonymous songwriters who, like worker ants, toiled away in spartan rooms, alone or in pairs, composing usually on piano.

Coming in from the outside a songwriter would hope to be signed up by a music publishing company as a staff writer. The alternative was to try to sell songs piece-meal to individual music publishers for, with luck, the then going rate of a few hundred dollars each. The number would subsequently be recorded by an established performer which, for a would-be singer-songwriter was not ideal. But it was a start and it put money in your pocket.

As a 14-year-old, still at school, clearly Paul Simon's only option was the latter. His was to be no slapdash approach.

Together with Artie, he had carefully genned up on which of the myriad record companies he felt would be most likely to appreciate their type of lyrics. And it was armed with a list of these addresses that they began knocking on doors. The principle had been sound enough, but it quickly became necessary to widen their scope. They would rap their knuckles raw as they made the endless rounds; sometimes finding it an achievement just to get past the office secretaries.

If they did make it through to an audience with the company boss, he was usually a fat, forbidding sight squeezed behind an overladen desk, half hidden by a blue haze of cigar smoke. From the second the boys entered, as boldly as their suddenly stiff legs would take them into the room, this character wore a discouraging expression. Time and again Paul Simon knew that they were dead in the water before they had even opened their mouths.

Admirably, repeated rejection, often without the courtesy of a proper hearing, was not enough to put the pair off. Looking back, Garfunkel candidly laid the credit for most of this stamina squarely at Simon's feet. Paul, he declared, undeniably possessed the lion's share of the drive right then. It was also Paul who would deliver spontaneous pep talks to his dejected friend as, closing yet another door behind them, they trekked doggedly on up to the next floor and the next door.

It wasn't only the Brill Building they tackled; any address that housed record company offices large or small was visited. And these days understandably made their mark on Paul, leaving him with the vivid memory of too many dingy premises and the unwelcome sensation of disturbed dust swirling up the nostrils as the boys pounded determinedly up musty, ill-lit staircases in their quest for success.

Even allowing for the buoyant optimism of youth, it must have been soul-destroying, but they managed to keep their hopes afloat. Indeed, Simon channelled the disappointment of rejection into a sharper spur to win out, for music now infiltrated every aspect of his life.

After leaving Parsons Junior High School, in autumn the previous year, Paul had started his tenth-grade education at Forest Hills High School. Artie Garfunkel did likewise, and both were far happier to be back on familiar turf. Here, Paul coped comfortably with the academic level, but he frustrated his teachers at times by becoming easily bored and restless. Artie and Paul sat near enough in class to pass notes to one another, and with their minds so much on music it was no surprise that they would be caught not paying proper attention to their studies.

The detention room was no stranger to either Simon or Garfunkel. But even so, because Paul carted his acoustic guitar to school most days, what was intended to serve as a punishment for the pupils usually ended up as a good opportunity to have a boisterous rock and roll jam session.

Paul and Artie's penchant for music had become well known outside school, too, where there were some like-minded teenagers to be found. In 1956 Simon and Garfunkel teamed up briefly with three locals, Johnny Brennan and Ida and Angel Pellagrini, who together formed the Peptones. The doo-wop style group was top heavy with singers. And although it's said that the five-piece privately recorded a demo disc of Paul and Artie's still unplaced co-composition, 'The Girl For Me', nothing came of it and the unofficial band soon dissolved.

For Simon, the Peptones had rated only as a mild distraction. Single-mindedly focused on chasing his dream, he continued to haunt the Brill Building in his free time, clutching the latest batch of songs he had written either by himself or in conjunction with Artie.

Lyrically, all these songs were firmly in the classic teen calamity mould, but he wasn't getting anywhere with them. And his intrinsic honesty meant that he was on the verge of examining whether he was on the right track when an exciting new sound seized his attention. In summer 1957 the Everly Brothers arrived on the music scene with the song 'Bye Bye Love'.

Written by Felice and Boudleaux Bryant, the song's impact lay not so much in its lyrics as in its radically new style of delivery – later designated by music historians as being close Appalachian harmonies accompanied by acoustic guitar work and jazzed up with a gutsy rock and roll beat. It was to become the Everly Brothers trademark sound. Paul Simon was knocked out.

Simon, who first heard it on the radio, later declared that 'Bye Bye Love' was 'the first thing that really killed me'. Before the last note had died away Paul was on the telephone to Garfunkel raving excitedly about this great new record that they just had to buy. Playing the single until the grooves nearly disappeared, Simon exulted in the enormous boost the arrival of this one song had given him. In the weeks immediately following its release the single rocketed to number 2 in the US pop charts, topped the national country and western charts, and also reached number 5 in the rhythm and blues survey, providing proof of its widespread appeal.

The Everly Brothers' newfound fame worked like an aphrodisiac on Paul and Artie who, as a harmonising duo themselves, immediately set about rigorously training their own voices to sing in a good imitation of the new stars. Paul also redoubled his practice sessions, playing pumping acoustic guitar rhythms with new enthusiasm.

Unquestionably, the Everly Brothers' sound had a major influence on Simon and Garfunkel. And 'Bye Bye Love' was exactly the shot in the arm the two needed to encourage them to take another run at Manhattan's music men. Only this time they planned to set about it by first making a demo recording of a new song they had co-written called 'Hey Schoolgirl'.

For $25 in summer 1957 they cut a professional studio demonstration disc of this song at Sanders Recording Studio on Seventh Avenue in Manhattan, plus a demo of a second number called 'Dancin' Wild'. They intended to woo the music executives in the Brill Building with this demo. But after all the time they had spent battering on doors to no avail, luck placed a record producer in a nearby room in Sanders Recording Studio just as the two 15-year-olds were harmonising, Everly Brothers-fashion, on 'Hey Schoolgirl'.

The producer was Sid Prosen, and when Paul and Artie stopped for a short break while everything was set up for them to record their second song, he approached them. It was his job to scout for promising new musical talent and he duly buttonholed the boys saying that he wanted a word with them when they were finished in the studio.

If Prosen didn't precisely use the corny call, 'Come with me and I'll make you stars!', his exuberant enthusiasm still, strangely enough, put both boys on their guard. Paul knew that he had nothing to be blasé about. And a great chunk of him wanted instantly to grab Sid Prosen's offer of a one-off contract for 'Hey Schoolgirl' with both hands. But caution kicked in, as it did with Artie. Keen they certainly were, but although not yet 16, both were aware that they should understand first everything that was or was not being offered to them.

But Sid Prosen was on the level, and he understood and accommodated the pair's stipulation that the disc must be recorded within two months. Paul and Artie's specific fear had been that they might sign a contract which in effect tied them up for a long time, and that this period might expire without them actually getting inside a recording studio to cut the disc. Paul and Artie also wanted a guarantee that the single would be released within that same 60-day span.

With these terms agreed, Simon and Garfunkel were happy. Sid Prosen promptly prepared to release the single on Big Records, one of the many new young record labels. As was still customary in those days, the record was to appear in two formats – the large breakable 78-rpm disc, as well as the newer 7-inch 45-rpm vinyl disc.

As Paul Simon turned 16 in October 1957 he was entering one of the most exciting phases of his life. He had dreamed of writing and releasing a record; over the coming weeks he got a glimpse of a different world entirely. A world in which, to begin with, plans were made to start promoting the upcoming single. Sid Prosen arranged for a set of stage clothes for the two boys – bright blazers and slacks: a smart, safe image to match their age and clean-cut style.

Prosen also suggested that they adopt a stage name. Art Garfunkel, years later, could not be specific as to why, but when he and Paul had entertained at school or at family get-togethers they had called themselves Tom and Jerry. On discovering this, the producer suggested that they think up surnames to match each forename. Tom was Garfunkel. And to it Art added Graph, perhaps because of his interest in mathematics and in keeping charts. Simon was Jerry. At this stage Paul was dating a local girl named Sue Landis, so he took her real surname to complete his stage name. They therefore became Tom Graph and Jerry Landis.

The publicity shots of the duo, which showed a pair of almost excruciatingly scrubbed-clean, grinning schoolboys, were very much in keeping with the popular style at the time. The glossy photographs proudly projected a youthful optimism.

Sid Prosen and Big Records invested genuine effort in this debut offering from a pair of unknowns when in November 1957 'Hey Schoolgirl' with 'Dancin' Wild' as the B side was released. Prosen used his business contacts to secure precious air time on Alan Freed's radio show, which gave a healthy injection of exposure to the single. Sales immediately began to take off. So much so that the record company pulled off a decided coup by managing to book Tom and Jerry on to the teen TV dance programme *American Bandstand*; this show, compered by trendy disc jockey Dick Clark, was transmitted all over the States live from Philadelphia each evening.

American Bandstand was totally oriented towards teenagers. Every day the live audience was composed of local high school pupils who rushed along to the ABC television studios hoping to be selected to dance to that night's guest performers. It was considered a kick to make it in as part of the crowd – let alone to be performing on the bill.

A nerve-racking experience, then, only partially described Paul's inner feelings as, along with an equally wired Garfunkel, he arrived at the ABC studios in Philadelphia. From the moment they entered the building they were conscious of being what they were – two gauche, neatly turned out, wide-eyed schoolboys from Queens, New York. Suddenly they were among busy television executives and experienced entertainers – household names who, until now, they had only seen on their TV screens at home.

Both Paul and Artie could also not help but notice the bulging sacks of fan mail stacked in one corner of the foyer awaiting dispersal, never knowing that worldwide fame and acclaim would be theirs one day. Then it was enough that they were to appear live on a show, which for months they had been rushing home from school to watch. Paul Simon revealed how strange it all felt to him when he reminisced, 'It was an incredible thing to have happen to you in your adolescence. I had picked up the guitar because I wanted to be like Elvis Presley and suddenly there I was!'

And no one can say that it was not a real baptism of fire. Performing on live TV is daunting enough – to do so for the first time on a top-rated, syndicated show takes a lot of bottle. On top of that, Tom and Jerry arrived to learn that they were to follow guest star Jerry Lee Lewis, who was to perform his explosive million-seller hit 'Great Balls of Fire'. Lewis was there in the flesh before Paul's very eyes. But Simon says that he felt too intimidated to introduce himself to the wild man performer, and it's hardly surprising.

In 1957 Jerry Lee Lewis was a mere six years older than Paul Simon. But the 22-year-old piano maestro, prone to abrasive and unpredictable stage antics, was already a bigamist and to many people almost the Devil incarnate. He had hit the headlines when it was revealed that he had married his 13-year-old cousin, pregnant with his child, while still legally married to his first wife.

Lewis's outrageous personal life was just beginning to shock America when in 1956 his 'Whole Lotta Shakin' Goin' On' was banned by most radio stations, the song's lyrics having been deemed to be sheer vulgarity. He had been on an extensive countrywide tour when he had made his TV debut on *The Steve Allen Show* only four months earlier. So he was hardly a veteran of the small screen, although from his brash behaviour on *American Bandstand* no one would have ever known it.

That late November evening, apart from being thoroughly overawed to be near Jerry Lee Lewis, Paul was acutely aware that he was going to be an extremely tough act to follow. But the pair performed sufficiently well to earn their first national review in *Billboard* magazine. Not only did they come away unscathed by the critic, but also, to Paul's intense pleasure, he and Artie saw themselves described flatteringly as being in the Everly Brothers mould.

News of the single's performance was also very encouraging. 'Hey Schoolgirl' sales, on the back of their national television appearance, had sailed beyond the 100,000 copies mark, earning Tom and Jerry their first US singles chart position of number 49. Topping an appearance on *American Bandstand* was almost impossible. But Big Records tried to keep the momentum going by using that TV moment and the creditable performance of the single to squeeze the inexperienced performers on to the bills at theatre gigs around the country before they returned to Queens.

When they did come home, they were local heroes and Paul intended to enjoy the sensation. He knew they were considered big stuff now at school, too. Unabashedly he declared of this change in circumstance, 'You can't imagine what it was like having a hit record at 16. It made me a neighbourhood hero.' In time, when the money filtered through, Paul used some of his $2,000 share of the royalties from the single to enhance his local celebrity status by buying a lurid red Impala convertible of which he was immensely proud.

When Paul returned to Forest Hills High School there was a decided tug of war going on between concentrating on his academic studies with a view to securing the successful business career he knew could be his, or focusing on a future in music. He wanted fame, he knew that. But of course, it could never be a clear-cut choice at this stage.

Simon, though, got to work to see if he could write a Top 20 hit next time. He still co-wrote songs with Garfunkel. But although Artie had also enjoyed the taste of the limelight, he was not at that time completely convinced that his own destiny lay in music. Garfunkel later reflected that while he'd always thoroughly enjoyed singing, he had for a long time assumed that he would make his way in life in a field far more reputable than popular music.

Throughout 1958 Paul Simon remained deadly serious about pursuing a recording career, and not only as part of a duo. There was certainly a distinct comfort and support to be found in a partnership. But a career as a solo singer-songwriter held an independence and freedom which strongly attracted him. Producer Sid Prosen tapped into this extra dimension in Paul and began working separately with him to produce a Paul Simon solo number called 'True Or False'. It was released early in the new year on the Big Records label, with the equally rockabilly-style B-side song 'Teenage Fool'. For this release Paul chose the new solo pseudonym of True Taylor.

'True Or False' failed to chart. Even so, it earns a highly significant place in Simon and Garfunkel's history. When Artie learned of Paul's intention to release a solo single, at a time when he considered them to be partners, he was hurt at what he felt was a casual betrayal on Paul's part. It could be argued that Garfunkel perhaps overreacted. But Simon would come to realise many years later that this one action of his as a 16-year-old was held against him for a very long time.

It caused the first faint tremor in the Simon and Garfunkel partnership, yet it was not confronted head on when it happened. Perhaps it might have been better if it had been, but instead of airing his grievance, Garfunkel chose to conceal his feelings of rejection and anger.

Maybe at that age Paul Simon would have wondered why it

went so deep with Artie that he had struck out on his own with a solo single. Simon had a clearly signalled determined streak in him, and beneath the surface he had long envisaged himself as a solo performer. His appreciably more assertive personality – essential for anyone who wants to succeed – always made it likely that he would be prepared to strike out on his own.

That same assertive personality might also have made Simon take the view that, if it came down to it, Artie – who was writing songs at this time – would have been just as entitled to break away solo if he had wished to do so. In any event, if Paul was privy to even a hint of his friend's disappointed hurt, neither of them was ready to rock the boat by bringing the subject out into the open.

Instead, the two carried on collaborating on songwriting. And in 1958 they emerged with Tom and Jerry's follow up to 'Hey Schoolgirl' with a quieter, less pacey number called 'Our Song'. The calypso-influenced 'Two Teenagers' occupied the flip side but it sank without a trace.

Despite the duo's inability as yet to replicate or improve on their modest debut success, Big Records went on to release a third Tom and Jerry single. But in 1959 the sweet love song 'That's My Story', backed by the rocking number 'Don't Say Goodbye' also flopped. Depressingly, the story was the same with Tom and Jerry's last attempt of the year – the single 'Baby Talk' on which they revived the previously used B-side 'Two Teenagers'. Reissued later on the bigger Bell label it still failed to chime with listeners.

Needless to say, with their track record to date, these four singles had only been released in America and had not been issued for the British market. The same applied to Paul's solo effort as True Taylor. And as he struck out for a second time as a solo artiste before summer 1959, the latest single likewise stayed within the confines of the US.

This time he had penned a song titled 'Anna Belle', which he paired on the reverse with 'Loneliness'. Big Records were now defunct and Paul's second solo single went out on the MGM label. Simon used the pseudonym Jerry Landis, but again it was to no avail.

The heady days of having appeared on *American Bandstand* were beginning to seem like fading skid marks down memory lane. Even the flashy souped-up car in which Simon was keen to be seen cruising around Queens had suffered a freak electrical fault and gone up in flames. There must have been moments when Simon thought that his abilities as a songwriter, which had shown bright promise, had somehow also turned to ashes. Yet he had a remarkably deep reservoir of resilience and a singular capacity to view repeated failure merely as something from which to learn, rather than an excuse to wallow in self-pity.

A rethink was needed. And Paul Simon was at a crossroads in more ways than one for by now he had graduated from Forest Hills High School and intended to carry on to college. After considering his options he had enrolled at the local Queens College. Part of the City University of New York and founded in 1937, it was a state and locally supported comprehensive establishment, offering bachelor and masters degrees. With a difficult entrance exam, less than 50 per cent of applicants were admitted. Simon intended to major in English Literature and would commence his studies in the autumn.

For his part, Artie Garfunkel had opted to enrol at Columbia University, an upper-class Ivy League college, to study mathematics. Unlike Paul who would remain living with his parents, Garfunkel took an apartment in Manhattan. Geographically therefore they were apart. Artie had seemed less consumed with a burning desire for a music career. He saw this time as a natural break point, when one phase of his life had ended and he stood hopeful on the threshold of another phase that was ripe with possibilities. A clever and inquisitive man, he was prepared to contemplate a life in which music played a lesser role.

Paul Simon was not. Also clever and inquisitive, he was interested in widening his horizons, aware that life experience would enrich him as a songwriter. He had also been analysing his failure to achieve chart success and had lately come to the conclusion that he had to approach the whole business from a different angle. He had somehow to understand the mechanics of the music business in greater depth, to get to know it from all sides, from the studio out.

He was in for the long haul and every scrap of his spare time was spent absorbing rock music, playing his guitar and endlessly writing songs. Paul Simon is a studier of life and over the years he was to draw direct inspiration for some of his most evocative songs from real-life situations.

In August 1959 he was gripped by a shocking story that was holding America in thrall when Salvador Agron, a member of a New York gang, which called itself The Vampires, was convicted of murdering two student boys. The 16-year-old Puerto Rican was widely sensationalised by the tabloid press, which gave him the nickname of 'The Capeman'. He was sentenced to death and remained harrowingly defiant in the face of overwhelming public outrage at his actions and his attitude.

Simon recalls the trial becoming a cause célèbre. But what struck him most was that behind the lurid headlines and the appalling circumstances of the killings, Salvador Agron looked the epitome of the rock and roll hoodlum. Paul later told *Rolling Stone* magazine, 'It was the summer between high school and college and the story was all over the newspapers and on the television. And I remember thinking, here was a kid who had the *look*! He looked like the fifties!'

The grisly affair made a vivid impression on Paul Simon, who filed it away in his subconscious for controversial revival decades later when he mounted a Broadway stage musical based on Agron's life called *The Capeman*. But right then, Simon was 18 years old and for the first time in a long while without the daily companionship of Art Garfunkel. They had gone their separate ways, but it would not be for good. In the meantime, Simon was about to embark on a very different working relationship with a fellow Queens College student. It would prove to be a stimulating experience and one that would ultimately take him closer to where he wanted to be.

CHAPTER 3

Musical Chairs

FROM A PURELY RATIONAL VIEWPOINT, Paul Simon knew that it made sense not to squander his academic abilities. After all, a fall-back career was a tidy safety net if his pursuit of success as a recording artiste failed to pan out. And it is not as if he had to particularly force himself to take an interest in the English Literature degree course on which he had enrolled at New York's Queens College. On the contrary, his strong artistic streak responded well to the depth and intellectual complexities in the works of renowned novelists and poets.

But songwriting was a passion never completely absent from his thoughts. It was no surprise, therefore, that he soon ran into a like-minded fellow student, a maths major named Carole Klein, who later found fame as the hit-making singer-songwriter Carole King. For a spell, Klein and Simon were to strike up an informal working relationship.

From Brooklyn, New York, Carole Klein had been singing and playing the piano since childhood. In spring 1959 she had released her debut single, 'Baby Sittin''. But her first taste of fame came second-hand at the end of that year when another Brooklyn-born, piano-playing singer-songwriter, Neil Sedaka, whom she had dated for a while at high school, had a Top 10 hit record with his affectionate tribute to Klein called 'Oh! Carol'.

As Paul Simon discovered, the music world revolved around connections, wheels within wheels. Until now he had managed to cut into the loop under his own steam but only temporarily, before being spun out into the cold again. His meeting with Carole Klein was an important step in beginning to change all that.

While attending New York's prestigious Julliard School of Music, Neil Sedaka had managed to make contact with successful music publishers Don Kirshner and Al Nevins, whose company Aldon Music operated out of the Brill Building. Sedaka's connection with Kirshner had led to Carole Klein making the music publishers' acquaintance. With a foot in the door to this world, Klein was now finding an outlet for her musical talents by making demo records for a variety of record companies. And it was a door that she generously now held open to Paul Simon as a fellow struggling artiste.

With Klein as his initial conduit, Paul was thrust into a whirlpool way of life. As well as studying hard for his degree, he was working long hours late into the night in Broadway recording studios making demonstration discs for record companies. He and Carole would record a demo together – she providing the piano and percussion parts, Paul laying down the guitar and bass work, and both singing lead and back-up vocals.

Sometimes extra session musicians might be required to achieve the best results and the combination of meeting their fees, together with paying for studio time could bump up the cost of making the demo to as much as a few hundred dollars. But, as Simon later reasoned, that extra effort and attention to detail could raise the standard of the end product so much that he and Klein could sell the demo to a record company sometimes for five times their initial outlay, thereby making themselves a healthy profit.

Paul also blanketed record companies with a note of his name and contact number, offering his services for hire to cut demo discs. Record company executives required demos to enable them to let an established star get the feel of how a song should sound. Within a short space of time his phone began to ring more and more often, as word spread of just how versatile Paul Simon was.

He had become adept at a variety of different styles of singing and playing. For $25 a session, Simon could lay down a demo on request, singing lead, overdubbing the back-up vocals and playing a range of instruments – a veritable one-man band.

He found time to make maybe four demo discs a week and the cash these sessions earned him came in very handy. But far more valuable was the fact that he was learning the full range of studio techniques. Years later he told *Life* magazine, 'That's where I learned to stack voices and to do overdubs – how to make records.'

It was also a time when Simon recognised the need to secure full payment up front on those occasions when he sold a demo to a record company (as opposed to the times when he was being hired by a company for a flat session fee). Simon revealed how imperative it was to see the money right away, because if a record company was successful and put the record out, the songwriter could not always be entirely confident of receiving any royalties. He discovered early on that not every record company operated strictly by the rules.

With all this activity for various record companies, it was natural that Simon would try to revive his own recording career. But none of his four singles released in 1960 made the slightest dent. ABC Paramount released first the Tom and Jerry number 'Surrender', backed by 'Fighting Mad'. Then again under the duo's banner they resuscitated 'That's My Story' but teamed it this time on the reverse with 'Tijuana Blues'. That, too, was a non-event. This latest failure pinpointed a permanent end of Tom and Jerry releases.

Not that Simon's solo work shone any brighter. Once more as Jerry Landis, he produced 'Just A Boy'/ 'Shy', and 'I'd Like To Be The Lipstick On Your Collar' with 'Just A Boy' rejigged as a B-side. Both went out on the Warwick Records label and both bombed.

These latest solo songs were delivered in a forerunner of the gentle, sensitive vocal style with which Paul would soon become synonymous. His preoccupation with writing the popular teenage love songs was certainly still there, but in his late teens Simon had begun to show in his writing the first hint of a sense of alienation; this was a theme which would come into its own during the second half of the decade.

The feeling of alienation flowing from his pen had its roots in part in his personal sense of self-esteem at the time. Simon has a lively brain, a dry wit and could never be described as being dull or boring to be around. He is too driven a person for that, but by the time he had moved into his sophomore year at university his personality had become overlaid by a distinct melancholy.

Apart from the fact that his recording career had not yet taken off, it should otherwise have been a riotous time in his life as a footloose student. But Simon, still acutely conscious of his lack of height, now tended to be dissatisfied in general with his appearance. As he would later write in 'Flowers Never Bend With The Rainfall', his mirror on the wall threw back an image dark and small, which to some degree depressed him. His feelings of alienation and disappointment with his looks would inevitably begin to infiltrate his songwriting as he developed into early manhood.

With the best will in the world, he would have been less than human if he had not also begun to become frustrated by his lack of chart success. It was made no easier to swallow when he had to stand back and watch his erstwhile songwriting colleague Carole Klein (now King) take off.

By now she enjoyed a songwriting and personal partnership with Gerry Goffin, who, for a while, was making ends meet by working behind a shop counter. Carole decided to drop out of Queens College to concentrate on a songwriting career in collaboration with her future husband.

Paul thought that she should reconsider dropping out and thereby passing up on obtaining her degree. But in January 1961 the Goffin and King song 'Will You Love Me Tomorrow' released by the Shirelles zoomed to the top of the US singles chart. What is more, nine months later Bobby Vee also hit number 1 with the pair's next composition, 'Take Good Care Of My Baby'.

Paul Simon dryly recalled how one minute he and Carole Klein had been producing demos for a few hundred bucks profit apiece, if they were lucky. Then, in the blink of an eye, as Carole King she was raking in hundreds of thousands of dollars a year as a red-hot hit maker. It felt, he baldly declared, downright demoralising.

There was precious little to perk Simon up as 1961 unfolded. From even a cursory recap of his endeavours he could see that, with the exception of scraping into the Top 50 once, some years before, the Tom and Jerry collaboration had died a death. And his solo singles, both as True Taylor and Jerry Landis had brought an equally dismal return. Jerry Landis had not quite seen the last light of day, but Simon now decided to have another go.

Paul's number one idol and inspiration remained Elvis Presley who, having emerged from his much-publicised stint of National Service in the US Army, continued to straddle the music world like a Colossus. The once rebelliously threatening rocker had melted into a tender balladeer and figure of romance, whose hits in the last few months included the number 1 multi-million sellers 'It's Now Or Never' and 'Are You Lonesome Tonight?'.

With this kind of corroboration of a market for such material, Paul Simon felt it made sense to stay with the trend. So he worked on a new collection of songs suitable for the popular genre. He would later, somewhat harshly, castigate these efforts as being yet more examples of 'dumb teenage lyrics'. But for the foreseeable future he pinned his fraying hopes on them.

Simon once said that he had never wanted to be in a band. But flying solo had thus far proved to be a lost cause. It was, perhaps, the next logical step to form a group and in 1961, along with two other students, Paul became Tico & The Triumphs.

Paul wrote the songs and it was he who secured this new band's first recording contract – originally with Madison

Records, though the company was subsequently acquired by Amy Records. He and his newfound cohorts began the drill, posing for publicity shots – three short-back-and-sides late teenagers, striking cool poses and trying to look the business.

Amy Records released 'Play Me A Sad Song'/'It Means A Lot To Them' in America only, but to Paul's disappointment it made not the merest ripple. Nothing daunted, he went knocking on doors and managed to nail a one-off contract with the Con-Am label, allowing the band to come next with 'I'm Lonely' backed by 'I Wish I Weren't In Love'. Again, it passed the charts by.

As Paul Simon neared his 20th birthday, he was still writing songs and producing records for other artistes; names long consigned to the forgotten annals of America's music history. Such backroom work continued to enhance his experience and forge more contacts within the industry, as well as filling his wallet. But Simon yearned to be making money from his own releases.

Returning to Amy Records at the end of 1961, to complement their biker-sounding name, Tico & The Triumphs released 'Motorcycle', of which the flip side was 'I Don't Believe Them'. This time the band reached the charts, but barely, as the record briefly blinked at number 99.

It was a meagre reward, but over the next 12 months Simon tried to build upon it. He secured three more releases with Amy Records for Tico & The Triumphs, and in 1962 they racked up 'Express Train'/'Wildflower', 'Cards Of Love'/'Noise', and 'Cry, Little Boy, Cry', which was teamed up with 'Get Up and Do The Wonder'.

The strange-sounding title of the latter song marked Simon's surrender to the rising tide of songs blatantly designed to be dance records since the runaway success of Chubby Checker's loud 1960 hit 'The Twist'. Dance crazes with weird names came and disappeared as quickly. And many songwriters jumped on the bandwagon, churning out ludicrously titled tunes with catchy, breathless beats to match.

There was nothing wrong with experimentation though, and

all Simon's releases this year reflected his absorption in his studio work on demos for contemporary artistes. Success in his own right, however, still eluded him and none of these latest singles came within sniffing distance of the charts. He acknowledged then that the group format was not working and he called it a day with Tico & The Triumphs.

Under his old pseudonym of Jerry Landis, he released 'The Lone Teen Ranger'/'Lisa' in December 1962, again on Amy Records. It slipped by a whisker into America's Top 100, stopping at number 97. This was two places higher than his last chart position but it wasn't enough, and Simon was almost ready to call time on Jerry Landis releases too.

Paul Simon was barely 21 years old and once more he was at a crossroads in his life. For the present he put behind him the various pseudonyms and attempts to emulate current chart fodder and graduated in February 1963 from Queens College, New York. Despite his heavy concentration on music, he left proudly clutching a BA degree in English Literature.

His years at university had seen him mature on a personal level, during a period of much turbulence and political change in American society. Student years are normally when an active interest in politics and social justice will seed, and they did so with the intense young songwriter.

Influential lyricists are products of their environment. In less than six months' time, leaving behind rock and roll and a forced attachment to mushy love songs, Paul Simon was to write the first of the type of meaningful song that would ultimately define him as a spokesman for an entire generation. And the backcloth to this lay in the socio-political climate in which he lived or had learned about at college.

For some years American politics had not enjoyed its finest hour. When President Harry S. Truman declined to stand for re-election in 1952, the Democrats' reign was interrupted and Republican Dwight Eisenhower took the reins of power the following year. Early into Eisenhower's first term in office,

Wisconsin-born Joe McCarthy, a former State circuit judge and now Senator, came to the fore and put a stranglehold on parts of American society in a way that would become a by-word for fanaticism around the world.

When McCarthy became chairman of the all-powerful Permanent Subcommittee on Investigations, he started a witch-hunt during which he arraigned a vast number of mostly innocent, ordinary citizens, as well as officials, accusing them of Un-American communist tendencies.

Many of these arraignments, during which McCarthy relentlessly grilled the person under suspicion, determined to establish guilt even by the merest association, were televised. And the effect on American citizens was oppressive and divisive, encouraging a culture of fear and mistrust.

By the time Paul, who holds Democrat political values, had been midway through his course at Queens College, a fresh wind of change had swept a young, charismatic, astute politician named John Fitzgerald Kennedy into the White House, thereby placing power back in Democrat hands. The handsome President, with his glamorous wife and young family, brought an atmosphere of hope and vigour, and perpetuated the feeling that what mattered to the youth of the day was what would create the driving force towards a better society.

But it was also a volatile time. The Cuban missile crisis brought the world closer to the brink of nuclear war than anyone in the wider public would know for decades. And not every level in American society felt liberated. During the early 1960s a head of steam was gathering as black people began to campaign for their human rights. Paul Simon was one of those who became attuned to this struggle.

Dr Stephen Perrin of Liverpool Hope University, a UK specialist in the 1960s/1970s counterculture explains, 'On 1 February 1960 there was the first spontaneous sit-in by black students in Greensboro, North Carolina. And as the years went on these incidents became more common, which brought about an increase in largely white, Jewish, young college-educated kids getting involved with black activists, a unique time in American history. Relations between the Jewish community and the black community have not always been that cordial. But the civil rights movement is where the two groups meshed together. So it is not surprising that Paul Simon was plugged into the movement.

'In fact, a lot of the people who were student leaders – young political activists around this time like Abbie Hoffman, Jerry Rubin, Bob Dylan if you want a comparison with Simon – were Jewish. And funnily enough, the leaders of the student uprisings in Paris later in 1968 were also Jewish, which was surprising because the Jewish population in France is about one per cent. In America, there is a small but significant Jewish population.'

Asked why many in the Jewish community would care so much about black civil rights, Dr Perrin goes on, 'Probably because these people grew up in politicised households because of the Holocaust. Among the white, Anglo-Saxon Protestant community there was almost a wilful desire *not* to take notice of politics in the 1950s.

'Eisenhower was in the White House and they were all doing very well because there was a major economic boom. They were trying to wipe out the memory of World War II and the Depression of the 1930s. That, I think, is very different to the Jewish community. They felt much more touched by the whole thing.

'As a result of the situation you got the Freedom Riders, who were again mainly white college kids going south in America to run Voter Registration Drives to try to get black people registered to vote.

'They would charter buses from college campuses up north and set off for Alabama, Mississippi and so on, where they would start agitating. They were very unpopular with the locals and often they were violently attacked. Sometimes they were shot. Sometimes people were killed. It was pretty much guaranteed that if you were a Freedom Rider you were going to get beat up, at the very least. Increasingly that became less and less the case as they gained successes and more people became involved. But for a long time they went into very tense situations and they were not welcomed by the white population down there.'

Picking up on these events, Paul began formulating an idea for a song. It would be a complete departure from anything he had yet written. Instead of squeezing his ideas to conform to the popular current trend, he would strike out in his own direction, a direction that, however, also owed a nod to another new influence.

When Simon graduated from Queens College in spring 1963, his feet took him not towards an academic career but instead of working full time for the New York based music publishers E. B. Marks Music. In effect, he became a travelling salesman. Armed with the company's catalogue of songs, the English graduate, immaculately dressed in a suit, collar and tie, plodded around all the record companies that would see him. He attempted to use his powers of persuasion to make record label executives agree to have one or more of the established artistes on their roster record one or more of the songs from the catalogue.

By day he was trying to sell other songwriters' work, but by night he had found a new source of excitement. 1963 would prove to be an explosive year in different ways on either side of the Atlantic.

In Britain, Beatle mania had taken hold like a bush fire. The debut album from the four Liverpool lads, *Please Please Me,* released in spring, powered its way to the top of the UK charts, where it took root for an unheard-of seven and a half months.

In America, meantime, the music that mattered was the burgeoning folk scene, which had its roots in its opposition to the rottenness that had been rife in McCarthyism. During those years it had been forced underground, but it was a potent form of expression. Paul Simon became acquainted with this scene during his student days and by 1963 had become a great admirer of Joan Baez.

Baez released her debut eponymous album of traditional folk songs in 1960. And a year later she was a regular turn at one of the best clubs in New York – Gerde's Folk City in Greenwich

Village. It was while she was performing there in April 1961 that she invited another 20-year-old folk singer-songwriter to join her on stage. He was Bob Dylan.

By 1960 Dylan, who was born Robert Allen Zimmerman, had been earning money by playing as a session musician for a variety of crooner-style singers. He also, though, became acquainted with Woody Guthrie, and as a result of the friendship that developed between them, Dylan became hooked on folk music.

He had changed his name in honour of the Welsh poet Dylan Thomas and was soon making his first recordings on crude, borrowed home recording equipment. Although his debut album, *Bob Dylan,* released in March 1962 failed to make the charts, as an artiste Dylan caused a major stir on the New York folk scene where, together with Joan Baez with whom he began a long-term personal relationship, he emerged as one of the leaders of the folk-music-led youth protest movement. For several years direct comparisons would be made between Bob Dylan and Paul Simon – something about which Simon would harbour mixed feelings.

Paul felt no such ambivalence towards Joan Baez. Always apparently oh-so serious, with her long curtain of heavy black hair framing her face and a guitar balanced on her knee as she sat on a stool, her unique vocal style could be extremely penetrating. It had a haunting, utterly worthy sound, and once more Paul as he put it was 'knocked out'.

Simon went wherever the music was playing, indoors and out. But on an almost nightly basis he haunted Greenwich Village, soaking up the atmosphere, which he felt plugged in exactly to the new direction of his songwriting. In June 1963 Simon finished writing 'He Was My Brother', which was unlike any other song he had yet penned. Years later, Art Garfunkel would pinpoint the exact moment when he first heard the song.

Just the previous month, Bob Dylan's second album, *The Freewheelin' Bob Dylan,* had been released, which featured such major compositions as 'A Hard Rain's A-Gonna Fall', 'Blowin' In

The Wind', 'Don't Think Twice, It's All Right' and 'I Shall Be Free' – all songs which Dylan would have tried out at the folk clubs. Over the years Dylan would influence countless performers and songwriters. 'He Was My Brother', according to Garfunkel, was cast in the typical Dylan mould.

The song speaks plainly of the waste of a young life, of a 23-year-old who is murdered while standing up for his beliefs. Identifying this central figure as a Freedom Rider pinpointed what that belief was. And the description of angry mobs issuing threatening ultimatums and of then taking the law into their own hands left nothing to be unsure about with regard to Simon's stance on the civil rights issue. The brother of the title need not have been taken literally; more appropriately he represented a brother-in-arms.

Art said of the song, 'There was no subtlety, no sophistication in the lyric.' The uncompromising content and nature of this, Paul Simon's first protest song, with its dark theme and conclusion nevertheless rose in spirit at the end. As Simon wrote of the young man's ultimate sacrifice – dying in the name of a cause from which others will benefit – the final lyrics are sung in an almost Christian-revival, hallelujah style.

The ending would find favour with Garfunkel who called it joyously optimistic after all. He would declare, 'I was happy to feel the way the song ultimately made me feel. It was clearly the product of a considerable talent.'

Indeed, after writing songs from the age of 14, Simon was at last on the right track. And it was *his* track – a product of his personality, his outlook, his keen observations on the less attractive sides of human nature, which are usually too uncomfortable for people to confront honestly or acknowledge. It was, of course, too early to confirm with absolute certainty that he had found his niche. After all, 'He Was My Brother' had not been recorded or released so could be no test of the water. But, in creative terms, Simon felt released and invigorated by it.

His parents were less sanguine about seeing their music-mad son squander a BA degree. And Belle Simon, in particular, who approved in principle of her elder boy's ambition to make it in music, still believed that he had time enough yet. And that he should nail down a fallback career for himself in something sound, challenging and respectable. She therefore steered him towards the law. Paul saw the wisdom of this and was not immune to the loving but insistent pressure. The upshot was that he enrolled at Brooklyn Law School.

Before the autumn semester began in 1963, however, Simon slipped the knot and took a vacation hitchhiking through Europe, ending up in the French capital. There is a great romantic myth about Paris and the bohemian arty sector on the Left Bank beside the River Seine. But like any large cosmopolitan city the reality is a great deal less friendly. Paris is riddled with seedy sections where not so far off the beaten track there lurks the distinct possibility of being mugged and the ugly face of poverty looms.

Playing his acoustic guitar, Paul busked on the Metro underground system and slept rough. He later talked of sleeping on the concrete embankment of the Seine under the Pont Neuf, having first ensured, of course, that his precious guitar in its case was well tethered to his body and that he was lying on top of his wallet. At one point, nuns gave him a bed for a few nights in their convent.

Living this kind of existence was part of the easy-come, easy-go student drifter scene right then. And it allowed Paul to witness at close quarters the underbelly of life. But while genuine down-and-outs sat for hours dejectedly holding up handwritten cardboard signs telling the world they were starving, and hoping to hear the clink of coins landing in their outstretched tins, if pressed, Simon could telegraph home to New York for money when funds ran low.

Still, it added to life's experiences and he often enjoyed busking in good weather. He soon realised that the more familiar the song he sang, the more likely he was to have money tossed to him. However, the public begging aspect of it did, at times, embarrass him.

The carefree life had its moments. Although a private man,

Simon enjoys communicating with like-minded types. Crowded parks or the large grassy areas around the Arc de Triomphe were places guaranteed to act like a magnet on a bright sunny afternoon to students and others. It was while Paul had given himself a break from singing in the Metro's tiled, cavernous corridors that he got drawn into a conversation on a park bench with a guy from England who was in Paris on holiday.

His name was Dave McCausland and Simon learned that he ran a folk club in the Railway Hotel in Brentwood, Essex. The British holidaymaker generously extended an open invitation to the American, saying that he would always be welcome at the club should he ever find his way to that corner of England. Bearing the invitation in mind, Simon soon afterwards returned to New York. Part of him was prepared to knuckle down dutifully at law school, but he also harboured inside one or two new exciting ideas for songs.

The first of these ideas that he committed to paper would become 'Sparrow'. As with many songs, interpretation of their meaning is (and ought to be, songwriters often argue) an individual thing. Particularly so, when the lyrics are strewn with Euphuistic references that are wide open to debate, as in this case.

With the starkly unequivocal 'He Was My Brother' already written, in 'Sparrow' Simon revealed his more subtle talent for conveying meaning. Presumably having absorbed the vulnerability felt by the true derelict, his awareness of the fragility of life was heightened; something, which generally speaking, tends not to occupy the thoughts of most 22-year-olds. The fragile, delicate and starving bird in the song stands as a poetic personification of life's vulnerable people.

He asks who is prepared to offer succour and protection to this needy creature, from the forces that are ranged against it, forces which lie in human traits. Again, these are Euphuistically alluded to; for example, the swan in the song represents vanity. The style of 'Sparrow' foreshadowed Simon's work to come.

Paul had not long completed this song and had settled back

to life in New York. He was performing at Gerde's Folk City and was about to embark on his law degree course when one day while out walking he met up with Art Garfunkel for the first time in what seemed an age.

Garfunkel was also newly returned to New York. He had taken time out from his studies, spent the summer in Berkeley, California and had now returned home to complete his maths degree at Columbia University.

In the years since he and Simon had parted company, Art's interest in music had continued. He had ditched the pseudonym Tom Graph for something closer to his real name – Artie Garr, under which he had released two singles. But like his friend's solo efforts, they had sunk into instant oblivion.

This failure had not dampened his passion for music, or for keeping abreast of the changes in the music scene. And at the same time that Simon had been absorbing the burgeoning folk scene at New York's Greenwich Village, Art had been mixing with the in-crowd on the west coast. He had enjoyed the flourishing folk scene in the small folk clubs that were dotted all around the fabled Bay area in California.

Art ran into Paul sooner, rather than later, after his return home because he had come back to live with his parents, having given up the Manhattan apartment before heading west. Years later, Simon remembered bumping into Art in the street near to their homes. 'I hadn't seen him for years,' he said. 'I'd been writing and we started to sing these songs and became fast friends again.'

It was remarkably easy for both men to tune back onto the same wavelength. Catching up with what had been going on in their lives was interesting and the unwitting parallels they shared in their separate experience of chart failure were sometimes funny. What mattered most, though was that they agreed that the most stimulating music lay in the folk scene.

As in the old times, Simon invited Garfunkel to come and hear the two new songs he had written. The unspoken hurt over Paul having recorded solo at the age of 16, while Garfunkel had considered them to be partners, had not vanished, but was buried deep. Although it would rise to the surface much later in life, for now Art was as pleased as Paul was that they had met up again and they happily headed back to Simon's parents' house.

Simon received a gratifying thumbs-up from Garfunkel when he showed him 'He Was My Brother' and 'Sparrow'. Art would state, 'I was greatly impressed and I arranged the two songs for us. We sang at Folk City that night and formed the partnership.' That night was the first time that Paul Simon and Art Garfunkel performed folk-style material. Still they were not yet billed as Simon and Garfunkel. Art used his stage name Artie Garr while Paul adopted Paul Kane.

The name Kane had not come out of the blue. While Simon had been working for E. B. Marks Music, in addition to doing his job for the company catalogue, he had at times also tried to interest the various contacts he was making in songs he had written under the pseudonym Paul Kane.

Soon after it was written in summer 1963, Paul Simon had taken 'He Was My Brother' along to Columbia Records and was thrilled to learn now that it had caught the attention of Tom Wilson, an influential record producer working with Bob Dylan among others. Nothing would come immediately of this interest, but Wilson would return to feature in Simon's life.

The stimulus of having reunited with Garfunkel energised Paul Simon and his creative juices were flowing. There was one highly significant difference, however. This time around the job of writing the lyrics as well as the melody was to be solely the preserve of Paul Simon.

This arrangement appears to have suited Garfunkel well enough. He later said that he had been conscious in 1963 that his own skills as a lyricist had somehow lagged behind his pace of maturity. He felt that, although like Simon he had broken free of the mushy love-song trap and would go on to pen material with more subtlety and depth, he did not feel that he had the requisite lyrical strength at that time to write the songs. He was comfortable, therefore, that that part of the partnership should lie with Paul Simon.

Paul Simon and Art Garfunkel – as was evidenced by the colossal success they were to achieve – clearly had a special symbiosis in which one man's particular talents and creative contributions complemented the other's and together created the whole. Garfunkel had great strengths when it came to harmonic arrangements.

That is not to say that Garfunkel's reaction to everything Simon wrote was instantly favourable. Such was the case when, in October, Paul came up with his third significant composition called 'Bleecker Street'. The astute psychological characterisation in this song was an extension of the poetic personification he had used in 'Sparrow'. The mental picture conjured up at the start by the dank, cold image of thick fog stealing in like blinding fingers poking up dark alleyways was a haunting alarm call to the listener to sit up and take notice.

Emotive words such as 'shroud' were also used to make a deliberate impact. This was no sweet song yearning for a better society. It was a harsh, stark jab in the eye that spoke of a world where the philosophy of every man for himself reigned, where communication between human beings was becoming spectral. And it takes no more than a heartbeat to associate the reference to 30 dollars paying the rent on Bleecker Street with the betrayal of Jesus by Judas Iscariot for 30 pieces of silver.

It was Simon's darkest work yet. Too dark initially for Art Garfunkel. On first hearing it he was dismayed at the heavy tone; he also believed that the symbolism contained in the lyrics was too dense. That said, Garfunkel genuinely praised the work publicly as being highly intellectual: the song was maybe not the easiest to understand but, he declared, it was worth the effort to try.

The clear beginnings of a strong lyrical direction was leading Paul Simon to pen what would become arguably one of his three best ever songs when, along with the entire world, on 22 November 1963 day-to-day life suddenly stopped with the shattering news that America's 46-year-old President, John F. Kennedy, had been shot by an assassin.

The horrific moment was captured on television as cameras were out on the streets in Dallas, Texas, to cover scenes of the President and his wife being driven through the streets in an open-topped car. As the Presidential motorcade slowly travelled between crowds of cheering people lining the streets, Kennedy waved and flashed his trademark white smile until the car drew level with the Book Depository building where, it would transpire, a gunman lay in wait at an open upper-storey window. The chilling pictures of the President's skull shattering as shots rang out would never be forgotten.

It was just over 1000 days since JFK had been inaugurated. Now he was dead and as his body was flown back to Washington, Vice President Lyndon B. Johnson was immediately sworn in as President.

Kennedy's callous assassination killed a dream in American society and plunged the country into one of its darkest hours. Even before the conspiracy theories reached their height, unrest was brewing with angry protests breaking out all over the country, some involving students on college campuses again.

Paul Simon was as affected by JFK's murder as anyone. And it was against this mournful atmosphere that he began work on 'The Sound of Silence'. The opening lines of the song – set initially against a simple finger-picking background – when the lone figure, who would often take centre stage in Simon's songs, welcomed the arrival of darkness as his friend immediately established the territory as being one of lost despair. And the figure's implied familiarity with this isolated state of mind is compelling.

In his element in this song, Paul painted a visual picture of a troubled individual tramping deserted damp streets while all around him people sleep snug in their beds. At other times, he again turned to symbolism to convey meaning: the brightly lit neon gods equalled commercialism, which in turn equalled the superficiality of an intrinsically shallow society. And once more his dramatic inclusion of almost taboo words like 'cancer' to describe the malignancy of lost communication was brave.

At three minutes, five seconds duration it would be slightly longer than the usual scale song of two and a half minutes. It also took Simon into the new year to complete since he was aware that it had the makings of a major work and wrestled with it conscientiously.

Garfunkel recalled that both he and Paul had been actively seeking a song that would raise the standard substantially higher than Simon was already achieving. He said of 'The Sound of Silence', 'But this was more than either of us expected.'

In time, the song's impact would be immense. Simon's mature lyrics appealed to many ages, but he connected particularly well with his own age group. 'The Sound of Silence' was tailor-made late-night, solitary listening material. The lyrics had a powerful effect on the young person brooding over anything from a broken romance to struggling to cope with the death of a close family member.

Youth is an intense time, when raw emotions are heightened to an agonising degree. Paul's appeal was not on a sexual level, but something that was infinitely more worthwhile. His voice and his words came in the darkness. He came as a friend – seemingly a young person's only friend in an isolated world – and he spoke to the listener personally of a loneliness out there in a wider world, a world of which he or she perhaps had no clear awareness yet. Nevertheless, this harsh environment was experienced by many people and somehow that knowledge was comforting.

In a peculiar way the young felt part of a select club, still cut off from an apparently uncaring society that was unable, or unwilling, to acknowledge their pain but now not so intrinsically alone. The invisible bond that this unique cerebral connection created would last a lifetime.

CHAPTER 4

Love, Loss and Living Free

PAUL SIMON DROPPED OUT of law school after just a few months. He had tried to do things his parents' way, but in his heart it was not what he wanted. His future, he was still determined, lay in music – not working in a large corporate office, wearing an expensive suit, and sitting behind a desk. He had done well in not allowing his lack of success to undermine his sense of purpose, and he was sure that he was on new ground with his latest compositions. But he was sorely in need of a lift, which came when, in spring 1964, Columbia Records producer Tom Wilson came back into the picture.

Wilson contacted Paul about the song 'He Was My Brother'. He was clearly struck by it. And if he had at first been considering acquiring it for someone else to record, he was soon deflected from that idea by discovering that Simon was now sitting on at least two other potentially exciting songs.

'Bleecker Street' was impressive. But Simon seized the chance to unveil his strongest offering yet – the recently completed 'The Sound of Silence'. On the spot, Wilson set about arranging for Paul Simon and Art Garfunkel (who Paul explained was his singing partner) to record a demo of a handful of Simon's latest compositions.

The recording sessions took place from March into April and it was now that Paul first made the acquaintance of record engineer Roy Halee, who would often work on Simon and Garfunkel albums; he also collaborated with Simon on much of his later solo material.

The resulting demo disc impressed Columbia Records well enough for them to sign Simon and Garfunkel to make their first album. At this point, Simon did not have enough newly written material to fill a whole album, so while he and Art laid down tracks of his original compositions, they also researched songs they would record as cover versions to complete the 12 tracks required.

The thrill of having finally arrived at the point of recording their debut album meant that there was no shortage of enthusiasm in the recording studio. Vastly experienced in this environment himself, Simon was still happy to be in the professional care of Roy Halee and Tom Wilson, and all too soon the album was done. The next item on the agenda was agreeing what to call themselves.

Both Paul and Art must have had their fill of pseudonyms, but to use their real names was now suddenly a matter for debate. Which side of the table initially raised the point is unclear. But it is true that in America, even into the early 1960s, there existed a very real anti-Semitism, which could potentially harm a record's chances of success. Particularly in middle America, obtaining a fair share of radio airtime for a disc recorded by a Jewish artist could sometimes prove difficult. After discussion, however, it was unanimously decided that the two new Columbia Records signings would go out as Simon and Garfunkel. It was honest and upfront, like their music.

Before that, 'He Was My Brother', backed by 'Carlos Dominguez' was released as a single around May. A Simon solo release, it came out under the Jerry Landis name in Britain on the Oriole label. It was using a pseudonym certainly, but it still stands as Paul Simon's first composition released in the UK. In America, Tribute Records released the single under the name of Paul Kane.

This single marked the last time Simon released a solo record under a pseudonym and, like its predecessors, it did not reach the charts on either side of the ocean. But somehow that didn't seem to matter too much, for Simon's thoughts were trained on Simon and Garfunkel's debut album release scheduled for later in the year.

With the official photographs taken for the album sleeve, it was now a question of waiting. Never one to be idle, Paul again had itchy feet. There was little holding him in New York City, so in early summer he headed back to Europe – this time to Britain.

One of his first ports of call was Brentwood, Essex, in southeast England. Paul had decided to pick up on the invitation he had received on a Paris park bench the year before from tourist Dave McCausland to look up the folk club held in the town's Railway Hotel. Over time, Simon would frequently perform at this popular folk club, where he was also to meet a pretty local girl whose name would go on to earn near mythical status in the Paul Simon life story.

She was Kathy Chitty who worked in an office and still lived at home with her family. Slender, with long brown hair, her quietly self-contained, low-key personality attracted Paul. Although girlfriends had featured in Simon's life before now, his overwhelming absorption in music had tended to squeeze out time for personal relationships. With this girl, things would be different.

For now though, Simon headed for London. It was *the* place to be in 1964: Conservative rule with Harold Macmillan had ended and a Labour government came to power under the stewardship of Harold Wilson. Voting the Tories out in the General Election gave Britain the heady, liberated feeling it had desperately needed, and a strong sense of optimism swept in like a tidal wave. Soon the whole social fabric of the country was about to tear at the seams as morals and inhibitions radically altered – clothes got brighter, hair grew longer and Sundays began to be less of a predictable drag.

It is a privilege to be the right age at the right time and for a particular generation this would be the beginning of a matchless era. An explosion was starting to happen in every field of the arts – fashion, photography, theatre and film – but spearheading this seismic shift was music. Music was entering its most glamorous period.

By the time Paul Simon set foot in the capital, London was rocking. The Who and the Small Faces had yet to break through. The Kinks were about to burst on to the scene, when their third single 'You Really Got Me' suddenly catapulted them from playing support slots to being number 1 hit makers. The Kinks's lead singer, songwriter Ray Davies from London's Muswell Hill, would on occasion, like a very English version of Paul Simon, vividly paint visual landscapes and everyday scenes in the social commentary of his songs and his rasping vocals added to the Kinks's highly distinctive heavy sound. But the big prizefight for chart supremacy in Britain was to be between the Beatles and the Rolling Stones.

In 1964 the Beatles proved that they had the Midas touch, producing an unending string of chart-topping hits, which consolidated the Fab Four's right to wear the crown. They were a phenomenon and they seemed unstoppable. However, the counterbalance to the smiley, lovable mop-top guys, coming up fast from the start of that year was the Rolling Stones.

Rhythm and blues-influenced, these five raucous rebels played hard-edged rock and expounded lyrics designed to send parents running to lock up their daughters. In stark contrast to the Beatles, any one of whom looked safe enough to bring home to mother, the Stones were sexual predators. Front man Mick Jagger was to earn his place in rock's hierarchy, but the Rolling Stones's dynamo was its founder, the brilliantly gifted musician Brian Jones.

Paul Simon arrived in London soon after the Rolling Stones's eponymous debut album had just toppled *With The Beatles* and for the first time in almost a year the Liverpool lads were not king pins in the charts. The liner notes on the Stones' debut album boasted, 'The Rolling Stones are more than just a group. They are a way of life!'

Music *was* a way of life and Paul Simon loved it. Taking in the colour of trendy Carnaby Street, the smell and bustle of crowded street markets where competing traders shouted in accents strange to him, and the excitement of Soho, he made a beeline to investigate the many thriving music outlets. There was a myriad pubs and folk and jazz clubs, usually claustrophobic cellar clubs down steep stone staircases, to choose from. With a suitcase in one hand and his guitar case in the other, even before he had found himself somewhere to stay, Paul talked his way into performing at one of the many sweaty venues. He was thinking no further than earning himself some money to pay for lodgings. Fortunately for him though, that night he made the acquaintance of a remarkably open-hearted older woman named Judith Piepe.

Judith's name had become a by-word for generosity in London's East End. Years before, as a refugee, she had travelled through Europe to escape Hitler's Germany and would carry for life the memory of being a lonely, hungry wanderer with no valid passport and finding most doors closed against her. She later said, 'That's why I don't close my door.' Her open-house attitude had attracted several waifs and strays over time and provided a comfortable, safe haven for people who, for their own private reasons, had launched themselves into the wide world, away from the security offered by friends and family. Paul Simon had nowhere to stay and that night, after performing in the club, Judith offered him lodgings at her place. He was happy to accept.

Judith already had a lodger staying with her, a friend named Joan Bata. Paul and Joan met that first night in summer 1964 and became fellow lodgers at Judith's. Joan recalls, 'Judith was one of those people who, if you'd got nowhere to live, she'd find a corner for you. Her place was a council flat just by Crisp Street market. It leads off Cable Street where I was working at the time in East London. It was quite a comfortable flat actually. Much nicer than the newer ones because they were thinking sensibly in those days that most people would have families. So they tended to be three- or even four-bedroomed flats. Everybody went to Judith's when something went wrong.'

In the overall scheme of things, Judith Piepe played a small part in Paul Simon's life. But she came into his world at a significant time, and in addition to providing him with a safe place to stay, she tried to help him further his career. Joan Bata explains, 'Although Judith did a lot of social work around the East End of London she wasn't an official social worker. She belonged to some religious organisation and she used to broadcast on the BBC radio service. She had a strange background. She was a Jewess. She had managed to get out of Germany and although some other people got out with her, some people didn't get out. She didn't like to talk about it very much.

'She ended up in England as a refugee and she was married. I never met her husband and neither did anyone else I knew at that time. He was in America. I don't think that there was anything wrong with the marriage as such. I think it was just that they lived very separate kinds of lives and got together when it was convenient. She was dark haired, very small and inclined to plumpness. Although she was Jewish, she was a practising Christian. She didn't spend all her time in church on her knees – she *lived* her Christianity. She would rope in all the local clergy to help her with the problems she was coping with for other people. Judith would do anything for anyone. And she was very fond of Paul. There's no doubt about that.

'But then, Paul was a very lovable person. He is an extraordinarily sweet-natured man. You never heard Paul be cruel about people. He was also very tolerant of all religions. He had respect for them. Whatever religion you were, Paul would have said, "Well, try and be a good one." And would leave it at that. It wouldn't have made a bit of difference to him. Paul was not what I would have called an Orthodox Jew in his behaviour. He didn't fast from Friday night, till Saturday sundown sort of thing. He might've done had he been living in his own home. But he would not have done so at Judith's place because she was a practising Christian.

'Paul was naturally a very mannerly young man. That's one of the things I found so nice about him because at that time the ill-mannered brigade was just beginning to come in. And he would have considered it wrong to have imposed his religion on company. If he had felt the need to give up food once a week, he would have said, "Oh. I have to go away every Saturday to see friends." Or something of the sort to cover it.'

Judith Piepe, although a practising Christian did, however, observe customs which Joan Bata put down to her religious heritage. And a particular custom made one day a week at her place very different. Joan recalls, 'Judith belonged to some kind of organisation which meant that on a Friday she did not speak. She would write notes for Paul or for myself and leave them all over the flat. You could speak to her. She just wouldn't answer you. If you wanted an answer, you would have to write down the question and she would write you back. It was all a bit stupid, I thought personally. I couldn't see the point of it. But if people want to practise those sorts of things, it's all right with me.

'Judith clearly got some satisfaction out of it. She used to say it was peaceful. If you forgot it was her day of silence and you rang her up on the telephone, she would tap the receiver in response to you. It was three taps for yes and two taps for no. It took an absolute age to say anything! You'd think to yourself, "Let's go outside and use semaphore. It's quicker!"'

Simon settled comfortably into Judith's flat. He was free to absorb himself in music and could pick and choose when he wanted to have company. Meanwhile he earned his keep by singing in clubs and pubs. 'Judith arranged quite a few of his early London gigs,' says Joan. 'She used to be on the phone constantly, trying to work on his behalf.' Other gigs Paul secured by himself.

Joan recalls, 'I used to go see Paul play at first at Les Cousins in Soho. It was a tiny club. He used to sing a lot there and he began to attract quite a local following. The normal fee for a pub gig was £3 a night. Except once, I remember Paul and Artie getting a much bigger fee when they played at a really big pub in the West End.'

It was a way of life which turned night into day as Joan explains, 'Paul slept a lot during the day. If he wasn't up to all hours writing songs, he was working at gigs and by the time he got back to the flat it would be about 4 o'clock in the morning. There was a Jewish bakers in Crisp Street market which stayed open all night. You could go in there any time after three in the morning and get stuff fresh from the bake house. Paul used to often come off of a gig and on the way home he would go in and buy ring doughnuts. They were his favourites – absolutely gorgeous, fresh and still hot.

'When he got back from gigs he would be on a high after playing, and he had to come down from that. He couldn't have gone straight to bed. So we would all sit up eating doughnuts and drinking coffee. Paul is really particular about his coffee. It has to be made with evaporated milk. But all in all, Paul didn't really need very much. Plain food did him just fine and he smoked, but I don't think we had alcohol in the flat.

'Paul brought back a bottle of champagne once for some reason. It was kept in the fridge in case anyone wanted it. Only nobody ever seemed to want a drink. Paul wasn't teetotal. But he would have been only, what you might say, a social drinker.

'It was all very harmless. Generally speaking there wasn't as much drug taking then, socially, as some people have suggested. Although, of course, drugs have been around since time began, they were a fairly new thing among the working class and the lower middle class. People since have been fed this idea that everyone at that time in London was high on drugs, but it really wasn't true.'

Simon would later own up to having smoked cannabis by this time. But even that, as Joan Bata recalls, was on a strictly limited level. She says, 'The smoking of weed used to take place just once a week, at the weekend. Paul used to consider it rather like going out for a Saturday night drink.'

Gigging at nights allowed Simon some space to cultivate a

personal life. And as he played the folk club in Brentwood, his relationship with Kathy Chitty had had a chance to develop. So much so that she now visited London and came to Judith's flat to spend time with Paul. Joan recalls, 'Kathy looked like hundreds of other young girls at that time and she was extremely quiet. I mean, after a month you didn't know her any better than you had done at the beginning. She was not at all outgoing, not like Paul. Paul was a mixer. Kathy was almost reclusive.

'It was probably a case of opposites attracting. I always felt rather sorry for the girl, in a way. But I also thought that Paul was wasting his time. I mean, that I didn't expect anything permanent to come of it. Paul was deeply fond of her. But, and I'm speaking purely from my own perspective here, I don't think you could've said that Paul was madly, passionately in love with her. At least, he never showed any outward sign of it that I could see.'

In the romance stakes, Kathy had a clear field with Paul – no worries that the nightly gigging musician's eye would stray. Her rival for his attention would never be another woman. The danger lay in his love of music. Joan confirms the situation as at summer 1964 in London. 'It was obvious to me that the number one thing in Paul's life would always be his music,' she states. 'In the end, it is everything to him. And that would not be easy to tolerate from a wife's, or from a girlfriend's, point of view.

'Kathy used to get a bit sulky sometimes because she felt that Paul was neglecting her. And he *was* neglecting her in a way. But he wasn't deliberately being hurtful by shunning or ignoring her. It was just that his mind was totally occupied with something else. There were times when he neglected all of us. But Judith and I, of course, were much older, so we didn't take any notice of that.'

Neither Judith nor Joan, of course, were romantically involved with Paul and so they were not so sensitive at being sidelined. But Kathy was. And it could not have been easy at times to be less appealing than the bit of paper he was poring over to the exclusion of all else. Songwriting, though, was Paul's passion and when push came to shove, when inspiration matched concentration, all else faded into the background. Irrefutably, songwriting is a solitary craft. Says Joan, 'Paul used to like to be alone for spells. If he wanted to stay in his bedroom for long stretches, fine. He was quite capable of coming out and going to the kitchen to fix himself something, if he wanted. So none of us went knocking on his door to see if he wanted a cup of tea or to ask if he was feeling well. Judith and I just left him to it and he would come out in his own good time. Yes, he had a very solitary side to him.

'In fact, it often struck me that Paul was a very unusual Jew in that one respect. Jewish people are usually very family oriented. Now, I couldn't imagine Paul as a family man. He would be good to a family of his, no question. He would do his best always to provide for them and care for them and all the rest of it. But it doesn't seem to me, his natural bent to be constantly surrounded by people. Paul likes his space. In fact, he *needs* his space. He's got an inventive, constructive mind and he needs quiet really. You can't write songs if you've got people bounding around you all the time.'

Simon's particularly insightful way of viewing life soon became apparent to his flatmates. Joan is firm, 'Paul watches a lot. He's an observer. He's also a listener and he's got a natural intelligence. But still I never knew where his grasp of human nature – which was quite remarkable – came from, especially as he was only about 23 at the time. Certainly he had travelled a bit and had gathered some experience. But somehow he had a lifetime of experience behind him. And it was astonishing just how well he *did* understand the many aspects of human nature.

'What particularly surprised me was that Paul seemed to have the capacity to look at life from a woman's point of view, if he needed to. Or he could see how an old person would feel about a particular thing. He had the imagination to pinpoint these feelings so accurately.'

Simon was indeed relaxed and in an environment in which he could let his talents grow. He had created a cosy nest for himself; he rapidly grew to adore Britain and was enjoying life.

Joan reveals, 'Paul can be very quiet. He would sit for ages and not say a thing. But you were always aware that he was there. He's not quiet because he has got nothing to say for himself. And unless you were a fool, you knew that right away.'

In contrast to these periods of companionable silences, he could also be good fun. Often other people visited the flat and Simon enjoyed the quick-fire and boisterous exchanges that would inevitably arise. Says Joan, 'Paul's got a very keen sense of humour, very dry and quick. You'll miss the point if you're not paying attention. He takes his music seriously. But he's not serious himself.'

One of the many things Simon was to take away from his experience of living in Britain in the early 1960s was an awareness of traditional English folk standards, songs like 'Scarborough Fair'. But not every longstanding English custom was palatable to him and he let his feelings be known. Joan remembers, 'He would stand up for himself all right. And if there was anything with which he disagreed, he would tell you straight, whoever you may be. He won't be rude about it. But he was not afraid to bluntly say, "Well. You've got that all wrong."

'I vividly remember him getting extremely cross once about the subject of hunting with dogs and just how much he would *not* let the matter drop. There were a few of us in the flat and the conversation had moved on, but Paul kept coming back to this issue because he was so determined that he was going to get his point over.

'He thought hunting with dogs was absolutely deplorable. He thought it was so unfair and cruel to have a pack of dogs chasing a fox. He considered it disgusting behaviour frankly. It'd come into the general conversation as being an example of an old English tradition and Paul heatedly argued back, "I don't care if it's traditional. In fact, in my view that makes it even worse!" And he went off on a real rant about it.'

Holding passionate beliefs is part of Paul Simon's character. It helps make him who he is and has dictated to great effect much of what he has written about. And these passions, though not to the forefront every minute of every day, are with him wherever he is.

In complete contrast to the all-pervasive groovy spirit abounding in Britain in summer 1964, back in America black civil rights was becoming a growing, compelling issue. It reached one of its hideous low points in July when, shockingly, three people were murdered during a voter registration drive in Mississippi. One of the three was named as Andrew Goodman and when Paul heard, he went immediately pale. He had known Goodman at Queens College in New York City. Simon would later reveal that the shock of hearing about Andrew's death on the radio had made him feel physically sick.

In tribute to the student he had once known, in later versions of 'He Was My Brother' Simon altered the lyrics slightly. In the original song the central figure is warned that an unnamed town would be his final resting place. In later versions Paul identifies that place as Mississippi; a fact that over the years would not go unnoticed.

Iwan Morgan, Professor of American History and Head of Politics and Modern History at London Guildhall University, says, "'He Was My Brother' is a song that came to reflect the 'Freedom Summer' voter registration drive organised by the Students Nonviolent Coordinating Committee and CORE (the Congress of Racial Equality). The murder in Nashua County of two CORE activists and a student SNCC volunteer became the subject of an FBI investigation, fictionalised in the movie *Mississippi's Burning,* and it aroused national condemnation of Southern racism. Two of those killed were, like Paul Simon, Jewish Americans, who were very active in support of the civil rights movement with which they identified because of the experience of Nazi racism.'

Paul had never experienced the death of anyone he had known before and it surprised him how deeply it affected him. In a happier vein it was sometime after that, in mid summer that Simon was joined in London by Art Garfunkel who was on holiday from Columbia University. Garfunkel moved into Judith's flat and naturally he and Paul thought much about their upcoming debut album. Although the tracks had been laid down, Simon continued to develop some of the songs.

Joan says, 'I can distinctly remember Paul working on 'The Sound of Silence' in the flat. Artie, Judith and myself were there and Paul had propped his feet up on the end of the couch. He and Artie were trying out chords, and Paul was experimenting with putting words in and knocking words out. He was writing down notes and this went on until about seven in the morning.

'That wasn't unusual though. Nobody went to bed in that house until the early hours. If Paul was working on a song, he never went to bed until he had the frame of the song worked out and then there was the building up of the song to do. Paul played the guitar *all* the time. He was never without his guitar. If he was sitting down doing something else, the guitar would be propped right next to him. It was almost as if it was part of him.

'And he was open to influences. His attitude to other kinds of music was, "I must listen to this. There must be something in this music, if it holds people's attention so much." Actually Paul taught me something. My introduction to modern music came via Paul and Artie. It gave me more respect for it because I could see the amount of work that went into making it.'

With both Paul and Artie in the flat, Joan Bata had the opportunity to observe the rapport between them. Says Joan, 'Artie could sometimes be quite sharp tongued. He and Paul struck me as being complete opposites. They had music in common, certainly. And Paul could now talk about his beloved baseball to Artie. Paul had probably often wished that he could have talked to Judith and me about baseball but neither of us could understand the game.

'But I never felt that Paul and Artie had much in common except their nationality and the fact that they had known each other for years and had gone to school together. They had totally different personalities. Artie's all right. He would never do you a dirty trick. And he wouldn't ever let you down. He's a nice enough chap. Artie with the fair halo of hair and pitch-perfect voice had an angelic image. But in my opinion, Paul was nearer the angel than Artie was. You couldn't compare the two.

'Artie might comment on something that had happened to someone and he would say, "Oh well, it served him right." And maybe that was absolutely true. But Paul would say, "Go on now. You can't talk like that. You don't know what sort of background he comes from. You have no idea what led up to this. You mustn't pass judgement on people when you don't know all the facts." Unquestionably, Artie took a more critical view. I didn't feel as comfortable with Artie as I felt with Paul.'

Simon, though, was pleased to have the company of his friend. When he went gigging now, Art performed with him. And not only for fee-paying gigs. Joan reveals, 'Paul and Artie did charity work. They would sing at shelters for down-and-outs in various parts of London and at Salvation Army Halls.'

Joan could not help noticing though that there was sometimes an edgy air around the duo. She says, 'I think there was competitiveness between Paul and Artie, even then. Paul was the songwriter and Artie had that voice. But there was something else that was hard to put your finger on. Everywhere Paul went he unwittingly overshadowed Artie. I noticed that it was always Paul and Artie. It was never Artie and Paul. People would say, "Have you met Paul Simon?" then add "And this is Artie." And possibly Artie found that unpleasant at times.'

If there were undefined undercurrents, Paul and Art were too focused on furthering their career to notice and Judith Piepe once again tried to assist. Joan recalls, 'Once Judith got her teeth into something, she was like a dog with a bone. So now she tried to think of anything she could do to get Paul and Artie on their feet.'

Circulating around the clubs in London, they were bound to meet many musicians but someone who came into Paul Simon's orbit around now was an old acquaintance, the singer Jackson C. Frank. Joan explains, 'Jackson was another American folk singer. He wrote some very good music, but he'd had a dreadful accident as a schoolboy. He'd been at school when the place went on fire. He got out safely, but then someone told him that his best friend was still inside and so he went back into the flames.

'I don't think he got his friend out. He barely got out that second time himself and by now he was appallingly burned. He'd received a big payout for his injuries and he ran around in this great big car. So when he was in London he started to run Paul and Artie to gigs. Jackson was very good to them. Paul had known Jackson before the fire tragedy because they came from the same district in New York. Jackson would sing, not actually with Paul and Artie, but often on the same bill.'

When the time came for Garfunkel to return to America, Simon continued with life as before and became ever more engrossed in writing songs. Their album release was coming close but Paul did not broadcast the fact. Joan confirms, 'Paul never told anyone about the records he had already made, or this debut album. He never hinted in any way about it. When people asked him, "What do you do?" Paul would say something like, "I sing for my supper." And that would be that. There was nothing of the showman in him at all. He didn't consider that he had anything exceptional. He had the attitude that anybody could sit down and do what he did.

'His music was what mattered to him, not attaining fame because of it. That was something that might come later on if he was lucky. I saw Paul perform at one of the big London venues towards the end of his stay in Britain and he was beginning to get a hearing. And I remember that night that he was so glad that his music was starting to be recognised. Again he didn't seem to be bothered if *he* was recognised. So long as his songs were.

'Paul will never consider himself a star. He's a chap who earns his living through music and he does it because he likes it. It isn't him being successful that counts. He's an instrument for his music. In many ways he is a purist. And he would probably not like to hear that in case it made him sound very dull, which he isn't.'

As the time rapidly approached for his return to the States,

Paul bent his attention to using what he had experienced, seen and read as material for more songs. Joan recalls, 'Paul wrote in his room a lot. After a while he would come out, sit down and play something and ask, "What d'ye think of that?" And I'd reply, "Don't ask me Paul." I was so much older and knew little about that type of music so I didn't think my opinion would help. And he'd just shrug, "Oh, that's OK." And he'd disappear back into his room.'

Simon described his time spent in the UK as the happiest days of his life. But by September 1964, having said goodbye to Judith Piepe and Joan Bata, he was on the move back to America. Kathy Chitty went with him for an extended holiday. Once on American soil, the couple did not immediately head for New York City. Instead, they embarked on a long trek, criss-crossing the States usually travelling by bus. Always jotting down commentaries on his surroundings, impressions of people he'd met or just seen in passing and of places, Paul steadily added to his cache of potential song material. This rootless wandering with his girlfriend would later inspire some classic hits including 'America'.

Not long after Kathy went home to England, Paul Simon at last welcomed the release on Columbia Records in October 1964 of Simon and Garfunkel's debut album *Wednesday Morning, 3 AM.* At this stage, the album was released for the American market only; it would be another four years, and on the back of other successes, before it came out in Britain.

The album cover was designed to stand out on the crowded racks in record shops and was certainly eye-catching for the casual browser. A black banner exactly covered the top half of the sleeve and against it stark white-stencilled lettering picked out the name of the album and the artistes. The lower half pictured Paul and Art standing on a deserted underground subway platform, a commuter train just speeding away in a blur.

Both young men sported cropped hairstyles and were dressed in conservative suits and ties. Garfunkel, standing to the right, strikes a casual pose with his left hand in a trouser pocket and his right palm placed on a nearby pillar above Paul's head. Simon, with his back to the pillar, is pretending to play a chord on the acoustic guitar, which he holds against his slightly forward-tilted body. In contrast to his partner's eager-eyed look and slight smile, Paul wears a worried expression.

The cover notes promised that the album inside contained 'exciting new sounds in the folk tradition'. And of the 12 tracks, five were original Paul Simon compositions. One of the other seven tracks was a restrained cover version of Bob Dylan's recent number 'The Times They Are A-Changin', and the remaining six tracks comprised five traditional folk standards, plus an ancient Latin hymn.

If a theme threaded throughout the collective work, it was one of negativity and a warning to mankind. One of the folk standards featured was 'The Sun Is Burning', its selection perhaps made on the strength of its being a cleverly deceptive song. Ostensibly it traces the path of the sun on a summer's day from sunrise to sunset and is almost an anodyne Sunday-school, singalong song until the mood of the lyrics alters to describe the deadly, destructive fall-out of a nuclear bomb devastating the world and blotting out life's light forever.

The sudden content change, however, is belied by the continued melodic delivery of the words – an incongruous contrast. Simon tended to ration the number of anti-war songs he recorded. And certainly, in contrast to the trend to make such songs rasping and obvious, 'The Sun Is Burning' is subtle.

A deft touch, too, came with the inclusion on side one, of 'Benedictus'. Paul and Art had written a new arrangement to accompany what was essentially a Gregorian chant – vocal music used in church in medieval times. Singing in Latin, Paul's lower register voice is overlaid by Art's high, delicate pitch. It may initially have taken the listeners by surprise, but it was to prove to be one of the tracks that made a lasting impression.

Of Simon's five original compositions the powerfully evocative 'Bleecker Street' and 'Sparrow' appeared on side one, which ended with 'The Sound of Silence'. The latter, carefully constructed song grew in stature with each hearing. When Simon declares that society's new breed of prophets were those who furtively scrawled graffiti messages on walls, it was a call to take heed of the angry hurt that was rising among the increasingly vocal disaffected youth in America's urban areas.

'He Was My Brother' opens side two and was bookended by the album's title song. Of all the original compositions on this album 'Wednesday Morning, 3 AM' was the shortest at just two minutes, 13 seconds. A tuneful melody, fluffed out by soft harmonies and perfect finger-picked acoustic guitar work, it also makes the least impact. It carries an unresolved narrative about a young man whose guilty conscience at having committed armed robbery keeps him awake at night, troubled and watching his lover, by contrast, sleeping contentedly in her innocence.

'The Sound of Silence' and 'Bleecker Street' alone gave notice that an impressive and very different songwriter had arrived. Journalist Ralph J. Gleason wrote for the album's liner notes that something new was happening in the field of American popular music, declaring, 'This generation is producing poets who write songs.' And he added Paul Simon's name to a list that already included Lennon and McCartney, Al Kooper and Bob Dylan.

Paul Simon would never be comfortable with being anointed as some fabled poet, but he wished that more people had taken notice of the album. Instead, prophetically, the dour expression on Simon's face on the *Wednesday Morning, 3 AM* cover just about reflected his disappointment when the album failed to sell in sufficient quantities to make the charts.

The year that had started out raising such hopes, when Paul and Art had signed to a major record label, was fizzling out on a flat note. While adrift is probably too strong a description for his state of mind at that time, Paul Simon did want to move fast to ease his disappointment. He came to a quick decision – musically, he would be back: it was a long road and he was not ready to drop at the wayside.

He did not know it yet, but the marrying of Garfunkel's

unique soaring voice with his own well-sculpted songs, and the precision and clarity of their harmonies would make Simon and Garfunkel one of the most influential acts in popular music's history, paving the way for a whole wave of minstrel-type singer-songwriters. Right then Paul's first step towards the next phase took him back to Britain – his spiritual home, where Kathy Chitty was waiting for him.

CHAPTER 5

Wandering Minstrel

RETURNING TO LONDON in early 1965 allowed Paul Simon to be reunited with his girlfriend, Kathy Chitty, whom he had been missing. It also enabled him to keep a promise he had made to Judith Piepe.

Piepe had a regular spot on national radio presenting the BBC series *Five To Ten*, a five-minute daily religious broadcast on the Light Programme. Judith had persuaded the programme's producer Roy Trevivian to let her focus, over eight shows, on a song each day from this unknown American singer-songwriter. She hung her hook on the fact that Simon's songs, although not religious, were about either the loneliness of man or the need for a brotherhood of man. Trevivian agreed and on 27 January at the BBC's Egton studios Paul recorded eight compositions.

Half were existing works, with brand new songs making up the rest, and they were subsequently aired in two batches of four. The first batch went out on consecutive days, starting at 9.55 am on Monday, 8 March 1965, in the midst of the Housewives Choice programme schedule. *Five To Ten* featured 'He Was My Brother', 'A Church Is Burning'. 'The Side of a Hill' and 'Sparrow'. The next four, 'The Sound of Silence', 'I Am a Rock', 'A Most Peculiar Man' and 'Bleecker Street', were transmitted two months later; this time, beginning on 1 May, one a week for four weeks on a Saturday morning, just prior to the hugely popular *Saturday Club* pop radio show hosted by Brian Matthew.

Paul appreciated any attempts to help bring him exposure. But a short, more or less fill-in, programme designed to remind people of Christian values could hardly be described as providing an ideal forum for his work. Nevertheless, Simon was interested to discover that after the first show in March, the BBC switchboard had received several enquiries about him and his music.

With music dominating his every waking moment, he kept on the move, hustling gigs. Although he had enjoyed staying at Judith Piepe's flat the previous year, this time around he consciously remained rootless, going wherever bookings took him. Of course, this largely involved playing in London, where he was making an impact in the folk and jazz clubs. Word of mouth recommendation began to swell his audiences, until it was quite common for him to be performing in Soho to crowds of more than 300 people.

The gentle American troubadour with the unassuming demeanour, who was also no mean acoustic guitar player, often turned a noisy, boisterous atmosphere into stunned, attentive silence. To his guitar accompaniment he sang original songs about life's trials in a way that his audiences had never heard before. And for some people Simon seemed to have interpreted their innermost anxieties.

Watching Paul Simon perform during this period in a packed Soho folk club one evening, Judith Piepe was transfixed by the expressions on the faces of the young people around her who were by now hanging intently on Paul's every word. 'With certain songs,' Judith said, 'one could see someone in the crowd suddenly recognise himself.' Thunderous applause shattered the reverential silence when Simon came to the end of his set; sometimes individuals were unaware, as they clapped enthusiastically, that tears stained their cheeks.

There is no doubt that Simon loved to elicit such reactions, since it validated his strong self-belief in his songs, but recording success remained his goal. Although *Wednesday Morning, 3 AM* had failed to ignite, Paul had kept in touch with producer Tom Wilson and was pleased to learn that Columbia Records were, in early spring 1965, branching out into Britain with a sister label, CBS Records, based in Theobalds Road in central London. On the strength of being a Columbia Records signing, Simon went to see them; the upshot of this was a contract to record a solo album.

Art Garfunkel had sensibly – particularly in view of *Wednesday Morning, 3 AM*'s non-chart performance – returned to his university studies. He and Simon adopted different approaches to living their daily lives and it was not at this stage a foregone conclusion for either of them that their professional futures would be linked. For one thing, Simon clearly still nursed the ambition of being a solo act, and with this first chance at his own album he was about to test the water.

Produced by Reginald Warburton and Stanley West, *The Paul Simon Song Book* was a low-budget, bare bones affair costing £60 to record. Working with a single microphone and playing his acoustic guitar, Simon laid down 12 tracks of songs, all of which he had written in the past two years. Some of these were to form the bedrock of Simon and Garfunkel's repertoire a few years later.

Today, the album would be classed as an unplugged early gem from an acknowledged music giant. In fact, because it was deleted in the 1970s, it is a rare album, valuable to collectors. But on its release in May 1965, Paul Simon was already distancing himself from some of the record's content. Surprisingly, from a marketing perspective, the record company allowed the singer to write liner notes for the disc where, in places, he disassociates himself from particular songs. These were honest comments on Simon's part and quite illuminating as to his character, especially when he patently views some of his former beliefs with scant patience.

Paul ends the notes by declaring, 'It is perfectly clear to me that the songs I write today, will not be mine tomorrow' – a poetic, but essentially inaccurate, statement. For, of course, songs once written and recorded remain *his* songs, although, his view of their validity or importance may fade or alter on mature reflection.

The Paul Simon Song Book lyrically represented those areas that were dearest to Simon's heart at that time: anger, loneliness, socio-political issues, a classic love song, and a perceived dig at Bob Dylan. All 12 tracks are Paul Simon compositions, although two numbers – 'He Was My Brother' and 'The Side Of A Hill' – are credited to his pseudonym Paul Kane. The latter number was another of Paul's select anti-war songs. In this song, instead of using broad brush strokes to lash out at war, Simon crystallised his meaning by drawing in sharp relief a single death, and that poignantly of a child, to personalise the human cost of conflict.

The version of 'He was My Brother' on this album was the revised one written after the murder of his friend Andrew Goodman in Mississippi. But Simon saved his strongest blast, in socio-political terms for the track 'A Church Is Burning'. He was not yet ready to let go of writing about the evil behaviour of white supremacists in America's deep south and this was an impassioned attack on the infamous and feared Ku Klux Klan.

Professor Iwan Morgan of London Guildhall University has this to say, "'A Church is Burning' holds multilayered references. A key leadership influence in the Southern civil rights movement was exerted by the Baptist ministry – hence Martin Luther King's Southern Christian Leadership Conference.

'Churches and ministers were subject to attack by the Klan, which had revived during the civil rights era and remained active in the South, and white racists generally. One of the most notorious racist actions was the bomb attack on the Sixteenth Street Baptist Church in Birmingham, Alabama, in September 1963 which killed four black children and injured 21 others.'

Dr Martin Luther King had recently preached in St Paul's Cathedral in London, attracting a 4000-plus congregation, mainly young people eager to hear his address which centred on demanding equality for all, regardless of their skin colour. Judith

Piepe recalled, 'When Paul first sang 'A Church is Burning' in a Soho jazz club he knocked us for six. It had the breathtaking shock effect of a fire alarm.' 'A Church Is Burning' was never to appear on a Simon and Garfunkel album.

The Paul Simon Song Book was, though, the first showcase for several songs that would become famous examples of Simon at his best, reaching out to the unloved and dispossessed. Paul's personal interpretation of a newspaper report on a real life suicide case had led him to pen the number that anchors the end of side one, 'A Most Peculiar Man'. In the space of a few minutes, giving very little back story in the song, Simon nevertheless hooks the listener on the sad isolated life of a man who, to end his bleak existence, gasses himself in his single room. But Paul's point was not so much the actual death, rather the tragedy of man's basic disinterest in his fellow man. In a song loaded with uncomfortably revealing imagery, the key word was 'but' – when the heartless epitaph for the suicide victim boils down to the phrase, 'shame he died, but wasn't he peculiar?'.

A forbidding isolation also permeated the album's opening track, 'I Am a Rock'. Simon sets a wintry scene and a person deliberately choosing to cut himself off emotionally from the world. The lyrics are obvious and unambiguous, but no less powerful for that. The theme of responding to past rejection by angrily building a mental fortress to harden oneself against the risk of loving and losing again was an interesting turn around. Simon frequently wrote eloquently of an unhappy state of hopeless solitude being foisted upon people. But in 'I Am a Rock', the lyrics talk of aggressively pursuing that very state of mind as a welcome form of protection. It is hard to know which represents the sadder case.

'The Sound of Silence' and the short, sweetly melodic 'April, Come She Will' completes the first side of the album, along with another peaceful number called 'Leaves That Are Green' in which Simon, in less profound mood, uses seasonal changes to represent the basic premise that time waits for no one and the fundamental truth that all things, including human life, come and go.

Of the songs joining 'He Was My Brother' and 'The Side of a Hill' on side two, the most obscure is 'A Simple Desultory Philippic'. While many wondered just what the title meant, it has since come to be considered to be a gentle, satirical poke at Bob Dylan, who in 1965 was on his way to attaining mythical status.

'Flowers Never Bend With The Rainfall' emerged as a thoughtful analysis of the struggle between choosing to confront reality or clinging to illusions in a blinkered fashion. Once more, Simon describes the lone figure wandering empty streets directionless in the dark. He also articulates an awareness of, and fearful acknowledgement of, one's own mortality.

Of the two remaining album tracks the darkest by far is 'Patterns'. This strong song, whose rhythmic pounding backbeat pointed to Paul's early interest in African sounds, holds the line of a dark atmosphere where shadowy shapes crank up the palpable tension. In lyrics that are almost hammered out, Simon first identifies, then comprehensively condemns, the preordained path of a life of drudgery that is the lot of most people. Using disturbing language, the life of the person described in the song is likened not so much to that of a mouse mindlessly treading an endless wheel, as to a rat trapped in a room whose only release is death itself. 'Patterns' was definitely one of Simon's earliest songs to leave a vividly uncomfortable imprint on the mind.

In an altogether different way, 'Kathy's Song' also made an instant impression and joined the slowly building ranks of Paul Simon classics. In his school days, he had tried to churn out love songs. This one owed its success to a mixture of maturity and real-life longing for his girlfriend, whom he immortalised with this tribute.

As the lyrics make clear, the song was written when Paul and Kathy were thousands of miles apart. Simon lays bare the extent to which he was missing her when he refers to the emptiness of his life being enough for him to lose the impetus to write songs; one of the worst fates Paul Simon could imagine. There was nothing oblique about the lyrics. This was a naked declaration of Kathy Chitty's importance in his life right then, and so it was appropriate that she should appear with Paul on the album cover.

The photograph taken by David Lowe shows Kathy on the left, with Paul opposite her. Both are sitting cross-legged on a wet cobblestone road. The pair loom large in the foreground and look like millions of ordinary young couples around the country. With her full-fringe, shoulder-length hairstyle framing a piquant face, Kathy is dressed in black knee-length boots, denim jeans and a V-necked sweater. Paul, so close to her that their knees are touching, is similarly clad in shoes, dark jeans and a brown, well-worn woolly crew-neck sweater which is turned back at the cuffs.

Neither one is facing the camera. Instead, they are both concentrating on the child's toy in Paul's hand, one of several toys that are lying around. The unsophisticated simplicity and almost domestic intimacy of the sleeve belied the complexities of the lyrics of the album's tracks. But Paul had been thrilled at having his girlfriend pictured with him on the album cover.

Following what must have begun to seem an unbreakable pattern, disappointingly the album failed to make the charts. Even so, in July 1965, CBS Records lifted a cut from *The Paul Simon Song Book* and released it as a solo single. 'I Am a Rock'/ 'Leaves That Are Green' nevertheless missed the charts and that was despite the song having been performed on *Ready, Steady, Go!*, one of Britain's top TV pop shows.

By now *Ready, Steady, Go!* was long established as being *the* influential focus for the beat boom in Britain's swinging sixties. Aired live early on Friday evenings, the show's slogan was famously "The Weekend Starts Here!". The presenters, Keith Fordyce, Michael Aldred and, particularly, Cathy McGowan became stars in their own right. Geared entirely towards the teen pop market, it was bubbly and informal. The delighted teenagers allowed into the tiny studios where the show was filmed, danced to the guest performers. And their infectious enthusiasm helped ginger up an excitable atmosphere.

On one occasion though it is said that there was a different kind of atmosphere behind the scenes when, in July 1965, Paul Simon appeared on this programme, performing his new solo single, 'I Am a Rock'. Vicki Wickham, programme assistant, editor and later producer at *RSG,* recalls that Simon had been originally booked for another programme which had been cancelled and that was why *Ready, Steady, Go!* had him on the show.

This was a great opportunity for Simon. But when he arrived at the studio he was asked to sing an abbreviated version of the number so that it would fit in with a time schedule designed to allow the other more established stars on the bill to perform their numbers in full. Vicki Wickham was the one delegated to ask Paul to cut the song, which she felt was ludicrous since it had a story and would be hard to edit. Paul is said to have agreed to concertina the number, but then at the last minute apparently he changed his mind.

Whether 'I Am a Rock' simply did not lend itself to being condensed, or whether Simon decided it would be an affront to chop his work down, when he came on stage, he performed the full version. It being a live show there was nothing anyone could do about his decision. But apparently it left one star performing his hit while the fade-out credits were rolling; a fact that seemingly left the star and the show's executives distinctly unamused. Paul Simon's confidence in the worth of his own material was justified, but not as yet recognised widely enough to let him easily get away with such an action.

Simon and Garfunkel as a unit was not faring any better either. In July in America, Columbia Records tried to float an EP by the duo, 'Bleecker Street'/'Sparrow'/'Wednesday Morning, 3 AM'/ 'The Sound of Silence'. But it did not register with the buying public.

It would have been understandable had Paul Simon begun to bang his head on the nearest wall in frustration, but in typically stoic fashion he held his nerve. He also utilised his skills to earn money, and so on top of playing gigs, he reverted to producing material for other artistes. In London, Paul produced an eponymous album by his friend Jackson C. Frank which was released in 1965. Simon also teamed up temporarily with Bruce Woodley, guitarist with the Seekers, to co-write a couple of songs including 'Someday One Day' which gave the Australian band a number 11 hit the following year.

His own objectives, however, remained paramount. There were enough music outlets in London and the surrounding areas to keep Paul in sufficient bookings to exist money-wise. But things felt a bit stale. He wanted a change of scenery and he decided to spread his wings and go on a solo summer tour of one-night engagements in different towns and cities around England. He preferred not just to hike off with his guitar case, arrive somewhere and take potluck. He needed to be more organised than that, so he asked around his various music contacts to see if anyone could put him on to a booking agent for venues in the north of England.

Simon's reputation as a club performer was pretty strong by this time. And not surprisingly, he soon came up trumps when Bill Fogg heard of him. Fogg ran a folk club every Saturday night called Barnacle Bill's at the Kings Hotel in Kings Lane, Bebington.

Bill Fogg recalls, 'I used to be part of the Merseyside Folk Federation and there were about 21 folk clubs in the area where musicians could get work. My own club offered a platform for not only pure folk music, but also contemporary folk music. The club was very popular and supported the local talent including the Spinners, Billy Connolly and Jasper Carrot who were all then unknown acts.

'Every Saturday a gentleman named Stan, surname unknown, came from Manchester to listen to the acts and in turn he would give me the names of his local acts in case I wanted to book any of them. But one Saturday night Stan came to me and said, "Have you heard this bloke?" And he played me a cassette tape recording of a young singer-songwriter performing. I said, "He sounds alright. What does he want?"

'Stan said the guy wanted work and would be prepared to come from London to Merseyside provided that I could get him two weeks of 'cash in hand' gigs. His fee would be £15 a gig. Stan wasn't his agent or anything. He was just trying to help a musician out. I said to Stan that if this man was prepared to work I would put him on. So sure enough I went ahead and organised a fortnight's worth of work in the clubs all around Merseyside at £15 a night, which in the mid 1960s was a lot of money per gig.'

Paul Simon would make an indelible impression on Bill Fogg. Bill goes on, 'When the day came for him to appear at Barnacle Bill's, Paul Simon arrived, a little man and very sure of himself. He wanted the whole night to be exactly as he wanted. Paul came over as being slightly antagonistic, I felt.

'When I first spoke with him before the performance, I was trying to tell him about all the work I had lined up for him. But Paul took a very commercial approach – and wanted to be paid up front.

'I introduced him on stage and he began performing stuff like 'The Sound of Silence', songs which were to make him a very famous artiste worldwide but that no one there had ever heard yet. He had the crowd eating out of his hand. You were listening to material that would not hit the charts for another year and more and he just *held* the audience.

'He played a 40-minute first half, had a break, then played for the same length of time for the second half. He played contemporary, not traditional folk songs. It was immediately clear that he very much wanted everyone in the audience to listen closely to him. In fact, you got the distinct impression that nobody dared even cough while he was singing.'

After that gig Simon would be moving on to sample other venues in this thriving musical community. Indeed it was such a thriving nest for musicians that Bill Fogg recalls, 'The Inland Revenue were after folk club performers in those days. It was a really prevalent time in the Sixties for folk clubs in Merseyside and there were a huge number of performers on the move. The tax man ended up setting up a special squad to try to catch these guys!'

Simon did not forget Fogg. Bill says, 'Paul wrote me a letter soon afterwards which I've still got. It reads: "Dear William, I enjoyed working at Barnacle Bill's. I'll be coming back next year. My fee this time was £15. But next year it'll be £18." Of course, there was no next year – he became famous!'

As he went round various Merseyside clubs, Paul Simon turned up at a folk club run by a married couple, Chris and Robin Sherwen. Chris recalls, 'Robin and I were part of a folk group called the Black Diamonds. John Finnan was our front man and we ran a club in Chester called The Tuning Fork in the George pub in the town's Black Diamond Road.

'Paul came to our club and gave an absolutely fantastic performance. We paid him 13 guineas for the gig. And we had never seen anything like him before. Folk clubs, truthfully, were very much homespun things usually. But we had had a guy playing some weeks earlier at the club who ran a coffee shop in Hampstead. And he actually spoke to Robin and I then about this fella in London called Paul Simon and one of the songs he sang called, 'April, Come She Will'.'

Chris goes on, 'I remember the first night we met Paul. Robin and I used to travel from Liverpool to Chester on the Friday night and we got there just as Paul arrived. I can still see him now as I first saw him. He is, of course, quite a small fella and he had on an olive-green polo-necked top. I remember we were almost exactly the same age, about 24. And it struck me because quite soon after meeting him, in conversation Paul said that he hoped to be a millionaire by the time he reached 30.

'That night he turned in this fantastic set. When I look back, it was pure perfection. Not that many people at that time had the opportunity to see him perform live. I'm talking of a different type of music to the type he sings now. He was a total perfectionist. He literally never missed a single note.'

Having arrived by train and gone straight to The Tuning Fork, Paul had not arranged any accommodation for the night. Says Chris Sherwen, 'Paul stayed with us over the weekend. We lived in Birkenhead in a flat in a big old Victorian house. We were on the middle floor and had this great big living room. No central heating. Not even a fridge! Robin and I had only been married the year before.

'Paul wanted to look around Liverpool, so on the Saturday we went there. He wanted to look at the guitar shops. In one shop we saw a special guitar and Paul said to Robin, "That's the guitar you should buy, man!" It was an American guitar – a Martin. It was something like £150 though. Well in those days, £150 was a deposit for a house! Robin told Paul, "Oh, we can't afford that." And Paul replied, "Yeah. But it would be a very good investment though." It was most unusual to see a Martin guitar in a Liverpool shop – I think they only had the one. Strangely, not that many months later we got the opportunity to buy a Martin which our son now plays.' Paul, Robin and Chris wandered about the bustling port city. Chris says, 'The Beatles were at their height so we took Paul to see the famous Cavern. It was his first visit to Liverpool and he was keen to see these places. After that we took him back home. He was singing in Birkenhead that night.'

Simon settled in at the Sherwens' over the weekend and to some extent he opened up to the couple. Says Chris, 'Paul spoke to us about Art Garfunkel and how they'd been good friends since childhood. He also told us about his father. I think Mr Simon had become a lecturer at a New York University although he hadn't started out as an intellectual. Paul was clearly very proud of his father.'

At close quarters in London in 1964, Joan Bata had not got the impression that Paul had been passionately besotted with Kathy Chitty. Now, in the company of strangers, Paul gave off very different signals. Chris states, 'When Paul spoke about Kathy it was obvious that she was the love of his life at that time.'

Simon, however, did not spend most of his time offloading his innermost thoughts. With Robin and Chris involved in a band, clearly music was the predominant topic of conversation in their flat. 'Robin was a nice guitarist,' says Chris. 'And a good banjo player too. He was learning all the time and to have someone of the calibre of Paul Simon staying over with you was a joy! Robin asked Paul, "Show me how you do this on the guitar?" and Paul did. They sat with their heads together over their respective guitars. I mean these things just don't happen every day!'

Feeding their guest stands out for Chris Sherwen to this day. Chris reveals, 'I wondered what to cook Paul for a meal that first night. One of my best dishes at the time was gammon and pineapple so that's what I prepared. But of course Paul is Jewish. But he was easy about it. He said, "Oh, it doesn't matter. I'm not Orthodox."

'And he wasn't concerned. He ate it anyway and looked like he enjoyed it. But I was mortified! I'd gone to a school where half of the girls had been Jewish so I should've known better, but I didn't think. I certainly didn't offer Paul bacon sandwiches for his breakfast next day!

'We enjoyed having Paul stay with us. He was very easy to get along with and music just filled our flat. As a matter of course, guitars were always brought inside. We never left them in the car. But over that weekend we could see that Paul treated his guitar like it was made of gold.'

Come Sunday it was time for Paul to move on. Chris recalls, 'We took Paul to a folk club that was being held at the Central Hotel in Birkenhead on the Sunday night and that's where Geoff Speed took over. Geoff was Robin's school friend. We stayed for that night's performance. Geoff wasn't married at that time and still lived with his parents in Widnes. After that gig he took Paul back home to stay because Paul was playing in Widnes on the Monday night.'

Here Geoff Speed picks up the story, 'I saw Paul Simon perform at Chris and Robin's club The Tuning Fork that first night actually and he impressed me very much. I hadn't known what to expect because a friend of mine had played at my folk club, the Howff, in Widnes and he had rung me some months after and said, "I've got this young man. He's American. His name is Paul Simon and he's very good. Would you consider booking him?" So on the basis of his judgement I agreed. Paul was booked for Widnes for the Monday night and he stunned the crowd so much that people still talk to me yet about that night. It's perfectly understandable – we hadn't ever seen anybody of his quality before.

'At the club he sang 'The Sound of Silence' and it was one of the most beautiful songs I had ever heard. It was an astounding work for someone of his age. To think that someone who was only in his early twenties could have felt like that and been able to communicate those feelings was incredible. That song still reduces me to tears sometimes when I hear it.'

In addition to making a professional impact, Paul created a favourable impression personally with Geoff Speed who goes on, 'Paul is a decent guy and great company – a very gentle sort of person. I'd just met Pam who became my wife and she and Paul also got on well together.

'He told Pam that if he had not made a million pounds by the time he was 30, then he would consider that he had failed. And he didn't say it with any bravado. It was just a matter of fact. He was a very determined young man but that was entirely acceptable because of how he carried it off. He wasn't in any way a braggart. He was obviously talented and extremely bright. He knew where he was going.

'After the show in Widnes Paul came back and stayed at my parents' home for almost a week. I was working during the day but my father, Arthur, was only working part time so he and Paul spent a lot of time together. My father was a Methodist and Paul is Jewish so they found a lot to talk about. They really enjoyed each other's company. Father told me that Paul spent much of his time writing a song but Paul didn't specify to either of us which song it was. As it turns out, it was probably 'Homeward Bound'.

'One day in the middle of the week I had to drop Paul off at Widnes railway station. He was going to the Granada television studios in Manchester to record something. That was our first trip to the station. Paul eventually left on the Friday because he was heading off to sing at a folk club in Hull. That last day when he was ready Paul rang me. I picked him up from my parents' home and again ran him to Widnes railway station and the train was nearly in the station already. As I recall, we didn't have much time. Paul subsequently said that he had written 'Homeward Bound' on Widnes railway station platform.'

Geoff adds, 'It can't have been much fun for Paul staying in a series of different houses with strangers over a period of weeks. He was very much a troubadour and on his own. He seemed well at home when he was with us. But still there was a feeling about him that he was missing his friends.'

Professor Iwan Morgan concurs with this last sentiment. He says, 'Songs like 'I Am a Rock' and 'A Most Peculiar Man' testify to the breakdown of old certainties. And there is also a sense of insecurity – with old values discarded, what really replaces them? I would suspect that Paul Simon went through a period of insecurity when writing these songs. After all, he still yearns for the security of home and by implication, family and friends, in one of his best songs of this period, 'Homeward Bound'.'

Ranking among Simon's all-time greatest hits, 'Homeward Bound' is straightforward in its depiction of the rootless tedium experienced by a performer on tour, and the resultant questioning of the worth of his own words. It struck a chord with an age group, which, in one sense or another, was itself obsessed with music.

The number made an otherwise common or garden railway station famous in music circles. And the song also added to Kathy Chitty's mystique, since it is widely interpreted after 'Kathy's Song', that it is she to whom Paul is referring when he talks of wanting to be home where the love of his life is patiently awaiting his return.

Geoff Speed reveals, 'I have unveiled two plaques at the station to mark 'Homeward Bound'. Harp Lager were putting up plaques at various places where certain events had occurred in a musical sense and the very first one they did was this one on Widnes railway station platform. The organisers had tried hard to get Kathy to unveil the plaque, but she kept away from them. So I was second choice. I unveiled it in 1991. Then it was stolen, so I unveiled a second one in 2000. This one is screwed in with chemical fixed bolts – the last I heard, it was still there.'

Geoff Speed has one other abiding memory of Paul's time spent there. He explains, 'I recorded Paul's appearance at the Howff. Paul kept saying to me afterwards, "Are you going to do me a copy of that tape Geoff?" And I would say, "Yeah. I'll get round to it." But I never did. On the morning he was leaving he said, "Let me take that tape with me and I'll send you a copy of it." So Paul took the tape but I never did get a copy of it.

'What I did get about four months later was a postcard from Paul which read: "Dear Geoff, Don't shoot! I just haven't had time to copy the tape. But I'll get round to it." He never did. By this time, though, 'The Sound of Silence' was riding high in the American charts and Paul's life was taking off.'

Chris Sherwen who remembered the business with this cassette tape wonders if Paul perhaps had another reason for not wishing to make a copy of it. She states, 'Although Paul only stayed those two nights with us we were left with the distinct impression of a very intense character and a very self-critical one.' The implication being that perhaps Simon, on hearing the tape, had decided that his performance that night had not been up to his own high standard.

One other person from this area remembers Paul Simon clearly at this time and that is Jack Froggatt. Says Jack, 'I ran the Minor Bird folk club in Warrington. We had an entry in the Folk Song Directory, which published a list of clubs along with the names and contact addresses of their organisers. So one day I got a letter from a Paul Simon saying he was looking for work. We were into more traditional folk music, but we agreed to book Paul for a fee of £12 although we didn't know anything about him.

'At that time we were getting audiences of a couple of hundred people at the club which was held in a room I hired over the Red Lion pub. Paul arrived and went down a storm. He was obviously a contemporary songwriter but he didn't really have a platform anywhere else. Folk clubs were his best outlets really, where people were guaranteed to sit and actually listen.

'*Wednesday Morning 3 AM* had by this time been recorded and when Paul was on stage at the club he came out with something that shocked a few people there. This was the sixties but still we weren't as free with our speech as we are now. And Paul was the first person we saw to use the F word on stage.

'He and Art Garfunkel had gone into one of the New York underground stations to have their photograph taken for the album cover. And it was only when the photo had been developed that they saw that the word "Fuck" was scrawled on the wall behind them – writings on the subway wall. Paul was telling this story from the stage and there was quite a gasp went up from the audience when he swore because it was almost offensive. Although in his case he had used it in the context of the story.

'Paul came back to stay with my wife Joan and I that night, after the club closed. It was fairly late and we gave him a bed in the spare room. Joan next morning found a hole in the sheet where Paul had been having a sneaky funny cigarette in bed. The remains of the cigarette was still in the room. I wasn't into that sort of thing, but I knew what it was.

'The wife brought Paul by bus into Warrington the next day. I met them and we went for lunch in a local restaurant before he moved on. I remember him though first going into the Army and Navy stores. He wanted to buy a woollen hat and he said to this shop girl, "Say! Do you carry bob hats ma'am?" The girl gaped then asked, "You wot luv?"'

As they said their goodbyes Jack Froggatt had something to ask Paul. He recalls, 'We had been so knocked out by his performance at the club I said we'd book him again. Paul said, "It's not worth my while coming all the way from London for one gig." Our club was a member of the Merseyside Federation of Folk Clubs and we had contacts with people throughout the northwest so I said to Paul, "If I get you a number of gigs, would you come back?" and he said he would.

'After he left I started to phone people about this American guy who was an absolute knockout. I got about four clubs to take him, so it was a sort of mini tour at the previous fee of £12 a gig. I contacted Paul about this and he wrote back to me and said, "If I come again, I want £15 a gig."

'I wrote to him and said, "Look. As far as I am concerned this was an arrangement. I've had difficulty getting these bookings. So I think you should honour the original understanding." I couldn't go back to the people and say this guy wants more money per gig. They would have all pulled out, I know they would.

'Well, Paul wrote me back again – a very long letter. Most interesting it was too, about four pages, all about how he had worked hard to perfect his art. And one of the things he said in the letter was, "I can't help living in a society that pays the Rolling Stones more than it pays its Prime Minister." And he added, "I don't think that £15 per gig is an outlandish fee." I agreed. It wasn't at all outlandish. It wasn't about that though. I felt it was the principle that was at stake and sticking to the understanding we had had.'

Paul Simon's brief but memorable tour of the north of England clubs had delighted many, but left at least one person uncomfortable as Jack Froggatt reveals, 'I went to one of the Merseyside Folk Federation meetings later in Liverpool and one musician from a popular band was at the meeting. I had Paul's four-page letter with me and this guy was saying – perhaps with more than a touch of sour grapes – "Paul Simon doesn't belong in folk clubs. He doesn't sing folk songs!".'

Soon after Paul returned to London in September 1965 he moved in with a musician he had come to know on the folk scene, Al Stewart. A Scotsman, born in Glasgow in 1945, Al Stewart was a burgeoning songwriter in the folk mould and so Simon felt at home in his company at the East End flat they shared. Stewart like so many others was strongly influenced by Bob Dylan. Dylan had caused a stir in Britain earlier in the year by playing a short but electrifying tour that had climaxed triumphantly with a string of sold-out London performances culminating at the Albert Hall. Throughout his stay he had been feted by the media as some sort of music Messiah.

Paul also slotted back into playing the London club scene,

which was brimming over with talent and future recording artistes, one of whom was singer-songwriter Ralph McTell. McTell's classic 1974 hit 'Streets of London' would eventually be covered by more than 200 artistes and in 2002 he received the Lifetime Achievement Award for Song-writing at the BBC Radio 2 Folk Awards.

Ralph remembers Paul in London in the mid 1960s. He says, 'When I first began to play Paul was over here listening to traditional English music, playing and absorbing all the sounds. I guess Paul's interest in other musical cultures began right back there in the 1960s when he came here to look at traditional British music and it would soon become evident in his early compositions. I used to see him occasionally around the Soho club area. He was very quiet. I suppose I felt he was a little bit unapproachable. But he had a good reputation as a young American singer going through the club scene and I played lots of places he played in that period.

'Our paths though did actually cross once when we shared a concert together. Paul was top of the bill and I was somewhere down near the bottom. It was at the Bexhill Blues Festival down on the coast. It had been put together by a guy I knew vaguely socially.

'There was a band on the bill called the Panama Jug Band, I always remember. But no one turned up! Well, hardly anyone. There were a few old-age pensioners slumped muffled in deck chairs, waiting to be entertained. But that was it.

'At the end of the afternoon the organiser came to me and said, "Ralph, I'm very sorry, there's no money." I said, "Well, I figured there wouldn't be." He went on, "I've had to pay Paul Simon because he's American. So he's had his £20. But I haven't got any money to pay you." I replied, "Oh don't worry about it." My fee was £7.

'The guy went on, "I want you to have my most treasured possession in the world instead." I said, "I don't want your most treasured possession! What is it?" And he gave me a record by Robert Johnson, the Delta Blues player. It wasn't available at that time in Britain and he had bought it in America. I've still got that record today.'

Viewing the immediate future, Paul probably knew his staying in England was not going to be a long-term arrangement. His two solo records hadn't cut it in Britain. He was almost too familiar now with the London clubs, and he had done the touring bit and was bored with it. His experiences in Britain had certainly enriched him lyrically. But the prospect of heading back to America, where he would have to determine his next move, was surely on the agenda. He had no idea that events unfolding on the other side of the Atlantic were about to change his artistic stature, and his world, forever.

In his pre-fame days, Paul Simon spent 1965 as a wandering minstrel in Britain. He was determined that his talent be taken seriously, and looking to negotiate a three-pound raise in his nightly twelve-pound fee at a folk club, he argued, “I can’t help living in a society that pays the Rolling Stones more than its Prime Minister.”
Harry Goodwin/Rex Features

Always politically active, Paul Simon joined other artists in New York's Central Park in 1975 to celebrate the long-awaited end of the accursed Vietnam War. Leif Skoogfors/Corbis

Yankee Stadium, New York, with Art Garfunkel. Paul Simon's passion for baseball took root at a young age, and he became a lifelong die-hard Yankees fan. And of course, he would immortalize the legendary center fielder Joe DiMaggio in "Mrs Robinson." Bettmann/Corbis

Friends from childhood, Simon and Garfunkel developed an intriguing, complex, and often fractured professional relationship. After their 1970 split, following the enormous success of *Bridge Over Troubled Water*, their reunion years later in New York's Central Park was a public triumph. But offstage, the harmony would dissipate once more. Rex Features

Paul Simon has divorced twice and married a third time, but has remained a devoted father to his children. Harper Simon is his eldest child, by his first wife, Peggy Harper.
Hulton-Deutsch Collection/Corbis

The high-maintenance relationship between the music superstar and the *Star Wars* princess Carrie Fisher peaked with their marriage in August 1983. Less than a year later, it was over. Carrie once said, "I figured out what he needed was an intellectual geisha."
Bettmann/Corbis

Paul Simon had enormous problems with his Broadway musical, *The Capeman*. The story of Salvador Agron, a real-life double murderer whose 1959 trial had become a cause célèbre, the show aroused heated public opinion and opposition from surviving relatives of the killer's victims.
Rex USA Ltd./Rex Features

The opening night of *The Capeman,* January 29, 1998, should have been a great moment for Paul Simon. Instead the show drew a plethora of poor reviews and small audiences, and lost a staggering $11 million.
Rex USA Ltd./Rex Features

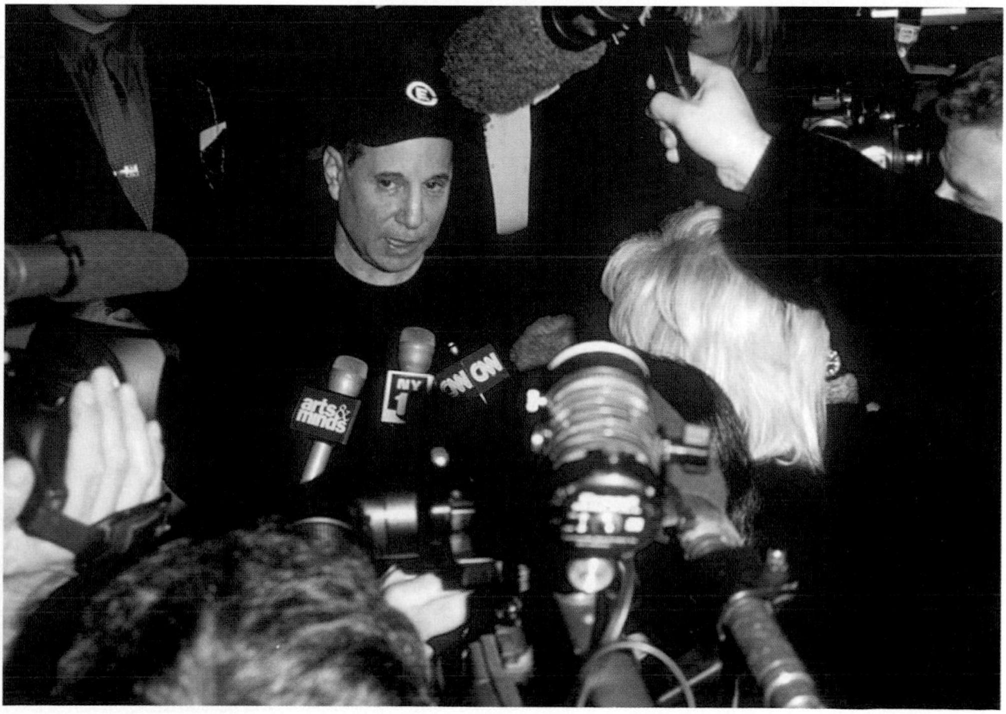

Paul Simon had a musical rebirth in the mid-'80s with his landmark, award-winning *Graceland*. He took his passion for African sounds out on international tour.
Penny Tweedle/Corbis

On May 30, 1992, 50-year-old Paul Simon married singer-songwriter Edie Brickell, who is approximately half his age. Determined to find lasting happiness this time around, Simon told reporters, "I'm in my life now, not in my imagination." The couple is raising a family.
DMI/Rex Pictures

Building on his incredible success in the 1960s and '70s, branching out into world music in '80s and '90s with *Graceland* and *The Rhythm of the Saints,* receiving worldwide acclaim, generating controversy and even death threats, Paul Simon retains his restless inquisitiveness about music. Lynn Goldsmith/Rex Features

In 2001 Paul Simon embarked on his fifth decade as a performer. He toured with Bob Dylan and received America's highest accolade for a performer, the Kennedy Center Honor, in 2002. He remains the timeless troubadour. Lynn Goldsmith/Rex Features

CHAPTER 6

Dazed and Confused

LIFE IS LITTERED WITH TEASING 'WHAT IFS'. Probably one of the most interesting examples of this in Paul Simon's life has to be – what if record producer Tom Wilson had failed to recognise and act upon the potential in 'The Sound of Silence'?

The song already lay dormant on albums *Wednesday Morning, 3 AM* and *The Paul Simon Song Book*. It also languished on the B-side of the Simon and Garfunkel EP, released just months earlier in July 1965. Yet the number's superior calibre was invariably acknowledged in live performances, when the lyrics sent a crackle of static electricity running up many a listener's spine.

Wilson's inspiration to take another look at Simon's song stemmed from the stimulus of a new trend in music that was coming out of California at the time. Traditionally there is a tendency to consider London as the capital of the popular music world in the mid-1960s, but an incredible West Coast sound was beginning to swamp all in its wake. For more than two years the chirpy clean-cut surf sound, mainly courtesy of the Beach Boys, had been riding the crest of the wave. Now, as summer 1965 sprinted on, with Bob Dylan rasping his warning that the times were rapidly changing, a new order was emerging.

Dylan himself, of course, was part of that process. His new album *Bringing It All Back Home* had already achieved international success. And its style was electric folk-rock – an exhilarating, full-bodied and skilfully produced sound that probably came to be most closely associated with another Columbia Records signing, the Byrds.

Formed in Los Angeles, the Byrds, with their immaculately honed harmonies bolstered by 12-string electric guitars and strong percussion, had stormed on to the scene with two number 1 singles in the space of four months: a cover of Dylan's 'Mr Tambourine Man' and 'Turn! Turn! Turn!'. And other exponents of what was an infectiously mellow, but never inane, sound were fast materialising. Absorbing all of this, record producer Tom Wilson went back to Paul Simon's acoustic version of 'The Sound of Silence' and overdubbed an additional rhythm backing on it that included electric guitar work, bass and drums. The resulting revamped folk-rock fusion worked wonders

All this had been done, as was Columbia Records' prerogative, without prior consultation with either Paul Simon or Art Garfunkel. It has been said that the first Simon knew of the single's relaunch was when he spotted that it had registered just inside the Top 100 in the *Billboard* chart. But Tom Wilson did send Paul, who was living in London in late autumn 1965, a copy of the newly pressed '45.

Simon had been ready to quit London anyway and this was reason enough to up sticks and return to New York City where, along with Garfunkel, he closely monitored the single's progress. It was a rewarding experience. Far from petering out, as Simon's few very early chart entries had done, 'The Sound of Silence' gathered pace state by state. Requests to radio stations for airplay began to rise steeply. By November, the momentum looked unstoppable. And, sure enough, at the turn of the year 'The Sound of Silence' hit the coveted top slot in the American singles chart. It went gold within weeks and became a renowned folk-rock classic

Paul has a vivid recollection of sitting with Art in a car parked by a kerbstone in Queens, listening on the car radio to the weekly pop music chart rundown. He could hardly believe it when the announcer declared that that week's number 1 single was 'The Sound of Silence' by Simon and Garfunkel. It was an understandable reaction. Simon had recently been singing for his supper around Britain. Moreover he had been pursuing success for a clear ten years already. Now, suddenly, because of the vision of a record producer, he had a number 1 hit to his credit.

What stood out for him right then was that it didn't feel any different. And, as he and Art stared out of the windscreen long after the song's last note had faded from the radio speaker, they could not help but reflect on the disparity between the public's perception of hit-making success and its reality.

On his return to America, Paul had moved back in with his parents. But although he enjoyed being with his welcoming family, such a move can feel like a retrograde step. Simon was naturally thrilled at topping the charts, but he was also confused – unsure how to react to this development; an unsettling combination of emotions. Columbia Records for their part had no intention of letting indecision set in. And soon Simon's nose was kept pressed close to the grindstone in the recording studio in an endeavour to capitalise on the single's success.

It was fortunate that during the previous December the record company, seeing the single zoom up the charts, had prodded the pair into starting to re-record some of Paul's solo compositions from *The Paul Simon Song Book.* For now they were given only a few weeks in which to complete a new album, for which half the tracks would still have to be new songs.

Although the pressure produced by tight deadlines can be stimulating, ideally the creative process does not lend itself to being rushed. But Simon and Garfunkel were in no position to do anything but comply with the record company's dictates. Paul was eager to progress to a second Simon and Garfunkel album, but the workload in the short time available was onerous. And there were other factors in the equation.

The existing numbers chosen to be re-recorded by the duo

first had to have new arrangements and extra instrumentation worked out for them. And the pair had been assigned a producer, Bob Johnston, who they had not worked with before. Because of the time restriction, they had to book studio time in a variety of locations spread over New York state, California and Tennessee. This meant much travelling and no continuity of working environment. Even the studio engineers, although proficient, were different from studio to studio.

For Paul there was an added problem. Granted it had flopped, but his last recording endeavour had been a solo album, and throughout the previous year he had been living the life of a solo performer. There was no arguing with the practically neon-lit signs that his musical career, for the foreseeable future, lay in partnership with Art Garfunkel. On a personal level Paul was pleased to be back with him, but to be part of a twosome again required a degree of mental adjustment.

It is often difficult to concede artistic points, to defer to someone else's opinion. Writing the lyrics and the music for the songs led Simon to the feeling that he held the reins. He had to remember, though, that this could not now be the case. As he'd had to acknowledge before, Art Garfunkel had much to give, not only with his tenor voice but also with his talent for musical arrangement.

That apart, a whirlwind of activity still produced Simon and Garfunkel's follow-up to *Wednesday Morning, 3 AM* with the album *Sounds of Silence*. The six re-recorded, revamped tracks from *The Paul Simon Song Book* were 'The Sound of Silence', 'Leaves That Are Green', 'Kathy's Song', 'A Most Peculiar Man', 'April, Come She Will' and 'I Am a Rock'.

Of the six new songs, the three additions to side one of *Sounds of Silence* began with 'Blessed', a song Simon wrote inside St Anne's Church in London. Appropriately, the lyrics took on a biblical flavour, but Simon knocks the spurious notion that the underdogs in life are somehow sainted, and points out that in reality they are people who are either abandoned or trampled on. 'Somewhere They Can't Find Me' revived a past theme of guilt over an illegal action, and the side ended with 'Anji', an acoustic guitar instrumental by Paul. The tune is credited on the album to jazz/blues guitarist Davy Graham.

'Homeward Bound' opens side two, with the jauntily, rocking blues number 'We've Got A Groovy Thing Goin' as the penultimate track. This high-energy song is a straightforward appeal to a girl not to walk out on a relationship and is the first fun number Simon had recorded in a long time.

Of the new tracks written for this album the strongest is 'Richard Cory', the second one to deal with a suicide. Unlike 'A Most Peculiar Man', this song tells of a handsome, successful playboy tycoon, seemingly with the world at his feet. It is viewed through the envious eyes of a worker in one of Cory's factories. When the playboy kills himself, Simon does not shy away from punctuating the lyrics with a sudden surprising brutality as he describes Cory putting a bullet through his skull. But Simon was making a more subtle point. Professor Iwan Morgan observes, 'The 'Richard Cory' song is a comment on the emptiness of the American Dream – a man who has vast material wealth, but who has nothing worthwhile to live for.' The fact that Simon has the factory worker, even after Cory commits suicide, *still* aching to fill such glamorous shoes is a comment on the heedless pursuit by many of a materialistic way of life.

Sounds of Silence was released in March 1966 in America, where it peaked at number 21. Weeks later in Britain it bettered that by climbing to a respectable number 13. Encouraged by this response, Columbia Records put a renewed push behind the duo's debut album, *Wednesday Morning, 3 AM* which at last managed to reach the Top 30.The new album had to be strenuously promoted and to help organise their busy schedule the duo now acquired an experienced manager, Mort Lewis.

In March the newly released 'Homeward Bound'/'Leaves That Are Green' had levelled out at number 5 in the States. And by April, it gave Simon and Garfunkel their singles chart debut in Britain by making it to number 9.

Although 'The Sound of Silence' had been a number 1 triumph in America, it had dipped out completely in the UK. In mid-April 1966 the British trio, the Bachelors, reached number 3 with their cover version of the song. Paul Simon seemed less than flattered by this development and was not slow to say so in interviews. If Simon's reaction to the middle-of-the-road Irish band's cover version of 'The Sound of Silence' had anything to do with a fierce sense of territoriality when it came to his compositions, who can blame him? His lyrics and their precise enunciation is an intricate matter of great importance to him. Any hint of their meaning dissipating into blandness was anathema to him.

Manager Mort Lewis knew that the natural live performance audience for his two new charges would be collegiate. His strategy was to book the duo primarily on the college and university campus circuit, rather than the clubs and theatres that he could have used, given their chart success. Success continued in America when in June 'I Am a Rock'/ 'Flowers Never Bend With The Rainfall' reached number 3, proving that alienation was a welcome theme.

With this third hit single there could be no doubting where Simon's lyrical preoccupation lay. Penning material that concentrated on the darker side of life and the stress of modern-day isolation played particularly well with college kids, who responded more readily to meaningful tales of life, than to hormonal yearnings. By concentrating on building a fan base in this market, Simon and Garfunkel began to gather an educated following: future professionals who appreciated the intellectual and subtle nuances which lurked in Simon's songs beneath the veneer of crystal-clear harmonies.

The personal satisfaction this afforded Paul was tempered by the fact that, while he was aware he was probing the depths of the possibilities available within the parameters of the three-minute pop song, he was conscious that there remained constraints in songwriting.

The college/university campus weekend gigs were nice

earners. And they also accommodated Art Garfunkel's new graduate studies at Columbia University. Indeed, Art managed perfectly well to juggle the separate strands of his busy life – music, studies, and a personal life. By early summer 1966 Paul did not. Recording success had not given him a secure frame of mind. He was apprehensive.

Much had happened in the last few months. Paul missed the footloose life in Britain. Although he had often found the itinerant existence frustrating, it had been stimulating, too, and he had enjoyed the independence.

Back in New York City, at 24 years old he naturally had not envisaged living long with his parents. Only now that he was in the financial position to have taken an apartment on New York's upmarket East side, he found himself cut off from the people he had grown up with. Paul had never set up home alone before and, by his own admission, he felt insecure. He was confident in the studio and in front of a live audience. But being a fast-rising recording star, expected to live in a certain style and to be seen in particular company, was alien to him. 'I didn't know who to be friends with,' he once confessed.

He had also lost the rudder of a steady girlfriend. His return to America and the subsequent recording success, with all the time-consuming demands that it entailed, had sounded the death knell for his romance with Kathy Chitty. 'I Am a Rock' made it to number 17 in the UK charts in July, around the same time as Simon and Garfunkel arrived in Britain for a short promotional tour. But Kathy remained a casualty of his success. Paul's life was in America, building the career he had worked so long and hard for. Kathy must also have wanted more out of life than to conduct a long-distance romance with a continually working musician. Her name was to feature in future Simon songs, but she no longer figured in his private life.

The 1966 summer tour was not Paul Simon's happiest time. He later admitted that he sank into a half-robotic state. 'I went into a daze,' he said. It was an isolating existence, and one which he did not feel particularly inclined to alleviate with female companionship. Like any on-the-road musician his was not then a life style conducive to establishing a new long-term personal relationship, and Paul was not attracted to the meaningless alternatives.

Simon and Garfunkel groupies tended not to be perfumed, promiscuous predators, dressed to kill and resourceful enough to lie in wait in the star's hotel room. They were instead doe-eyed soulful types who hung trustingly on the duo's every word on stage. Paul was not the sort of man who got a charge out of pretending to care for a besotted young fan. He felt that was tantamount to taking advantage and was also disrespectful to the girl. And so, apart from occasions when he and Art wound down by dissecting the night's performance, Paul usually left the stage and headed alone to his hotel room.

Simon's close collaboration with Garfunkel meant that they spent a great deal of time in each other's company. Music was the pivot of Paul's life. If he was not writing songs and melodies, he was working on arrangements with Art and adhering to the record company's requirements by recording, again in various cities around America. While an important part of his work as a lyricist relied upon deep introspection, Simon never failed to keep a finger on the pulse of what was happening around him musically – and 1966 was proving to be a vintage year.

In spring, greatly inspired by the Beatles' *Rubber Soul*, lyricist Brian Wilson had reached new heights of ingenuity with the Beach Boys' masterpiece album *Pet Sounds*. Around the same time, the Rolling Stones were basking at number 2 in the American album charts with *Aftermath*.

By August Bob Dylan's critically acclaimed double album *Blonde On Blonde* arrived, soon spawning the single 'Just Like A Woman'. And the Beatles were trying to calm the furore John Lennon had unleashed when he told a London *Evening Standard* reporter that the Beatles were now more popular than Jesus. This remark, when repeated in America, produced a frenzy of righteously motivated opposition to the group. At a televised press conference in a Chicago hotel, Lennon awkwardly apologised for any offence he had given. At the end of August, the Beatles, road-weary, played their last ever concert at Candlestick Park in San Francisco. Only weeks later *Revolver* topped the US charts.

An invigorated Paul Simon, part of this whole scene, told the *New York Times*, 'Pop music has become the most exciting area of all today.' He added that it was fast becoming *the* forum in which it was possible to get through to people and make a valid point about what mattered in society.

At that time Simon's lyrics reached another unexpected mass forum when English literature teachers at several academic levels began using Paul Simon songs as a teaching tool. As an entertainer, Simon shied away from the notion of his songs becoming classwork, but part of him must also have been flattered. All he would say in response to this development was that if his songwriting provoked debate then that could only be constructive. 'We are just creating doubts, raising questions,' he maintained.

The question that was uppermost in Simon's own mind come September 1966 was why Simon and Garfunkel's latest single 'The Dangling Conversation'/'The Big Bright Green Pleasure Machine' had flunked out disappointingly at number 25. It missed the UK charts altogether and Paul felt abruptly halted in his tracks. Unable to conceal his amazement, he openly declared that he could not understand why 'The Dangling Conversation' was not a smash hit. His only possible answer was that it was perhaps too heavy a number. The song certainly used complex imagery, but its central theme was failed communication between lovers who have slowly lost connection in their dislocating lives. As such, it was not an obscure concept for anyone familiar with Paul Simon's style.

In any event, the single's parent album soon dispelled his disappointment. Released in America in October, *Parsley, Sage, Rosemary and Thyme* would eventually level out at number 4, Simon and Garfunkel's highest album chart position yet – which made up for the fact that it did not perform in Britain. *Parsley, Sage, Rosemary and Thyme* was the first album on which the duo had been able to exercise a degree of creative control. In the first place, they had been allowed a more realistic time span within which to make it.

Once again, working alongside them was Columbia Records engineer Roy Halee, and the three men became a tight-knit team. Paul was keen to explore the possibilities to their limit and was a perfectionist in the pursuit. He could be brilliantly spontaneous too. Roy Halee later reflected that Paul often wrote great material on the spot in the studio under pressure. In this album Simon also sought to experiment with a wide range of styles, from sombre songs to the airily ebullient.

In the interests of fairness, the three men decided at the outset to operate a democratic system whereby, if a unanimous agreement was not forthcoming on any issue, whoever was outvoted had to give way.

Paul had occasions when he fought his corner on a point but was overruled. He had agreed to this system, but deep down it never really sat well with him, no more probably than it did with Art Garfunkel when he lost. It takes confidence to pursue a certain path in a song's construction or development, and cemented beliefs are hard to budge. Paul was not forever arguing, but if he did and he lost, it sometimes left a dissatisfaction that was never entirely overcome, banking up trouble ahead.

Parsley, Sage, Rosemary and Thyme once again used re-recorded existing numbers, including 'Patterns', 'Flowers Never Bend With The Rainfall' and 'A Simple Desultory Philippic'. An unwieldy and bracketed sub title of (Or How I Was Robert McNamara'd Into Submission) had been added to the latter song.

The suspicion that Paul Simon was having a low-key poke at Bob Dylan with this number continued. Indeed, some sections of the music press had for some time been comparing the two artistes, a habit which Simon, in 1966, described as 'unfortunate' – in his eyes Dylan's philosophies were totally different from his own.

Like 'Patterns' the mood was dark in the ugly urban angst reflected in 'A Poem On The Underground Wall', while the contrast could hardly be greater with 'Cloudy'. The pure clarity of the tone on this number is instantly evocative of the refreshing outdoors and airy, drifting summer clouds. The four remaining tracks were each remarkable in their own distinctive way. The album's opener, 'Scarborough Fair/Canticle' conjured up olde England and the traditional folk song was given a Tudor inflexion with the use of the delicate harpsichord. On this song, Simon and Garfunkel's voices gave a lesson in perfect harmony.

Writing 'The Sound of Silence' had taken Paul three months, but conversely he sometimes wrote songs in a single night. Such was the case with the love song 'For Emily, Whenever I May Find Her', one of Simon's most rapidly written songs. The dreamlike sequences bring an imaginative depth to the emotion that pours from every line; here is a man grateful to be in love and the romanticism extends even to descriptions of a figure clothed in a crinoline.

One of his most unusual compositions has to be '7 O'Clock News/Silent Night'. It is in effect two merged tracks. One is a straightforward melodic version of the traditional Christmas carol. The other is a newscast that details a series of events reflecting the seriously turbulent times in America. The newscast increases in volume from being barely audible until, symbolically, the headlines about politics, murder, war and civil rights all but obliterate the carol's message of peace on earth and goodwill to all men.

With crisp diction the newsreader touches on the trial of a notorious serial killer, the dangers inherent in the swell of anti-Government feeling over the already thorny issue of the Vietnam War and the death from an accidental drug overdose in Hollywood of the young iconoclastic comedian Lenny Bruce.

Parsley, Sage, Rosemary and Thyme hit home with many and in a deeper than usual sense as Professor Iwan Morgan explains, 'Simon and Garfunkel shared the growing alienation of the student movement. For example, it was not until 1967 that segments of the media began to go sour on the war [in Vietnam].

And the Tet offensive of January 1968 [when the world was stunned that the Viet Cong, essentially a Third World peasant army, could inflict such grave damage on the mighty American war machine] caused further disquiet. But the *Parsley, Sage, Rosemary and Thyme* album contains several songs recorded much earlier in 1966 that refer to disillusion with the war. Paul Simon's antagonism, therefore, was well in advance of the mainstream.'

The album was intriguing and whetted the public's appetite to know more about music's fastest-rising duo. For one thing, there was no clear picture of the role each man played in the successful partnership. It was a PR decision from the outset deliberately to blur the lines about who did what in the working process. Of course, there was a whole area where it would not have been possible strictly to separate the two anyway, but the fact that Paul Simon wrote the songs *and* the melodies was to be fudged.

The music press, therefore, speculated or made assumptions as to each of the two's responsibilities. The picture became even more muddied when the record company's PR department seemed to allow the thought to grow that while Simon was the lyricist, both Paul and Art wrote the music.

Since it was a PR policy to avoid making clear distinctions, both Paul Simon and Art Garfunkel uncomfortably participated in this image. But it led to frustration for both men, an underlying tension at or after press meetings. It also reawakened the long-standing competitive edginess that lay at the foundation of the duo's professional relationship.

The strategy, if it was defined enough to call it that, had been to deter the music press from making Art Garfunkel appear in any way irrelevant beyond vocal duties, because that plainly was not the case and would have been unfair. Paul admitted that he disliked it for his friend's sake when a journalist would buttonhole them about who specifically wrote the words and the music of their songs. But although Paul went along with the fudge, it was something that would later begin to trouble him.

In December their single, a new upbeat number 'A Hazy Shade of Winter', which was backed by 'For Emily, Whenever I May Find Her', reached number 13 in America. But again the British remained unmoved. To some extent that was also true when three months later Simon and Garfunkel came to the UK for a short tour. When they played in regional English cities there were signs that people had not yet quite cottoned on to the Americans.

This was not true, however, of their Royal Albert Hall dates in London which were a huge hit. Immediately afterwards they returned to New York City. Garfunkel was working on his master's degree and needed to go back to university, while Simon wanted time to write.

Soon after, in April 1967, 'At The Zoo' was released and stalled at number 16. The bouncy, bizarre number, in which different zoo animals are equated with human traits such as honesty and integrity, again did not click in Britain. To some, bizarre lyrics suggested the influence of drugs on songwriting, which was prevalent by then. The B-side to this latest single – 'The 59th Street Bridge Song (Feelin' Groovy)' projected a kind of high, too. Only, in this instance, the high had come from a pure happy-to-be-alive moment, which Simon had experienced just before he had written the number. This B-side was the fourth remarkable cut from *Parsley, Sage, Rosemary And Thyme*. In a few months time it would reappear as the lead track on an EP and Simon later said of 'Feelin' Groovy', 'I knew that record was a hit as soon as I wrote it.'

'Feelin' Groovy', with its soaring notes and West Coast laid-back attitude certainly fitted very much into the mood of this time, when artistes often referred directly or indirectly to drugs in their songs.

By early summer 1967 psychedelia was the word. Dressing had been elevated to an art form and it was important to make a visual statement. Garish colours and complex patterns were in, as were mind-altering substances.

Two years previously, in the search for excitement and experimentation, a select group of people at the cutting edge of this movement held Acid Test parties when they had tried out a man-made drug which was so new that it had not yet been declared illegal – Lysergic Acid Diethylamide, a hallucinogenic drug, abbreviated to LSD and more commonly known as acid. By 1967 its use among the younger generation had been increasing steadily the more they saw their music heroes indulging themselves. In Britain, celebrity drug busts had hit the headlines when the authorities, worried at the deepening drug culture, went all out to try to crush the Rolling Stones by arresting Keith Richard, Mick Jagger and later Brian Jones on drugs charges.

Since his days living in Britain in 1964 Paul Simon had occasionally smoked marijuana. LSD was in a different league altogether, but he had his views on the matter. Like many of his contemporaries, Simon did not discount the theory that creativity could potentially benefit from chemical assistance. He spoke to Britain's *Melody Maker* about how scientists were currently exploring the possibility that a stimulant such as LSD *could* turn a clever man into a genius. At the same time, he aired the warning that if such drugs were used in an uncontrolled fashion who knew what lasting damage they could cause? According to Paul he knew a few people who were already on LSD. 'I don't think there's too much wrong with pot,' he mused. He would not be beyond a spell of experimentation on different ground himself in the not too distant future.

CHAPTER 7

Flying High

BY AND LARGE PAUL SIMON did not enjoy his experimentations with LSD, which began in spring 1967. In a creative sense, like many of his contemporaries, he had been interested in exploring the argument that the drug could unlock the door to hidden depths. On a human level, he was just curious to discover what all the fuss was about. First timers often chose to drop acid in the supposed safety of the company of friends. But, having no way of knowing how LSD would affect him, typically, Simon opted for the privacy of his New York City apartment.

The experience would leave him lurching through endless hours of paranoia – something he could well do without. He later admitted that the trip was weird, but he added, 'I wasn't going to let an acid trip throw me just because it was bad.'

The drug culture was widespread. For Americans it was mainly focused on California, specifically the Haight-Ashbury area of San Francisco, where the extent of the breakdown in inhibitions as, in 1967, the summer of love approached, was enough to bring Paul Simon's eyes out on stalks when he and Art Garfunkel visited the region.

At one open-air musical gathering, Paul turned up to discover that everybody was naked and completely blasé about it. Certainly the West Coast psyche had always been different from that of New Yorkers, but even so, Simon was staggered at the scene. He quickly sensed that a strange air hung about almost everyone he encountered. People wore slow, lazy, knowing smiles that he found infuriating and the unnatural atmosphere spooked him. At times he must have felt like the only sober man in a room full of drunks all of whom shared an in-joke. He revealed, 'I felt hopelessly out of touch.'

Someone who can vouch for the existence of this unique inner world is Noel Redding, former bass player with the Jimi Hendrix Experience. Says Noel, 'In the sixties, Haight-Ashbury was classified as *the* hippy area and everyone who hung out there had long hair, wore brightly coloured clothes and, of course, smoked dope.When I went there in 1967 it was a bit grotty but the hippy thing was really getting started. It's a great area – all restaurants and little bars.

'But it was a grand atmosphere. Everyone was having a wonderful time and there was never any bother. The police were walking about and they weren't bustin' anybody. People were openly smoking and obviously taking LSD but the cops were very laid back about it all. But then, that's the whole thing about 'Frisco. It's a very laid-back place. In 1967, though, you had to be careful there in one sense. If you went into a bar, when you weren't looking somebody would throw a tablet of LSD into your beer.' The LSD, obtained knowingly in Noel's case, came from a character called Owsley, who assumed a semi-legendary status.

Noel Redding explains, 'Owsley was a professor of chemistry. He came from a very well-to-do family and he was a brilliant chemist who used to make LSD. He used to make special stuff and give it to special people – the Beatles, the Stones, the Hendrix Experience. He got busted at the end of the day but he wasn't a nasty person and he wasn't doing it for money. It's just that he knew how to make it. I think Owsley did a bit of time. But as I say, he did not make LSD for profit. He did it because he was hanging out with rock and roll stars.'

During that visit Paul Simon obtained LSD. By now, of those in the music scene who were interested in the drug, few would own up to not yet having tried it. Indeed, at that time there was almost a climate in which one came close to being odd if one didn't experiment with drugs. The influence was everywhere.

Once back in his New York apartment, Paul picked the early hours of one morning to take the tablet. It was several hours before he came out of the trip, some stretches of which had clearly been frightening. Simon later spoke openly of how he had tried to apply his normally reliable grasp of logic to rationalise why he felt that something was seriously messing with his head, but it didn't always work. Simon had been half intrigued by, and half concerned at, the thought of losing control – not a natural state for him. But he had believed it would be worth the experience. Now he had discovered that on this first occasion, very little of the mind-blowing trip had felt good, nor had he enjoyed the hoped-for moments of clarity. Disappointingly, there had been no burst of astonishing insight into life's colour and complexities. All in all he must have felt short-changed. He was certainly left emotionally and physically drained by the acid trip. He repeated the experiment with future trips, however, still seeking the promised sensation.

Paul Simon had been used to keeping his drug indulgence (which thus far had been restricted to smoking pot) under wraps by surreptitiously puffing away in the confines of a hotel room on tour, making sure that no incriminating smell wafted out into corridors and led to his being busted. He would keep his trials of LSD equally private.

Later he publicly recounted these experiences and his ultimate disappointment with the stuff. With hindsight, he frankly deemed it 'stupid behaviour', particularly because, as he also acknowledged, the cost can often be your health.

Paranoia was a commonplace consequence of taking LSD, often leading to depression. Paul suffered frequent bouts and worried that, far from gaining a short cut to increased creativity, he might lose the ability to write songs altogether without the stimulus of drugs. If that had happened, it would have been a high price indeed for experimentation.

Paul Simon was always in command of how he used the substance. But it is true that he felt himself retreating into a sometimes troubled world. He confessed that he was for a substantial time during this whole period, 'as stoned as anyone'. He was never stoned, however, in performance or in the recording studio.

Paul's main reason for going to California during spring 1967 was that he had become involved in organising an event that would put down a marker in pop music history.

The first international open-air pop festival was to be held in mid-June at the County Fairgrounds in Monterey, California. The three-day event was to be filmed by D.A. Pennebaker for the movie *Monterey Pop.* The brainchild of a collection of music industry people, it had originally been conceived as a business proposition. But the idea rapidly developed and changed, until soon the showcase for artistes, both established and new, was envisaged as a project that could raise money for charities.

John Phillips, from The Mamas and The Papas, was approached and asked if the group would headline the event. Phillips, in fact, took a prominent role in planning the project and he roped in the band's manager Lou Adler, who was also a record producer and owned the new Dunhill label. He approved of the charity idea and together a group of interested parties bought out the one man who remained in favour of it being a business venture.

In 1966 Simon and Garfunkel had once played support to The Mamas and The Papas and had since remained friendly with the group. Paul and Art agreed to join Phillips, Adler and a couple of others in putting up a sum, said to have been $10,000 each, to finance the festival, monies to be repaid from the profits. To run the growing project, a steering committee was set up which read like a Who's Who of rock and included the likes of Paul Simon, Paul McCartney and Brian Wilson.

For his part, Simon devoted much time to promoting the event. It was at his personal persuasion that the Grateful Dead agreed to appear. They joined the Who, the Jimi Hendrix Experience, Jefferson Airplane, the Indian sitar player Ravi Shankar, Otis Redding and Janis Joplin. Simon and Garfunkel were to close the show on opening night.

Thousands were expected to flock to the event, which began on 16 June 1967. To facilitate a general spirit of love and harmony John Phillips had written a song called 'San Francisco (Be Sure To Wear Some Flowers In Your Hair)' which he passed to singer Scott McKenzie, once part, with Phillips, of a folk trio called the Journeymen. Scott McKenzie had a number 4 hit with the song, which came to epitomise this fabled period in 1960s culture.

The County Fairgrounds were overrun as upwards of 70,000 young people arrived by every available means of transport. The stars likewise began to show up. The hippy bivouacs, colourful stalls and quickly erected sideshows all added excitement to the general camaraderie.

Noel Redding recalls, 'It was amazing to walk around and see all these stars everywhere. Booker T and the MGs, Otis Redding and, of course, Brian Jones who had travelled over to the States with Jimi and me. It was an incredible weekend. The performances started in the mid-afternoon and carried on until 10 o'clock only, because in those days there were curfews imposed on events.'

Simon and Garfunkel closed Friday night's proceedings with a set that blended some new material with standards 'Homeward Bound', 'The Sound of Silence' and of course, 'Feelin' Groovy'. Noel Redding recalls, 'I watched Simon and Garfunkel from backstage. It was the first time I'd seen them and I thought they were excellent. Set against bands like the Hendrix Experience, Janis Joplin and the Who, yeah Simon and Garfunkel was a different act. But it was a great situation. Everyone went down well at Monterey. But they went down *extremely* well. And that was the first night, which is a pretty hard gig to do.'

Otis Redding was the closing act on Saturday. And Jefferson Airplane had delivered a passionate performance that evening, too. But for anyone taking stock of the upcoming talent the one to watch was the brash and powerful Texan-born singer Janis Joplin who, fronting the blues band Big Brother and the Holding Company, gave a show-stopping performance.

Sunday's show on 18 June, ended with the headliners The Mamas and The Papas. They faced a crowd that had been left breathless by the American live stage debut of the Jimi Hendrix Experience. In addition to Hendrix and Redding this band featured drummer Mitch Mitchell. Their debut album *Are You Experienced?* was held off the top slot in Britain only by the Beatles' watershed album *Sgt. Pepper's Lonely Hearts Club Band* and Hendrix's wild-man image usually spilled over into outrageous stage antics.

At Monterey he played his electric guitar at one point with his teeth, before dousing the instrument with lighter fuel and setting it ablaze in front of the astonished crowd. Noel Redding remembers, 'It was my first gig in America, at 21 and in front of 70,000 people. It was quite a freak out. We did 45 minutes and we went on after the Who. That was a hard job, but it was a great gig. We worked our asses off – it was an incredible feeling.'

The memorable Monterey International Pop Festival was also a financial success. Paul Simon was pleased when the hoped-for profits meant that charities benefited as planned, including those schemes which set up music workshops for would-be musicians living in deprived inner-city areas. Simon later told *Mojo*, 'They gave me $50,000 to start a little guitar programme in Harlem which gives guitars away to kids.'

After that electrifying weekend, Simon moved back into the recording studio. Soon afterwards, the single 'Fakin' It'/'You Don't Know Where Your Interest Lies' was released. It did not quite connect, however, and pulled up in August at number 23 in America. Simon's mind, though, was elsewhere. He needed time to write material for another album. It was hard going, but in the next few months the duo laid down a couple of new tracks. They also took time out to appear for the second time that year on US network television as guests of the hugely popular *The Smothers Brothers Comedy Hour.*

It was always smart to maintain a regular public profile. But the most interesting development to come Paul Simon's way in the last quarter of 1967 was when he was approached by Mike Nichols to write a music score for his latest movie.

The 36-year-old Berlin-born stage and film director, whose later credits were to include *Postcards From The Edge* and *Primary Colors,* had, in 1966, already earned an Oscar nomination for his work on the Richard Burton/Elizabeth Taylor acclaimed classic *Who's Afraid Of Virginia Woolf?*

Nichols's new project was *The Graduate.* From a screenplay by Calder Willingham and Buck Henry, based on the Charles Webb novel, the movie starred Anne Bancroft and Katharine Ross, with actor Dustin Hoffman appearing in his first major screen role. The fast-paced sex comedy told the story of a naive graduate who is seduced by Mrs Robinson, the glamorous wife of a family friend, only for him to fall in love with the older woman's daughter. Such a film about contemporary youth needed a sympathetic musical soundtrack and Mike Nichols was convinced that Paul Simon fitted the bill. Simon himself was initially less convinced. On reading the novel he had not exactly been swept away, but after long consideration, he agreed to write the score.

Problems, however, began to pile up. Not least because Simon already had a heavy commitment writing songs for the duo's next album, which had to be carried out while they were continuing to play some live gigs. His impetus for the film score slightly wobbled when two numbers he did come up with, 'Overs' and 'Punky's Dilemma', were turned down. Simon found that little buzz was to be had from the experience of working in this potentially exciting new medium. He had assumed that the recording facilities in film sound stages would be vastly superior to those in his regular environment of the record studio – they were not.

Neither was he happy at the pressure being placed on his output for the film score. The filmmakers, with their own deadlines to meet, had no choice but to apply this pressure, but it was not something Simon had ever appreciated. The success he and Art Garfunkel had recently achieved had permitted them more slack when it came to making albums. So it was doubly unwelcome to the songwriter now to have anyone breathing down his neck.

The record company at least were in a win-win situation. They eagerly awaited Simon and Garfunkel's next offering and they accepted the encroachment on time that was being placed on this new album by the forthcoming film soundtrack work – such tie-ins usually made a mint. For Simon, though, work on the two projects sometimes conflicted. Faced with delays in receiving material from Simon, Mike Nichols – appreciative of the fact that it was stressful for both sides – had to rethink as time moved on and he still did not have the necessary songs from Paul. He began to sift Simon's existing catalogue of material to see if there was anything he could use. At this stage, he probably anticipated replacing any existing tracks he did select with Simon's new compositions as they became available. He chose 'The Sound of Silence', 'Scarborough Fair/Canticle', 'April Come She Will' and 'The Big Bright Green Pleasure Machine'.

Nichols also enlisted the services of experienced musician Dave Grusin to provide some incidental music. The looked-for replacement Paul Simon tracks for one reason or another were not forthcoming. And the more the editing process on the film evolved, the more the director saw that his choices from existing material worked.

It certainly eased tension. But the director was adamant that he had to have at least one brand-new Paul Simon composition for the film score. Nichols came to yet another Simon and Garfunkel recording studio session to check on progress, desperate for a chink of light.

When Garfunkel suggested that Paul let Mike hear the song 'Mrs Robinson' (the name of the film's female central character) the director launched himself to his feet shouting, 'Do you mean to tell me that you have a song called 'Mrs Robinson' and you haven't told me?' When the director calmed down and listened to the track he was blown away. It was a strong, upbeat driving number. Moreover, as Mark Kriegal for the *New York Daily News* would later state, 'Mrs Robinson' contained some of the best-known lines ever in American popular music.

The lyrics in question come mid-way through the song when Simon poignantly ponders just where wholesome, decent, respected heroes like baseball legend Joe DiMaggio have vanished to in today's less civilised world. With Simon's lifelong passion for baseball it was easy to assume that he had been looking for a sporting metaphor when coming up with these lyrics, but that was not the case.

Thirty years on Paul revealed that he still has no idea where those two famous lines came from. He has concluded that rather than racking his brains to come up with something inspirational, that thought, in those words, actually found him and he knew instantly it was right. He said, 'It made the song feel like it was about a larger subject.' While the song and those lyrics caught the collective imagination of millions, in differing degrees it upset two baseball legends.

Simon's baseball hero was still Mickey Mantle, who later took the songwriter aside backstage at a live US chat show and asked Paul point-blank why he hadn't referred to him in the song instead of Joe DiMaggio. Paul patiently explained that it all came down to syllables and Mantle was mollified. But the other baseball giant was in more militant mood – at least for a while.

It has been reported (and Paul Simon himself has, over the years, referred to this) that Joe DiMaggio considered suing the celebrated songwriter over these lyrics thinking that he was being made fun of. Joe DiMaggio must have been the only person in the world to fail to understand that it was one great big glowing tribute to him. But Paul Simon disliked the idea that the sportsman felt upset and when an opportunity arose to clear up the misunderstanding he took it. Sitting in a swish Central Park restaurant he spotted Joe DiMaggio across the room and went to join him, explaining that he was the man who had written 'Mrs Robinson'. DiMaggio invited Simon to sit down and explain the lyrics to him.

The Graduate opened in New York City and Los Angeles in December 1967 before going on general cinema release the following March. It was a box office triumph. 'In terms of sheer connection with us, *The Graduate* is a milestone in American film history,' wrote critic Stanley Kauffmann. Its soundtrack also catapulted Paul Simon's standing as a lyricist, and Simon and Garfunkel as artistes, into a new hemisphere. This was one of the first major movies to incorporate a rock soundtrack. The album, released in spring 1968, grabbed pole position in the States, as well as number 3 in Britain months later when the film opened there.

The soundtrack album was instantly certified gold, just before the newly released single 'Scarborough Fair/Canticle'/ 'April Come She Will' peaked at number 11 in the US charts. The single 'Mrs Robinson'/ 'Old Friends/Bookends' hit number 1 in America during the summer and was to peak at number 4 in Britain, thus restoring Simon and Garfunkel to the British singles charts. Later, in December, and only in the UK, 'Mrs Robinson' was released again, this time as the lead track in an EP along with 'April Come She Will', 'Scarborough Fair/Canticle' and 'The Sound of Silence'. By February 1969 it peaked at number 9.

Nevertheless, back in late spring 1968, amid the plaudits over *The Graduate*'s success, Paul Simon was preoccupied with the performance of the soon-to-be-released new Simon and Garfunkel album. It had always been his main priority. Called *Bookends*, its first side was a concept song cycle in that the theme of the tracks ranged from youthfulness through to old age. The second side contained released singles.

Much more attention this time had been paid to applying advanced studio techniques that enhanced the end product. Paul was proud that he and Art were among the forerunners of recording artistes who were exploring the use of multi-tracking vocals. He called it recording by layers.

Released in America in May, followed about two months later with release in the UK, *Bookends* was the first album to give Simon and Garfunkel a dual number 1 hit on both sides of the Atlantic. In the States it took over at the top from *The Graduate* soundtrack album and enjoyed a seven-week run, which meant that for approximately four months solid the number 1 album in America was a Simon and Garfunkel product. *Bookends* was no slouch in Britain either, hogging the top slot for five weeks.

After years of acknowledging Simon's penchant for writing about introspection and alienation, critics seemed to view *Bookends* as different. Yet Simon's observation of human nature and a strain of pessimism were still there.

Following the opener 'Bookends Theme', came 'Save The Life Of My Child' – a caustic tale of a window-ledge suicide jumper, but seen through the eyes of the assembled crowd below as they witnessed the drama unfold. The song's electronically discordant first note acts like a wake-up call and the harsh enunciation of lyrics that seem to spit out the story makes for intentionally uncomfortable listening.

Just before side one's poignantly reflective last track 'Old Friends/Bookends', 'Voices of Old People' makes perhaps the oddest addition to any album. In an attempt to snag an insight into the sentiments of life's senior citizens, Art Garfunkel had tape-recorded conversations between old people. Sometimes he had surreptitiously walked about public parks with a concealed microphone; other times he openly recorded the elderly discussing life. Not unnaturally, it lent a certain voyeuristic tinge.

In tandem with the fuller version of 'Mrs Robinson' on side two, the album's most famous track was 'America'. This number racked up another all-time Paul Simon classic. Not just a unique love song, the lyrics somehow correlated a man's deep-down inner emptiness, with a comment on the state of America's social fabric.

Professor Iwan Morgan says, 'Many of Paul Simon's 1960s' songs have a sense of alienation and loss of identity with the values that American kids had been taught to respect. 'America' is the best example of this – where the singer goes off in search of America but is aching, lost and empty and does not know why.

'For the college-educated segment of the 1960s generation this was the result of their alienation from their parents' values of material gain, personal advancement in the workplace and a hierarchically structured society. I have always felt that Simon was trying to say something about age in many of his songs – a peculiar preoccupation for a minstrel of the youth generation. A number of songs on *Bookends* suggest this.'

Bookends, which also used the two songs previously rejected as soundtrack material for *The Graduate*, was the first Simon and Garfunkel album in 20 months, an eternity in the record business. But even as the album's commercial success was complemented by critical acclaim, it was not without its down side. Simon had had reservations about the wisdom of releasing *Bookends* hard on the heels of *The Graduate* soundtrack, since the risk of diluting potential sales was obvious. On top of that he had deemed (wrongly as it turned out) that Columbia Records' decision to stick an extra dollar on the price of *Bookends* would handicap sales.

Columbia Records had included a giant poster with each album and they were also implementing a new policy of experimenting with variable pricing. But both Simon and Garfunkel had disliked the higher price mark. Even though the album was a runaway success, it marked the start of a strain in Paul's relations with the record company.

Following the launch of *Bookends* in Britain, Simon and Garfunkel arrived there in July to play some sell-out gigs. It was their second UK tour of the year – they had carried out a short regional tour in March. This time the gigs included triumphant nights at London's Albert Hall. As summer 1968 rolled on, previous Simon and Garfunkel albums hitched a lift on the explosion in the duo's popularity. A re-released *Parsley, Sage, Rosemary and*

Thyme made it to number 13 in the UK album charts. And, belatedly, their debut *Wednesday Morning, 3 AM* was finally issued in Britain and reached number 24.

Gigging continued on their return to the States with an appearance in late August at the prestigious Hollywood Bowl in California. Two months later, the duo returned to their old Queens stomping ground as heroes when they performed at the packed-out Forest Hills Stadium.

By this time, certain aspects of Paul Simon's personal world spilled over into his professional one. It was scarcely surprising. For a man for whom politics is important, 1968 was a vital year as November heralded the presidential election after months of rigorous campaigning by the candidates.

Throughout 1967 and into 1968 there had been growing anti-war activism as the Vietnam conflict worsened. This had led to a tumultuous political campaign in what was anyway a crisis year in many respects. America was a tinderbox. On 5 April the civil rights leader Dr Martin Luther King was shot dead in Memphis, Tennessee by a white rifleman who got away. In grief and rage, militant black Americans rioted in the streets and mob violence spread to so many other cities that civil unrest seemed endemic. Tension was already at breaking point when the Democratic Party lost its best hope. Exactly two months after King's murder, Senator Robert Kennedy (JFK's brother) was ambushed leaving a Los Angeles hotel and shot dead by a young Palestinian, Sirhan Sirhan.

The Democratic Party Convention in Chicago at the end of August was another powder keg. Brutal police tactics were plastered all over the nation's television screens when cops wielding batons beat anti-war protesters outside the venue, leaving several hundred hurt.

John Lennon is probably the pop star most associated with taking an overt political stance against the Republican presidential candidate Richard Nixon. But Paul Simon's intense dislike and distrust of Nixon and his running mate Spiro Agnew led the songwriter to make his contempt public knowledge when, from the stage at Forest Hills Stadium, he referred to Agnew, the soon to be disgraced politician, as an idiot.

Simon and Garfunkel also took part in a benefit gig for the Peace Candidates in October at the giant Shea Stadium in New York. Top acts were included on the bill, but alas poor organisation in publicising the event let it down and Simon was disappointed when the stadium turned out to be less than half full.

Disappointment, however, could not compare with the devastation Paul Simon experienced when on 6 November 1968 Richard Milhous Nixon became America's President. Simon was aghast as he watched the election coverage climax on television. His intrinsic distrust of Nixon would, of course, prove to be justified when the Watergate scandal exposed and brought him crashing down in the 1970s. But right then, in 1968, the new incoming Republican regime hammered one more nail into the coffin of the dying decade.

Dr Stephen Perrin, a specialist in the 1960s/1970s counterculture understands Paul Simon's despair, which mirrored that of so many of his peers. Says Dr Perrin, 'Basically, in 1968 Lyndon Johnson decided he was not going to stand for re-election. So the Democrats put up Hubert Humphrey who refused to take a stand against the war. Because of this, the young protesters were outraged.

'Obviously they couldn't vote for the Republicans – they were always right wing and pro-war. But they felt that they couldn't vote for the Democrats because their candidate would not come out against the war. The Chicago Democratic Convention then was a complete debacle. And effectively what happened was that the student protesters decided that they could not vote at all. Richard Nixon therefore sneaked in with a very small majority, which was very likely as a direct result of people not voting.

'It was like all this youthful optimism, the campaigning and so on, had gone completely the wrong way. The result of it had been Nixon and Agnew. Part of the problem too had stemmed from disillusionment with the system.

'Some had even tried sending up the system. The American radical Jerry Rubin leader of the revolutionary yippes (the Youth International Party) had tried to run a pig for President called Pigasus because they felt that they couldn't trust Hubert Humphrey.

'People were left not knowing what to do. The result ended up as increased bombing of Vietnam. The sixties' counterculture had pretty much become moribund. People still knew what they wanted. They just didn't know how to achieve it.' Gloom, with the new incumbent ready to take office in the White House, greeted the New Year's arrival.

Politics aside, come March 1969, Simon and Garfunkel's work received its highest public recognition yet when at the 11th annual Grammy Awards ceremony, held in Los Angeles, 'Mrs Robinson' won the trophy as Record of The Year, as well as the Award as the Best Contemporary Pop Performance Vocal by a Duo or Group. Candidly, Paul expressed his surprise at the honour. One of the other nominated singles, the Beatles' 'Hey Jude', had been, in his view, the record of 1968. Nevertheless he was pleased with the prizes. The 27-year-old star then added to the haul when *The Graduate* soundtrack album picked off the Grammy for Best Original Score Written for A Motion Picture or a TV Special.

Away from the glow of public acclaim, life at this juncture for Simon was a mixed bag. Financially he was clearly now fixed for life. He lived in a desirable part of New York and had not lacked the opportunity to form personal relationships. He was young, eligible and, although he had resisted the trend to grow his hair long, he sported a natty beard, which stretched like a chinstrap from sideburn to sideburn. For a time he had dated Denise Kaufman, formerly the girlfriend of *Rolling Stone* founder/editor Jann Wenner. In due course he was to become romantically involved with an acquaintance named Peggy Harper.

Marriage though till now had not particularly entered his mind. As a very wealthy young man, advisors around him had tried to point out the advantages in him getting wed. Typically, Simon had not been slow to counter with the unromantic but highly realistic consideration that it can equally all get messy if the union goes awry. In any event, he was in no hurry to tie the knot. He still had to work through a few demons, which could do without the pressure of making a full-time emotional commitment to a wife.

Despite basking in the great glow of *Bookends*, a part of Simon managed to glimpse a down side. It *is* possible to become a victim of one's own success, and it was in Simon to want to use the latitude that success ought to have given him to experiment with diversifying musically. But instead, he felt locked into a genre in which he was expected not only to repeat his last performance, but also forever to outdo it.

Tangled up in all of this, an old resentment had begun to seep to the surface. Because of the PR fudge when Simon and Garfunkel had first come to the fore, with regard to who did what in the partnership, Paul felt that there was not a clear enough understanding even now among the public of the fact that it was he who wrote both the words and music for the duo's hit songs.

Simon later stated that he believed that because Art could, and often did, look the more confident, the less worried, of the two that that aura of confidence made people assume that Garfunkel must be the more talented member. That was Simon's assumption and it was enough to reignite a slow-burning fuse.

There was also another bone of contention. In spring 1968 director Mike Nichols's new project was the film *Catch 22*, to be based upon the Joseph Heller novel of the same name. Garfunkel had been asked to consider making his professional acting debut by playing a significant role in the intense black comedy about services life in World War II.

Paul had also been invited to take the smaller role of Dunbar and like Art, he had eagerly accepted, after reading one of the film's preliminary script outlines. However, as the project passed through the various development stages for budget considerations, certain characters were culled. One of those was Dunbar.

Paul was upset and the fact that Garfunkel's role survived led to an air of tension. It is slightly ironic that Paul should have felt the way he did. As a 16-year-old he had gone ahead with pursuing a solo career, leaving Garfunkel who'd thought of them as being partners at the time, feeling hurt. Now, 11 years on, Garfunkel's decision to go ahead with the film role – to pursue a separate path for a while – left Simon alone.

Principal filming for *Catch 22* started in January 1969 and was expected to take three months. Art's acting commitment would unavoidably make a serious dent in the time he had available to collaborate with Paul on new recordings. He had not abandoned their recording career, but right then his priorities were different. Paul's allegiance remained firmly with music and he had already started to create the songs that would form an album to eclipse all of their work to date.

Bookends' sleeve had featured a shot of the two famous faces tilted together in a friendly fashion. But the reality was that their professional closeness would soon be at an end.

CHAPTER 8

All Things Must Pass

FOLLOWING THE 1969 GRAMMY AWARD CEREMONY, Art Garfunkel immediately returned to location shooting in Mexico for *Catch 22*. Soon afterwards, Paul Simon enjoyed the honour of throwing out the first ball at the packed Yankee Stadium in the Bronx, New York on the opening day of the season in April. Hopes were high for a good new season for Simon's favourite baseball team, but his own road stretching ahead looked to be fraught with difficulty.

The original time frame for filming *Catch 22* had been three months. But not unusually this had had to be doubled. Songs had to be written and recorded for the next Simon and Garfunkel album, but Garfunkel would be primarily tied up with his acting commitments until way into the summer. As Paul put it, psychologically he was not comfortable with their recording career ranking second in importance to Art's film work.

Simon did publicly stress that his partner was keen to make a new album. It was true though that Art's film interests were very strong. Both men had their own perspectives. But when one is working full-time on a project while the other party only flits in and out, it is a recipe for serious discord.

Already feeling that he did more than his fair share in their musical partnership, Paul was faced with a colossal workload to produce the new material virtually alone. This often darkened his mood in the coming months.

It was a very human dilemma for Paul Simon. He *wanted* to be the sole songwriter and to write the music – even if the fact that his work was not sufficiently acknowledged irked him. And he knew full well that his material was the main reason for Simon and Garfunkel's success, regardless of how Garfunkel's input in the studio subsequently enhanced the songs and melodies. Nevertheless, he frankly disliked being left to get on with it alone.

Two new songs had already come together and were released as a single in April 1969. 'The Boxer'/'Baby Driver' soon peaked at number 7 in America, while managing one place higher in Britain. 'The Boxer' had evolved over time – Simon had started work on the enigmatic number the previous November – and some say that it is Paul Simon's best song.

Renowned lyricist Sir Tim Rice declares, 'Paul Simon is top flight, no question. He's one of the very best songwriters of his time. You've only got to listen to him. There are plenty of songs to choose from, but I think 'The Boxer' is my favourite song. That's the one I *really* like more than all the others.

'It's very hard to analyse where a songwriter's strength lies. Paul Simon writes songs that usually say what a lot of people think, but he articulates it better than most. And of course, he sticks a great tune to it usually. His melodies aren't half bad! I wouldn't say he's the world's greatest singer although he's got a very good voice on record. But that doesn't matter really. It's like Bob Dylan. It's the way Paul interprets that counts.'

'The Boxer' is a complex composition. In places it is clearly autobiographical, when he recalls the routine loneliness of waiting around at train stations. But what is more intriguing than his glancing references to his wandering minstrel days, is the emergent strain in the lyrics which gives a personal glimpse into his state of mind.

Simon seems to say that having come through turbulent

emotional times, he is left standing more resolute – bloodied but unbowed would be too clichéd. Rather it's that, having worked off stored-up resentments, he has come through ready to move on – but alone. This implied 'warning' that he was thinking of going solo would permeate more songs on the forthcoming album. 'The Boxer'/'Baby Driver' was Simon and Garfunkel's only release of 1969. The other songs were still in the works.

As summer arrived Paul ploughed ahead and the pattern of work turned out much as he had suspected. He concentrated on developing songs, working in the studio with a group of assembled new musicians, and waited for opportunities to familiarise Art Garfunkel with the material when his busy schedule permitted. It could not have been an easy situation for either man. Garfunkel's screen commitments meant that he could only snatch time to link up with Paul. He undoubtedly gave his all to the work when they were together, but to do so he had to make some deft mental switches. Fresh from the film set, with his head swirling with all that carrying off his acting role entailed, it must have been difficult to downshift from that exciting fantasy world and lock in at the required level with Simon's newly written material. And all of this often happened in bursts of only a few days' duration.

For Paul, these songs had been his entire professional focus on a daily basis so it is easy to imagine how a defensive possessiveness could creep in at any hint of a challenge to them from a 'visiting' partner. But in mid-1969 managing to cope with this situation was not Simon's only pressure.

After all these years he chose now to come off drugs altogether. It took a great deal of willpower, particularly as he feared that his songwriting ability could suffer or desert him altogether without drugs. To shore up his willpower and help him make the necessary adjustments Paul turned to analysis. Americans' preoccupation with psychiatric analysis was to explode in the coming years, but even in the late 1960s it was not uncommon for celebrities to visit a therapist regularly.

Simon started seeing his therapist several times a week. He

had acquaintances in therapy who were making a mockery of their efforts by continuing to take drugs while seeking professional help. The biggest help to Paul was his own attitude: he said, 'I *wanted* to stop and I took that as a good enough reason.'

Reflecting on this cold turkey period, Simon admitted that he retreated even more into himself. He explained how he had been determined to end the cycle that he had often endured, when he had plunged from giddy highs to dark, depressing depths that inevitably had left him in a mental turmoil.

Never one to do things by halves, in the midst of a heavy work schedule and while making important life changes, Paul also became deeply involved with a woman slightly older than he was.

Peggy Harper was a vibrant Southern beauty, originally from Tennessee, who had been among Paul's inner circle of friends for years. He was comfortable in her company and she had been on the periphery of the music industry long enough to recognise and appreciate the special stresses and strains involved in that world.

Peggy was married. Subtly, and probably slowly, the friendship between Paul and Peggy had been altering and reshaping itself into a romance that eventually became a full-blown love affair. So much so, that around July, when Simon rented accommodation on Blue Jay Way in Los Angeles, Peggy went to live with him.

Paul's move to LA came because *Catch 22* was now being filmed in California. Garfunkel could now leave the set at the end of a day's shooting and join Paul and Peggy at their house. He made his home base with them, which made exploiting Art's free time to the hilt much easier for Paul.

Simon turned part of the house into a den of musical instruments – a work place kitted with some home recording equipment. And when they were all together for workout sessions, some songs came off spontaneously, raising enjoyment levels considerably. Even so, Paul Simon dubbed the new album in the works as a Simon and Garfunkel record that 'wasn't really'

– essentially because it was still proving necessary to work separately much of the time.

In doing the lion's share of the work, Paul had now to make decisions by himself which he and Art had once chewed over together. Part of Paul didn't mind that, but it didn't stop the fault lines in this working environment from widening further when the time arrived to start recording the new songs.

Paul had been rehearsing for some time with the session musicians who were to feature on the album. They were Hal Blaine on drums, Joe Osborn playing bass, with Fred Carter Junior joining Simon on guitar. The strings came courtesy of Jimmy Haskell and Ernie Freeman, while Larry Knechtel took charge of keyboard duties. The constant rehearsals had honed the session team into a tight unit. That was true, too, of the blend between the session team and Paul Simon. But between Art and Paul tension arose almost from the moment they entered the studio and bickering began.

Inevitably there were two ways of looking at it. On the one hand, it was entirely natural that Paul, having been so much in command of this album's material, found it extremely hard to relinquish even part control over how it would finally appear on record.

Equally, this was to be a Simon and Garfunkel product on which Art was entitled to make suggestions regarding aspects of the material and how it ought to be developed. The experience of acting in a movie, trying though it had proved to be in terms of putting an album together at the same time, had probably given Garfunkel extra self-confidence. At any rate, he was not slow to put his case.

Paul Simon did not want to defer to anyone else. He later admitted that he had found it hard to take criticism, and the last thing he was prepared to do was to almost audition his songs, hoping that approval would be forthcoming. In all, more than 800 recording hours went into completing this album under these conditions. What was more, it was not uninterrupted time even when Garfunkel had completed work on *Catch 22*.

Despite the existing workload, the duo had also agreed to make their first television special. In September recording the album was suspended for work to commence on a one-hour programme called *Songs For America.* If they had thought that a break from the album would alleviate stress levels, the notion was soon dashed.

The duo were not, however, to butt heads with each other; their argument was with the TV special sponsor AT&T. The communications company had envisaged 60 minutes of magic material delivered to perfection by two hugely popular, polished performers. Paul and Art saw the special differently. AT&T wanted a show that said 'America' and they imagined a warm, tuneful, family-friendly show. What they got was an unvarnished look at the USA at that time and it made for uncommonly frank viewing. America had been changing as the decade died, and the looming 1970s presented a lot of problems.

1960s/1970s counterculture specialist Dr Stephen Perrin explains, 'In 1967 you'd had Scott McKenzie singing about people coming to San Francisco wearing flowers in their hair. But then the original hippies moved out of Haight-Ashbury and the mafia moved in and controlled the drug supply. They caused an LSD famine and flooded the place with speed and heroin. So where we had the flower children before, we now had a bunch of very strung-out people.

'In 1969 came the Charles Manson murders. All of the associations of the young people had gone. Even if the mainstream population had not agreed with the hippy students' messages of love and peace, still they could see the point of it and they had not considered these people to be a terrible threat.

'On top of the horrific Manson murders, the Rolling Stones' Altamont concert went hideously wrong. And it turned the whole hippy thing on its head. Suddenly you couldn't even hitch hike anymore. Paul Simon had written about young people going off to look for America. Before they could have done that and been picked up easily, but the murders ended that overnight. Now nobody would pick up anyone with long hair for fear that they were a murderer or a psychopath in the Manson mould. It all got very dark, very fast.'

Acutely aware of that darkness and the state of the country under the Republican regime, Paul Simon was passionate about exactly what the TV special ought to say about his country. Art Garfunkel was in agreement. And so the programme they put together included footage of the violent fall-out from Martin Luther King's murder. It covered Robert Kennedy's assassination with scenes of his funeral cortege. The hounded Lenny Bruce featured, as did pictures of injured victims of the Vietnam War. In all it delivered a blistering attack on the Nixon/Agnew political administration and sent out a defiant anti-war message.

It was brave, unorthodox and controversial and when unsuspecting AT&T executives gathered to enjoy a private screening before its scheduled transmission on 30 November 1969, they froze in their seats within minutes. Deeply alarmed at the political content, they requested Simon and Garfunkel to tone it down. Paul and Art refused. A short, tense stand-off ensued but the duo would not alter their position and in the end the two sides went their separate ways.

The stars immediately looked to CBS who rapidly found another sponsor, allowing *Songs For America* to go on the air as planned. Standing their ground had been a point of principle, but there is little doubt that Simon and Garfunkel could have done without the added tension it created, especially as they were booked to tour America in October.

Needless to say, these were not the best circumstances in which to hit the road. Both were tense, tired and consequently short-tempered. Paul Simon admitted that it was obvious that a head of steam was building. There was no spectacular bust up, but there was a continual underlying antagonism between them, which was hard to pin down. They also faced a return to complete the album, the creation of which had already assumed mammoth proportions. When the tour ended, after two nights at New York's

Carnegie Hall, they ventured back into the studio in early January 1970.

By now two significant things had happened. In late autumn 1969 Paul had married Peggy Harper after she and her husband had been divorced. She was very supportive of Paul's ambitions to draw a line under Simon and Garfunkel and go it alone. Then Art Garfunkel had his own news to impart, announcing that before the year's end he had agreed to work with Mike Nichols on a new film called *Carnal Knowledge*. This role would be more prominent than his first, so more time-consuming, and shooting would begin in May 1970.

Despite all that was happening, early in the new year the two got to work in the studio and the short time left was spent finalising matters. By the end things were so fraught that their threadbare patience had almost run out. Both had had enough and needed to step back. Paul declared years later, 'In my mind I said "That's the end".'

The true strained state of the working relationship between these famous figures would not be known for a long time. All the public knew was that in February 1970 Simon and Garfunkel launched their masterpiece, *Bridge Over Troubled Water*, on the music world.

The title song was released first. In Britain 'Bridge Over Troubled Water'/'Keep The Customer Satisfied' entered the chart at number 2 initially but then mercifully dislodged Lee Marvin's 'Wand'rin' Star' from the top. In America, the single entered at number 9, only to rocket to number 1 also, giving Simon and Garfunkel pole position on the singles charts on both sides of the Atlantic. The song, which Simon had recognised instantly as being very special, was to have astounding longevity. Covered by hundreds of artistes over the years, including Paul's hero Elvis Presley, the song and its parent album made an enormous impact.

'Bridge Over Troubled Water', a song about the redemptive power of healing, is a masterpiece in its own right, in which Paul Simon delves into the hearts and souls of the abandoned and the lonely. The combination of lyrics that offer unqualified selfless devotion with Art Garfunkel's angelic soaring tones and a gospel-flavoured solo piano accompaniment never fails to connect. Towards the end of the four-minute, 52-second song its simple, solemn sound builds to a crashing crescendo in a way that was influenced by Phil Spector's famous 'wall of sound'. But its beauty had already by then been captured by a piano accompaniment that had taken four dogged days to work out.

The song had originally been written with only two verses. In the studio it became obvious, however, that a third was required, so Paul composed the final verse separately there and then. Consequently, he never quite saw it as fitting seamlessly with the rest.

Simon wrote 'Bridge' on guitar in the key of G, which, for Art to sing it, had to be transposed into E flat. Arranger Jimmy Haskell did the honours and later picked up a Grammy Award for doing so.

The vital piano work was entrusted to multi-instrumentalist Larry Knechtel, a much sought-after Los Angeles session musician. Knechtel's patience and skill with the piano accompaniment for 'Bridge Over Troubled Water' crowned Simon's lyrical achievement. But during those four days, unused to handing over the baton, Paul restlessly paced the recording studio control room floor, itching to find out what the experienced pianist was doing with the song.

According to Simon, Garfunkel had not instantly leapt at the chance to sing solo on 'Bridge' feeling instead that Paul should have done so. Simon revealed that often in the future he wished he had done just that. Certainly the reaction Art received every time he performed this number live, when people cheered, clapped and rose delightedly to their feet, came to be like a burr under the saddle for Simon.

Having left the stage for the number's duration, he would feel sidelined in more than the obvious sense. Paul has not hidden the resentment he felt during those moments, aching as he was for people to acknowledge that the beloved 'Bridge Over Troubled Water' was *his* song.

The album *Bridge Over Troubled Water* hit number 1 in Britain first in mid-February, quickly equalled just over two weeks later in the States. This placed Simon and Garfunkel in an elite corp of recording artistes to have simultaneously topped the American and British singles *and* album charts.

Their string of achievements, however, was only just beginning. *Bridge Over Troubled Water* was to become Britain's top-selling album of the 1970s. Staggeringly, the album topped the British charts for a total of 41 weeks and held a Top 10 position for 126 weeks, far outstripping all rivals. What is more, nearly all the reviews were glowing.

'Bridge Over Troubled Water' still ranks among the all-time favourites for many. Chris de Burgh, whose own songs such as 'Don't Pay The Ferryman' and 'The Lady In Red' have established him as an international songwriter of strength and sensitivity, is happy to nail his colours firmly to the mast with regards to Paul Simon and his work.

Says Chris, 'I've been an enormous Paul Simon fan for many years. He caught my attention when I was at school in the sixties. He's a very literate songwriter who wrote so well about feeling lonesome. I would describe him as a poet who has written so many of the great classic songs of our time.

'As a songwriter, I can look at his work and fully appreciate him. But although it seems odd to say so, Paul Simon hasn't, I believe, been lauded near as much as he should have been. To me, he is in the top three songwriters of all time, alongside Lennon and McCartney.

'I listen to 'Bridge Over Troubled Water' and wonder what was it that inspired the gospel-type background to the writing. I'm not talking gospel, as in black Alabama gospel. In this case I mean the spirituality of Paul's writing. It has a very strong Christian value to it. The song could almost be a national anthem.'

The title song was also the album's opening track and was followed by 'El Condor Pasa', which featured an instrumental backing by the group Los Incas – Paul had been familiar with their work for a few years now. The unusual song, basically sticking with the premise that it is better not to be the one in life left hurting, was an 18th-century Peruvian folk melody to which Simon had written English lyrics.

'Cecilia' next bursts into life. A breezy pop song, it tells of a guy being so unimportant in a woman's life that he is picked up and dropped at a whim. The jaunty number featured virtually no instruments other than rhythmic drumbeats, augmented by hand clapping. Maintaining a high energy level, the penultimate track on side one was 'Keep The Customer Satisfied', the bright, fast pace of which belies the fact that it sees Simon again taking a bite at life.

Essentially, it's about the rigours of a musician on tour, compelled to sing what punters want to hear. Unlike 'Homeward Bound', 'Keep The Customer Satisfied' has an almost rascally element – a feeling of staying just a step ahead of the law. That inference opened the door for the songwriter to conjure up all those nightmare movie scenarios in which middle-America small-town sheriffs can be a law unto themselves and love to run strangers out of town.

'So Long, Frank Lloyd Wright', which closes the first side, appears to refer to the late famous architect. But like 'The Boxer', which opens side two, this track seems laced with a personal double meaning. Lyrics talk of endless hours harmonising together which points more closely to home and to Paul's long-time partnership with Art who himself studied architecture at college. If reference to Garfunkel is meant, it is almost a goodbye – Simon waving Art out of his life with the footnote acknowledgement that he will occasionally miss and think of him.

In track two of side two, the upbeat 'Baby Driver', Simon reverts to a hint of autobiography. The family bass man is a reference to his father Louis Simon, and the picture is established early on in the song of a boy born in winter into a musical household.

The song on *Bridge* most usually assumed to be a direct message to Art Garfunkel is 'The Only Living Boy In New York'. When Paul opened the number by urging Tom to catch his flight to Mexico it was widely interpreted as him encouraging Art (whose early pseudonym had been Tom Graph in their Tom and Jerry days) to go with his blessing and knock 'em dead on the film set of *Catch 22*, the first scenes of which were shot in Mexico. Paul being left behind in New York would also have tied in.

Over the years this inference has stopped at Paul, in song, wishing his partner well with this new dimension in his life. What perhaps has been overlooked is the point midway through the song, when the lyrics go on to mention the one left behind smiling. Is that a twist? Does that mean that he is happy to be left on his own – a state he covets – going solo, for instance?

Likewise, it leads one to wonder if the lines that query whether either party precisely knows where he is at, is a significant pointer to indecision about their professional future. 'The Only Living Boy In New York' is a personal song and could be a window in more than one way on to how Paul Simon was feeling when he wrote it.

Once embarked on this train of thought, it is tempting to look differently, too, at 'Why Don't You Write Me'. With a blatant Everly Brothers influence, the song ostensibly has a guy waiting for his absent girlfriend to remember his existence. But certain lyrics can be interpreted as Simon perhaps feeling abandoned, while his erstwhile partner explores a new life without him. When the lyrics state that even a letter cutting all connections would be welcome, was this a plea for one of them to resolve an unsatisfactory situation?

Asked once to comment on how, in a practical sense, things changed for Simon and Garfunkel while recording *Bridge Over Troubled Water,* Paul pointed out that Art's contribution to 'The Only Living Boy In New York' had been to sing a small amount on the background. And that he had not featured at all on 'Baby Driver'.

'Bye Bye Love', the 1957 Everly Brothers song, was a Simon and Garfunkel live track and therefore full of atmosphere. The album ended with 'Song For The Asking'. If 'The Boxer' at five minutes, eight seconds was the album's longest track, this was its briefest at one minute, 39 seconds. The simple song with its self-effacing lyric was a promise to bend over backwards for someone, even to the point of the singer changing his ways. Was this a final turn around appeal to see if he and his long-time friend couldn't heal what was driving them apart?

With the magnificence of *Bridge Over Troubled Water* and its attendant acclaim, which had only just begun, it's hard to imagine many music stars going to ground at the height of this moment of fame. But Art soon headed off to join the film set of *Carnal Knowledge.* With Mike Nichols at the helm, this study of the sexual obsessions of two men over a span of years starred Jack Nicholson, Candice Bergen and Ann-Margret.

Garfunkel was in experienced company and keen to blossom in this bigger role. His first film, *Catch 22,* opened in June 1970 but did not perform well at the box office. Critics described the plot as 'long', 'laboured' and 'heavy handed'. The actors were credited with having tried their best, but Garfunkel's acting debut was largely unremarked upon. He had higher hopes of *Carnal Knowledge.*

Paul Simon, in the midst of being bombarded with the most lavish praise yet as a lyricist, disappeared into the halls of academe. In April 1970 he turned teacher for one semester at New York University, tutoring students in a songwriting class. To Paul it is not actually possible to teach someone to be a songwriter. This workshop was for already budding lyricists. Simon saw his primary role as one of 'been there, done that'. In other words, one of the best things he felt he could impart to his attentive class was his experience of the many pitfalls in the music industry. He also, of course, helped the students to dissect what made a song work or not – valuable advice from a celebrity master of his craft.

While Paul rolled up to take class at New York University in May 'Cecilia'/'The Only Living Boy In New York' reached number 4 in America where by mid-June, it was certified as a million-selling single.

The colossal success of *Bridge Over Troubled Water* meant that the duo could not continue to keep out of the musical limelight. Pressure began to grow for a tour to take the new much-loved numbers out for a spin on the road. In contrast to their enormous show of strength in the charts, an odd unsettled air hung over the pair's future.

The media found it hard to pin them down to definite plans, which fuelled the unease. Asked whether they planned to tour, Simon had earlier in the year answered that it was possible. 'Probably', too, was his suspiciously lukewarm response to whether he and Art Garfunkel would make another record

It was all too vague to satisfy and it wasn't a fantastic leap to think that each had his eyes on a different path. But no one would come out and say so. The unease settled somewhat when Simon and Garfunkel set off around America in the summer. Unknown to anyone, it would be their last tour for more than ten years and heralded the slow dissolution of the fabled Simon and Garfunkel partnership.

The tour ended in mid-July 1970 with sold-out appearances at Forest Hills Stadium. The crowd on both nights gave the pair from Queens a great reception and in return they received their money's worth of entertainment. However, throughout the tour, the niggling tension had begun to break out in disagreements that left a sour aftertaste.

By the end of the second night at Forest Hills Stadium, time was up. Paul Simon recalled them walking backstage at the end of that last night, shaking hands and parting, not talking for several months. It had become too much of a strain trying to keep the partnership alive. But although the two knew that they were, at least for now, going their separate ways, no one else knew officially.

Unlike today's often very public band bust-ups, when colourful, sometimes savage, recriminations ricochet all over the press, Simon and Garfunkel publicly ceased more by dint of simply having no plans to work together in the foreseeable future. Neither star would be drawn on the matter.

In September 1970 the next single from *Bridge* was released.

'El Condor Pasa'/'Why Don't You Write Me' stopped at number 18 on the US chart and was not released in the UK

By this time Paul had already taken his first step towards renewing his solo career. He had put his toe in the water by performing alone as part of a marathon anti-war gig called *Concert For Peace*. Held on 6 August 1970 at New York's Shea Stadium, it marked the 25th anniversary of the first atomic bomb dropped on Hiroshima in Japan. Other acts on the bill included Janis Joplin.

The night was not an enjoyable experience. The nature of the crowd was different – restless, inattentive and unresponsive to Paul Simon's material. The concert had a depressing effect on him and he came away dispirited.

Not nearly as dispirited, however, as the executives at Columbia Records felt when one half of their golden goose arrived at the company's offices towards the end of 1970. Paul explained that Simon and Garfunkel as an entity was now, at least mothballed if not over, and he was seeking a solo recording contract. Columbia Records was shocked to the core to see their phenomenally selling artistes apparently dry up as a financial asset. When the initial shock receded, they made a concerted effort to dissuade Simon, perhaps feeling that after all the strain of making *Bridge* he only needed a rest and would regret making any hasty changes.

Paul Simon, on the contrary, having thought it all through and being resolute, did not appreciate meeting with such resistance. He took amiss, too, the implication of some of the executives that he was going through a phase from which he would awaken and return to his senses. Whatever arguments were put to him he didn't want to hear, and there ensued a deeply frustrating impasse.

Simon has admitted that one of the reasons he and Garfunkel did not stoutly declare that their partnership was defunct was because neither of them knew that it was that final. What Simon did know was that he wanted – needed – a change, a *frisson* of risk back in his working life. It was a need that few people around him understood. With only certain exceptions, all those Paul told in confidence that he was branching out alone, shook their heads in gloomy discouragement.

It's quite likely that this lack of support steeled Simon all the more. From Columbia Records' perspective, he stuck alarmingly to his guns. In the end, before December they capitulated and signed a solo recording contract with him.

Three months later, in March 1971, at the 13th Grammy Awards, *Bridge Over Troubled Water* won Album of the Year. The record walked off in total with a sizzling six trophies, when the single 'Bridge Over Troubled Water' also scooped Record of the Year, Song of the Year, Best Contemporary Song, Best Arrangement and Best Engineered Album.

Collecting their armful of prestigious trophies Art and Paul stood smilingly side by side. Garfunkel wore a dinner suit with bow tie. Paul, sporting a moustache and beard with his dark hair now scraping his collar, was more casual in a dark suit and open-necked white shirt. With the applause thundering in their ears and blinded by what seemed like a million popping photographer's flash bulbs, they looked to be king pins of the music world – an inspired partnership, stemming from friendship and cemented by incredible success.

There was a certain ironic twist to the scene which Paul Simon succinctly captured when looking back he said, 'Paradoxically, as *Bridge Over Troubled Water* was selling ten million copies, our relationship was disintegrating.'

CHAPTER 9

Renaissance Man

THE NEXT STEP IN Paul Simon's journey to expand his musical vocabulary meant stepping back from the showbiz pool of light into a private realm that allowed him the space to think. Solo ambitions were nothing new, but Simon and Garfunkel's record-breaking success was a tough act to follow. Paul's plan was not to try to outdo it. It was more important to him to find a new individual identity.

He did not want to be fossilised in a particular musical stratum, and was keen to break out and see what happened. In the interests of widening his experience he was prepared to be totally flexible, so he spent months studying music theory, as well as listening to music in a variety of styles. He dissected and analysed them, endeavouring to discover why he was receptive to certain sounds and which of those would be good to explore.

As a boy, standing by the stage watching bands play at his father's gigs, Simon had developed an appreciation of South American music. He already had an interest in African sounds and he was now drawn to the lilting, hypnotic rhythm of reggae. Simon was fascinated by the intricacies of this distinctive musical genre, which would go on to exert a major influence on popular music. A near relative of ska – itself a blend of calypso, jazz and rhythm and blues – reggae's bounce came down on the second and fourth beat of every 4/4 bar. It had an almost addictive sound and Paul became hooked.

The authentic home of reggae was Jamaica and in summer 1971 he hot-footed it to the capital, Kingston, where he settled in at Dynamic recording studios. With an open mind and a genuine thirst to learn, he gathered about him a clan of experienced local musicians with whom he worked in a stimulating partnership. Initially, the musicians were not used to the way Simon worked, since normally they were hired for a set fee for a set output.

Paul was concerned with experimentation, not volume of output. To settle the specifics upfront, therefore, he arranged a generous pay rate for the musicians, leaving everyone free to focus on evolving music in the studio. Simon's patience was limitless as he set about getting to grips with these new sounds. He was in his element with these people who had music running in their veins.

That time was also blessedly tension-free. He could indulge in trial and error and lose himself in daily jam sessions that might or might not yield anything. He also celebrated the refreshing situation of having only himself to please. He respected and admired his fellow musicians, but at the end of the day they were hired hands. He was in sole charge; he could work as fast or as slowly as he wanted and was in complete command of the direction he wished to pursue. No stage of the work was dependent on anyone else; indeed, he found many unsuspected freedoms in his new working world and it was a liberating feeling.

In time, however, he had to rein in his enthusiasm for experimentation and, gathering up his mass of recorded material, he headed home to America. Back in the studio he began to separate the wheat from the chaff. He was joined in this task by Roy Halee, with whom he would produce the next album.

Simon's travels were not yet over. Before the year's end he flew to Paris where he had arranged to record with a very special guest musician, the famous French-born jazz violinist Stephane Grappelli, who had agreed to play on one of Simon's new songs,

'Hobo's Blues'. Although a man who adores the company of talented and dedicated musicians, Paul Simon was understandably a little intimidated at the thought of working with this music maestro. But he rose to the occasion and returned to New York pleased with the result.

As 1972 arrived and his album had all but taken shape, Simon felt happy enough with life to let contentment offset much of the anxiety attached to the launch of his solo career. By now he had managed to cut down the number of therapy sessions per week with his analyst and his life was straightening out. He had the support of an encouraging wife who, at the turn of the year, pleased him further with the news that she was pregnant with their first child, due in September. He felt ready to face the public with his new musical product.

Paul Simon was released roughly two years on from *Bridge Over Troubled Water.* By mid-March 1972 it had topped the UK album charts before dropping anchor at number 4 in America.

Stylistically diverse, with a multicultural emphasis, its 11 tracks kicked off with the Jamaican-reggae-flavoured 'Mother And Child Reunion'. Famously Simon later let out that the song's title had come from nothing more profound than the name of a chicken and egg dish on a restaurant menu in New York's Chinatown. The number's cheerful beat, however, belied the fact that lyrically Simon was touching on the devastating experience of a close bereavement. It marked a departure from the way he normally wrapped up and presented such intense meaning. This was entirely in keeping with his intention now to move away from what he called past simple stuff. He wanted his words to be less literal in the future.

'Duncan' followed – a ballad, punctuated by ethereal flute work, which depicts innocence lost as a young boy explores his sexual inquisitiveness. The sombre 'Everything Put Together Falls Apart' dealt with the more dramatic scourge of drug abuse and at the same time offered a glimpse into Simon's own withdrawal from his past drug taking.

Simon called for a more positive attitude to health in 'Run That Body Down', which he unashamedly personalised by references to his own name and a wife called Peg. Notably though, the interesting track from Paul's viewpoint came with the final song of side one – the heavy blues number 'Armistice Day'.

Knowing the star's stance on the Vietnam War, listeners could be forgiven for assuming that he was making a plea for a cessation of American military action there. In fact, the conflict was closer to home. His meaning lay more in an admission that he had been left weary from the struggles over making *Bridge Over Troubled Water.* In a wider sense, though, he did highlight the general need for people to stop creating misery for others.

Side two opened with the jaunty 'Me And Julio Down By The Schoolyard', a Latin-style street song, which revolves around vague references to an illicit underage liaison between two teenagers and subsequent attempts to evade its repercussions. The bluesy 'Peace Like A River' and the jazzy instrumental 'Hobo's Blues', in which Simon's chugging, rhythmic acoustic guitar work kept pace with Stephane Grappelli, sandwiched the more complex 'Papa Hobo'. This song uses the motor car as a symbol of something which expands people's opportunities but has the downside that rising carbon monoxide emissions (he calls this Detroit perfume) are going to poison the planet; still a hot topic of environmental debate 30 years on.

Finally, after the self-explanatory 'Paranoia Blues' with its strong bluegrass appeal, came the melodic but moody 'Congratulations', which sadly wonders whether lasting peace can ever be found in a relationship. *Paul Simon*'s cover, front and back, could not have proclaimed his new solo status any more clearly – it features extremely close-up face shots of Simon.

Simon's solo career had begun, but it was a risky and anxious time. He said that he could live happily enough not performing, but his professional pride was at stake and his competitive spirit meant that he would have hated this album to flop. In the deepest recesses of his mind, he may also have been slightly haunted by the thought that maybe he needed to be paired with Art Garfunkel to be successful? He could not forget that his previous attempts at going solo not so many years ago had foundered – and that it was when he had teamed up with Art again that the magic had struck.

Paul Simon would not be the first artiste to fall prey to the anxiety that he had too much to live up to. Getting to the top is hard. Staying there is a pressure all of its own, a pressure that increases substantially if the star at the same time is bold enough to tamper with a proven successful formula.

Realistically, Simon knew that, in some ways, he was starting all over again, and he anticipated that it might take his fans some time to adjust fully to his different musical direction. But despite this rational thinking, he was a feted star who, on a human level, hoped his fame would be enough for him to be greeted with just as much enthusiasm as before. In the end, this first solo album since breaking from Garfunkel went gold in Britain and America. It had never been on the cards that any solo effort of his could match the massive commercial success of *Bridge Over Troubled Water*. Simon knew that. But it seemed unfair that an album which in its own right sells a million copies in each of at least two different markets can still be perceived as a flop because it is ten times less successful than his last work – the best album of the decade.

Music critics were not on the whole ecstatic about *Paul Simon*, although they remained respectful. Simon, however, looked for more. Inwardly, he was convinced that he was writing his best material yet, certainly from a personal perspective, and that counted for a lot with him.

Spin-off singles from the album began with 'Mother And Child Reunion'/'Paranoia Blues' in March, which checked in at 5 in Britain and nudged one place higher in the States. Two months later came 'Me And Julio Down By The Schoolyard'/ 'Congratulations', which fared less well and stopped at 15 in Britain and 22 in America.

Despite the big emphasis on going solo Paul did not tour to back the album. He was not ready to face a live crowd alone, night after night. He pointed out that people like to criticise and he knew he would have cared if comparisons implied that he was reaching something less than his previous best. He preferred instead to start writing material for his next album.

Simon only deviated from this path when, in the summer, politics intervened – 1972 was an election year in the US. Paul Simon openly backed the Democratic Presidential candidate George Stanley McGovern and agreed to take part in the latest in a series of fundraising benefit gigs held to aid the 50-year-old South Dakota-born Senator.

The stellar event was organised by a friend of Paul's, Hollywood actor Warren Beatty, and was to take place at New York's Madison Square Garden. Paul Simon and Art Garfunkel had agreed to reunite for the evening. Although they had gone their professional separate ways, the two had recently resumed personal contact

On the night, Simon and Garfunkel were one of a number of high-profile acts and although the spotlight was not primarily on them, it undoubtedly felt odd. They had not performed in public as a duo since that taut last night at Forest Hills Stadium. Fortunately, familiarity soon kicked in and led to them delivering a nostalgic treat of resounding crowd-pleasers. Politically, it would be all to no avail. For in November, to Simon's despair, Richard Nixon was returned to power, again by a slim margin. Following the Madison Square Garden fundraiser Simon was faced with clear evidence that the appetite for Simon and Garfunkel was still voracious when in July 1972 Columbia Records, quick to capitalise on the duo's albeit brief reunion, issued *Simon and Garfunkel's Greatest Hits.*

The compilation album, which contained one knockout number after another, reached number 5 in America and stopped just short of the top in Britain. The subsequent speculation that almost every household in the land owned a copy of this album does not seem too wide of the mark when the facts show that in the UK alone its chart tenure racked up a mind-boggling 283 weeks – almost five and a half years!

In contrast, in August, Paul Simon's solo single 'Duncan'/ 'Run That Body Down' stalled at number 52 in America. Undaunted, he concentrated on steering his solo career and returned to song-writing in a happy home environment. Personal contentment can be a lyricist's worst enemy. Like a successful boxer who has left the mean streets behind, no longer being lean and hungry can lead to losing an edge.

Simon, who seems to distrust happiness, was already on his guard against this, acknowledging the sobering truth that some people can only be happy when they are struggling. But he chose to use his present joy to light his way and he let it infiltrate his new material.

Paul Simon had been an interesting album in terms of musical expansion, but its tone had remained largely moody and intense. The material he was now working on already signposted a brighter, more optimistic album. In the closing months of 1972 Paul devoted himself to moulding this material in the recording studio. In the same period, Peggy gave birth to a son whom they called Harper – Peggy's maiden surname. Both parents doted on the boy. Paul adored spending time with the baby and was inspired to write a special lullaby for the new arrival.

On the domestic front the Simons purchased a plush triplex apartment in Manhattan, as well as a farm in Pennsylvania – a get-away-from-it-all bolthole. Simon is a city dweller – indeed, he could happily hibernate in the recording studio. And by spring 1973 his solid commitment to work was starting to place a strain on his marriage. This was magnified when in May he set off on his first solo tour. He was naturally nervous at going back on the road, this time as a solo artiste. There was a lot to live up to, and he was concerned that if people came expecting too much they would be disappointed.

The backing vocal groups Urubamba and the Jessy Dixon Singers joined Paul Simon on his trip. It's hard for one man to fill a stage, so their colourful style, musical expertise and vocal harmonies enhanced and fleshed out the act each night. Ultimately, though, Simon had to carry the can himself – after all, it was he whom the crowd came to see.

The tour wound its way around America, boosted by an encouraging start when the first single 'Kodachrome'/ 'Tenderness', from the forthcoming new album, sailed to number 2 in the US charts. In Britain 'Take Me To The Mardi Gras'/'Kodachrome' stopped at number 7. Some performances on tour were recorded and would later provide atmospheric material for a live album.

In June 1973 Simon's next solo album arrived, called *There Goes Rhymin' Simon.* Generally upbeat in tone, it immediately demanded attention and reached number 2 and 4 in the US and UK charts respectively. The album had primarily been recorded at Muscle Shoals Sound Studios in County Sheffield, Alabama, where Simon had revelled in finding a resident group of musicians to work with. Instantly at home with these men, Paul had benefited from their professionalism and intuitive ingenuity.

Simon had also used Malaco Recording Studios in Jackson, Mississippi, and, while in Britain, he had worked on a single song at Morgan Studios in Willesden, north London. Over the course of the album he had called on the services of a variety of musicians as well as the six-man, black vocal group, the Dixie Hummingbirds. And along with engineers Jerry Masters and Phil Ramone, plus Roy Halee, he had brought in the Onward Brass Band.

'Kodachrome' and 'Tenderness', already released as a single, set up the album. The former song, backed by a strident combination of piano and horns, uses references to a colour camera bringing warmth and brightness to the world. While the other, a late-night listening type, lamented the lack of compassion that can creep unwittingly into a relationship. The urge to stop the rot and find a solution makes 'Tenderness' a soft romantic ballad.

'Take Me To The Mardi Gras' midway on the first side jolts proceedings. The number shrieks 'The Big Easy' – New Orleans, the undisputed home of jazz and the world-famous Mardi Gras festival, when round the clock partying is the order the day. The sounds of Bourbon Street, the bohemian French Quarter and the image of grand steamboats cruising down the Mississippi are all captured by Simon's lyrics and music. The song is appropriately punctuated by horns from the Onward Brass Band and some falsetto singing by the Reverend Claude Jeter.

'Something So Right' earned special attention when it emerged that the love song was a tribute to Peggy. In it Simon praises her, crediting her with having a calming influence in his life and being his touchstone. He admits his propensity to spot what is wrong and his downright distrust of happiness when life goes right. The featured strings are the work of Quincy Jones.

On older terrain, 'One Man's Ceiling Is Another Man's Floor', which ends side one, was a reminder of how insular society has had to become. Simon illustrates this via a depiction of everyday apartment life and the philosophy of keep your door closed and your nose out regardless of what may be going down outside. Sad, but practical. Another interpretation altogether has also been put on the song.

Singer-songwriter Ralph McTell says, 'One of my favourite Paul Simon songs is 'One Man's Ceiling, Is Another Man's Floor'. I really loved that one. I'd never heard the expression before. And I thought it was just perfect about aspiration – and where some people's aspirations begin, someone else's is ending. It was typical of Paul. He is brilliant at coming up with these short incisive comments, which he expands into songs. And he gave it that lovely jazzy feel.'

A joyous spirit elevates many of side two's tracks. The calypso style 'Was A Sunny Day' is a breezy boy meets girl ditty. The lullaby for Harper 'St Judy's Comet' was the work of a very proud dad, and reverting to blues, 'Learn How To Fall' maintained the same lighter tone.

'Loves Me Like A Rock' took Paul deep into gospel country and featured the Dixie Hummingbirds. The song's particular appeal was to be proved later that year; when released in October 1973 as a single, backed by 'Learn How To Fall', it peaked at number 2 in the US charts and became Simon's first solo million-selling single.

But Paul Simon's personal favourite from *There Goes Rhymin' Simon* was 'American Tune'. Recorded in London, this is certainly one of Simon's big songs. It is long on narrative, which he handles with flair. Fearful for his country's future under what he saw as Richard Nixon's oppressive policies, Simon had written this number, which deeply queries the direction in which the US was heading. In it he talks eloquently of how wearying the continual struggle to keep picking oneself up feels. As well as harking back to the country's idealistic founding fathers, he uses symbolism to conjure the prospect of the Statue of Liberty breaking loose from its moorings and drifting away, thereby deserting Americans.

Chris de Burgh singles out 'American Tune' for praise. 'The lyrics are phenomenal. One of the key words in the song for me is 'uncertain'. It's such a sad observation on American society and its values at that time. If Paul had written that song after September 11, what an impact it would have had.'

Returning to the past practice of making blunt references to dying, in 'American Tune' Simon emotively paints the scenario of a surreal out-of-body experience. It is a song that emanates fear, sadness, idealism, but it ends by holding out hope for America's rebirth one day.

Simon's own rebirth as a solo artiste received a significant thumbs-up when *There Goes Rhymin' Simon* attracted a Best Album of 1973 Grammy Award nomination. Surprisingly when 'American Tune'/'One Man's Ceiling Is Another Man's Floor' was released late 1973, its chart best the following February was number 35 in the US singles chart and it failed to chart in Britain altogether. By then, though, Paul had more important matters on his mind.

The strain on Paul's marriage had been worsening to the point when, in early 1974, the couple decided to separate. Paul later commented that he had been too young for marriage. He certainly acknowledged that being married was not a state that can best thrive when one party has such a close commitment to something else – in his case a solo recording career.

Paul moved out of the marital home and into a Manhattan hotel suite. His personal life lay in tatters just as his solo work was starting to receive acclaim. It seemed that there always had to be a choice between one or the other, and that depressed him. Life was not like songs. If something is not working out in the studio, there is always a solution to be found. His marriage to Peggy would never be fixed.

In spring, in this lonely, unhappy state, circumstances drew Paul's longest-standing friend back into his life. Art Garfunkel had in the intervening years released his first solo album *Angel Clare,* and in 1972 he had married his girlfriend Linda Grossman. Sadly, by 1974, Art was in the same boat as Paul – his marriage was on the rocks. Their parallel experiences brought the old friends together.

They made arrangements to take separate bachelor apartments in the same building and gradually they began to socialise among New York's music fraternity. It helped, but not all of the time. Paul was alone and unhappy. And trying to look back and figure out what could have been done differently might not have helped. For writing songs, recording and touring when necessary *was* his life.

When involved in a project he was always totally plugged in to it, which was not a state ideally suited to responding to other calls on his time. But then, creative work can never be a timetabled affair. Paul Simon acknowledged that a wife and child have their needs and a perfect right to expect their share of attention, but it had not always been possible for him to give enough to satisfy.

As the year unfolded there was precious little to cheer him. *Live Rhymin'* released in April 1974 reached number 33 in America and did not chart in the UK. Seven months on, the single 'Something So Right' backed by 'Tenderness' failed to score a hit in either market. There was something sadly ironic in the fact that this meaningful ballad, written in tribute to his wife, should be released when the couple's divorce was a foregone conclusion.

CHAPTER 10

Swings and Roundabouts

PAUL POURED HIS PAIN at the failure of his marriage into songwriting throughout the first half of 1975. It had a cathartic effect, but, with his and Peggy's lawyers at the same time negotiating the terms of the divorce settlement, Simon's emotions sometimes overwhelmed him when alone in his New York apartment.

The songs reflecting this crisis were seasoned with a maturity that further sharpened his cynicism about life; they were to benefit, too, from his continued study of music theory. His interest had centred on jazz and to assist him in acquiring a better understanding of style and structure within that discipline, he sought specialist advice from the experienced jazzmen David Sorin Collyer and Chuck Israels. He later credited these two men with having helped him greatly.

Collectively, this material made up Paul Simon's most deeply personal album yet. Called *Still Crazy After All These Years*, its themes dealt with relationships disintegrating, rejection of various kinds, hopes for redemption, and even touched on ritual murder. It was in places dark, edgy, brittle and sad. It was released in autumn 1975 and though it would be Simon's last album for five years, by December it gave him his first number 1 solo album in America.

The entire record was about the aftermath of his marriage. The opening title track conveys the loneliness of a man uprooted from home, leaving his wife and child and planted in a plush but impersonal hotel suite, where he has nothing to do but miserably watch others go about their lives. Simon said of this time, 'I was pretty depressed.' A jagged edge juts into the song when he speculates that he could quite possibly snap violently one day. Interestingly, tucked in behind that is a confidence that if he did snap, he would escape the consequences because people would sympathise with his plight; this perhaps hinted at having been hard done by.

For Chris de Burgh, the song 'Still Crazy After All These Years' stood out particularly. He says, 'If you look at it closely, the first verse is very simple. But by the time Paul's at the middle, it becomes complex. He knows what he's doing and he's skilled at employing within the same song different time signatures, different keys, then returning to the familiar. So you have repetitive melodies which suddenly disappear when he goes some place else then comes back – very clever.'

With more defiant self-assurance '50 Ways To Leave Your Lover' is a wry, snappy number promoting the pleasures of staying footloose. 'Night Game', on the other hand, produces a tangible chill – the song turns out to be about ritual death. Simon uses sporting metaphors and the eerie stadium setting to twin today's cut-and-thrust of competitive play, where there is a victor and a loser, with barbaric Roman times when life and death contests were fought in similarly packed arenas filled with bloodthirsty spectators.

Remaining with dark thoughts, 'Gone At Last' establishes immediately the dismal attitude of a man down on his luck. It's also reflective, though, and offers the chance of redemption. Phoebe Snow joined Simon on vocals for this number, with extra backing from the Jessy Dixon Singers.

The pattern continued when typical Paul Simon musings on the fact that most people get a raw deal in life while others idly prosper, created 'Some Folks' Lives Roll Easy'. So it was almost inevitable when a stream of paranoia infiltrated 'Have A Good Time', in which desperation leads to uncharacteristically reckless behaviour.

This window on to Simon's inner thoughts revealed the tumultuous emotions he had put down on paper before he added 'You're Kind'. A feeling of hurt abandonment had so far permeated his lyrics. Here he sang of being cared for by someone at last, only, paradoxically, to lust after his freedom, which he represented by his preference to have a window kept open not closed.

'Silent Eyes', featuring the Chicago Community Choir, about the state of Jerusalem and Judgement Day, anchored a most unusual album, on which two more tracks stand out. The first of these is the starkly simple ballad 'I Do It For Your Love'. It reeks of sacrifice and the hardship faced by a struggling young married couple, particularly the man trying his hardest to provide for his wife. Yet his efforts all come to nothing when the union dissolves.

Simon's tortured thoughts were laid out here with excruciating clarity. But, he put them beyond doubt when he told journalists during the promotional round of interviews that he had wept at times while writing parts of this song. He backed up this extraordinarily public admission by stating, 'I don't know how good a song it is, but it's really about my life.'

No confusion there, but such frankness usually has a price. That Simon was prepared to reveal something so intimate to the media meant that he was still vulnerable. His candour left him feeling very exposed and embarrassed over speculation about his private life.

The other most notable song from *Still Crazy After All These Years* was 'My Little Town'. Simon's solo album had been long awaited, but this three-minute, 51-second song caused the biggest stir. The dynamic number poked a sharp stick at the mentality of narrow-minded people, unwilling to imagine a world outside the confines of their own lives and who never put a foot wrong. Again a patent violence entered the song when its protagonist finds his pent-up frustration turning him into a time bomb just waiting to blow. The blast for everyone, though, was that 'My Little Town' was a new Simon and Garfunkel number.

Although Paul and Art were known to be back on friendly social terms, it still had not seemed likely that they would record a song together. It came as a great surprise to faithful watchers of the duo, and the music press, when they went public with this song, which had been recorded back in May.

Originally Simon had penned the number for his friend to include on his solo album *Breakaway*. But it emerged that while Paul was familiarising Art with the words that they had spontaneously begun to harmonise. It struck Garfunkel forcibly that the number was perfect for them both. When he asked his ex-partner to duet with him on it, Simon happily shrugged his acceptance. Now that casual decision sparked soaring speculation that a full-blown Simon and Garfunkel reunion was on the cards.

Some time before *Still Crazy* was released, Paul Simon had returned to the public arena. 'Gone At Last'/'Take Me To The Mardi Gras' had charted in America at 23 in October – the same month in which Simon had agreed to take part in *Saturday Night Live*; an innovative weekly television show then only months old. Produced by Toronto-born Lorne Michaels, the programme featured the regular talents of Chevy Chase and John Belushi, among others, and it often invited celebrities to guest-host individual shows. Hollywood comic actor Chevy Chase, whose string of movies include *National Lampoon's Vegas Vacation* and *The Three Amigos*, recalls roping Paul Simon in on the show.

Says Chevy, 'We first met properly in 1975. Paul was recording the *Still Crazy* album. Lorne Michaels and I went to the recording studio to convince Paul to do the show. *Saturday Night Live* is a satirical show that pokes fun at pop culture and at the media. And it makes use of being live on television. It has a cast of impressionists and improvisational actors and it's always got a very interesting musical guest on who is promoting an album that week.

'We knew that Paul wanted to promote *Still Crazy After All*

These Years, so it worked out well. In fact, he sang 'Still Crazy' on that show. If my memory serves me correctly, that was the first time Paul appeared on *Saturday Night Live* and he was quite something.'

In Lorne Michaels and Chevy Chase Paul found two new close friends. Chevy goes on, 'Throughout that year the three of us were very, very tight friends. And we had one heck of a time – it was a lot of fun. Paul is a very funny man, but not in an overtly physical way. By and large he's funny verbally. He's intelligent and articulate. He reminds me of Buster Keaton.

'Paul is often sitting with his guitar. Even when he is just talking to you he's picking away at it. He probably writes and plays his guitar every day for some period of time. He has a very ironic view of things with a touch of cynicism and scepticism. He's not a sarcastic man. He enjoys the silly in things and he's really quick on the uptake.'

Paul Simon hosted *Saturday Night Live* on 19 October 1975. He performed solo material first, before introducing Art Garfunkel as a special guest. Together they then revived some of their oldest favourites as well as performing the new 'My Little Town'. Each man must have known that they were playing with fire, tantalising people with this re-teaming after a five-year hiatus. But the strength of the commotion in the press next day still took them by surprise. Scenting the reunion that people still clearly hankered after, the pressure began at once.

In a way, the whole 'My Little Town' thing had been an odd step for Simon. He had striven hard to establish himself in his own right and had finally managed to emerge from the very long shadow cast by the duo, to be recognised and rewarded in his own right. This one song seemed wilfully to wreck all that work. When the single 'My Little Town'/'Rag Doll' (which was an Art Garfunkel solo number) came out, it charted at number 9 in America. The track also appeared on Garfunkel's recently released solo album *Breakaway*.

Ignoring the clamour it caused, Paul began serious rehearsals for an upcoming solo tour to back *Still Crazy*. But when he emerged from these, it was to find himself still beating back the media who were on his trail with virtually only one question in mind.

Nothing daunted, along with the Jessy Dixon Singers, Simon set off around the States and people flocked to see him. If his and Garfunkel's intention had been to tease folk further, they stoked the flames when at New York's Avery Fisher Hall, Art strolled on stage unexpectedly to the stunned delight of the crowd and joined Simon for a handful of numbers. After that night rumours flew that he would appear at other Paul Simon gigs.

The US leg of the tour ended in late November when Simon flew to Europe. After a few gigs there he landed in Britain where *Still Crazy After All These Years* was to reach number 6. After fulfilling dates in the north of England, he headed to London for three consecutive nights at the Palladium starting on 11 December 1975. Paul Simon had good memories of Britain, but this time he came to the UK capital at a very tense time as terrorist activity on the British mainland had created a jittery state of high alert.

Above the doors of the famous London Palladium hung a huge yellow banner board proclaiming in large red lettering "Tonight: Paul Simon". Tickets were priced at around £3.50, but touts circulating furtively among the crowds outside were getting ten times that for tickets for the subsequent performances. Paul Simon was in superb form for these Palladium gigs. Performing each night for two hours with precisely a 15-minute interval, he punctuated the evening with occasional flashes of his quiet droll humour.

One night he remarked over the mike that he'd always thought the mark of being truly famous was when an audience applauded in recognition of a song's opening note. He then picked out the start of 'The Boxer' only to stop when nothing happened and prompted, 'I said. . .' Belatedly taking the hint, the audience erupted with happy laughter, which echoed to the high ceiling, and applauded loudly.

That weekend Paul Simon was the top guest on the popular

UK chat show *Parkinson* hosted by Michael Parkinson. It was recorded at the BBC's Television Centre studios in the afternoon of 13 December before a small live audience and was aired that evening. Veteran comedian Arthur Askey and Formula One motor racing driver James Hunt were fellow guests, with Paul coming on last.

It had been a successful stay in London and by the time Simon returned to the States to fulfil the tail end of the tour's bookings the single '50 Ways To Leave Your Lover'/'Some Folks' Lives' Roll Easy' was out. In Britain it stuck at 23, but just weeks into 1976 it graced the US top slot, this time giving Paul his first number 1 solo single in America.

Simon's only other solo placing that year would come in April when 'Still Crazy After All These Years'/'I Do It For Your Love' made the Top 40. But by then his achievement with his new album had been recognised at the 18th annual Grammy Awards held in Hollywood at the end of February.

Still Crazy After All These Years won Best Album of the Year, and Paul was awarded the trophy for Best Male Pop Vocal Performance, which surely strengthened his sometimes wobbly belief in himself as a singer. 'My Little Town' had been among those nominated as Best Pop Vocal Performance By a Duo or Group. But 'Lyin' Eyes' by the Eagles made off with it instead.

That summer, Simon put his career on the back burner. He had come through a maelstrom of emotions and activity and needed a breather. He had brought order to his life that he wanted to capitalise upon. His elegant apartment with views over Central Park was close to where his ex-wife lived. Harper lived primarily with his mother but was near enough to visit his dad easily, often sleeping over. Paul and Peggy had established a communicative, non-hostile rapport, which helped their son to enjoy both his parents.

When Paul didn't have Harper staying the night he enjoyed the bachelor life. He, and several regulars from the *Saturday Night Live* crowd, had become a common sight in the social whirl of the trendiest New York nightclubs. Chevy Chase confirms, 'We were very much a crowd. Absolutely. We're friends so we tend to get together in the summers when people are available. A good deal of the time one person's touring, another person is making a movie so it can make it more difficult. But we get together when we can. Lorne and Paul live in the same building so they see each other every day.'

Occasionally Simon returned as a guest on *Saturday Night Live* when he would gamely throw himself into hilarious comic sketches. Normally his deadpan face made him the straight man, but he could goof it up with the rest when required. Another memorable highlight on the show came in November 1976, when Paul Simon duetted with ex-Beatle George Harrison on the song, 'Here Comes The Sun'.

Producer Lorne Michaels had hoped to pull off the coup of getting the four Beatles to reunite on *Saturday Night Live*, a prospect that would have ensured that his programme smashed all TV ratings. Paul McCartney was in New York City where John Lennon already lived, and with Harrison in town three of the four were in place. But it never happened.

What had occurred for Paul Simon before the year's end was that he had made his screen-acting debut. Despite being cut out of *Catch 22*'s cast he had retained an urge to try out the silver screen. Even so, when Simon's friend, actor/director Woody Allen had approached him to take a cameo part in *Annie Hall*, he took a while to be convinced. He did, however, and he shot his scenes for this romantic comedy in New York and LA.

Centred on a Jewish comedian's affair with a girl from the mid-west and concentrating on the neuroses prevalent in American society, *Annie Hall* which went on to bag four Oscars, starred Woody Allen, Diane Keaton, Tony Roberts and Carol Kane. The witty, intelligent comedy contained brief appearances from actors Sigourney Weaver, Beverly D'Angelo, Jeff Goldblum and Shelley Hack. Paul Simon's cameo was rather more substantial, although still a small role. He played Tony Lacey, a slick, designer-suited, drug-taking record producer tycoon, with a hackneyed chat-up line and a belief in the casting couch.

The actress Laurie Bird played Lacey's on-screen girlfriend, but it was another cast member, Shelley Duvall, with whom Paul would become involved in real life. Duvall played a rock critic and although she and Simon had no screen time together, their mutual attraction meant that they were often seen in each other's company around the set.

Her exuberant bubbly nature seemed at odds with Paul's lower-key persona. Still it quickly became obvious that they had bypassed platonic friendship and gone straight for romance. Shelley Duvall confirmed as much by relocating from Los Angeles to move in with Paul Simon in New York once their filming commitments ended.

As this was Simon's first love affair since his divorce from Peggy, the gossip columnists were poised, but while Shelley commented that it was 'real nice to be in love', neither one was prepared to be garrulous about their relationship to the press.

With a new love in his life, Paul also had the satisfaction that the political landscape had finally changed with Democrat Jimmy Carter's victory in the recent elections. An Inaugural Eve Gala concert was held for the President-elect on 19 January 1977, and Paul was honoured to join the line-up of guest artistes taking the stage at the Kennedy Center For The Performing Arts in Washington DC.

As 1977 progressed Simon found that although he was happier and on a more even keel, he wasn't writing. His only single release of the year would be 'Slip Slidin' Away' – a downbeat number about the problems that riddle relationships on different levels. With 'Stranded In A Limousine' on the B-side, it ground to a halt outside the Top 30 in the UK. By contrast, it notched up number 5 in America.

On 18 October in London at a special awards ceremony, held to mark the Queen's Silver Jubilee Year, the rock band Queen's 'Bohemian Rhapsody' and Procol Harum's 'A Whiter Shade of Pale' tied as the Best British Pop Single 1952–1977. At that same event the *Bridge Over Troubled Water* album and single won the category of Best International (Non-UK) Album and Single 1952–1977. Simon and Garfunkel attended the ceremony at Wembley Conference Centre to receive the honour.

To emphasise the success of his solo career to date, at the end of the year Simon released *Greatest Hits, Etc.* Commencing with 'Slip Slidin' Away' and 'Stranded In A Limousine' the further 12 tracks were handpicked selections from his three 1970s solo albums. This compilation piece peaked at 18 in the States and 6 in Britain, earning a platinum disc.

For some time Simon had found himself less drawn to writing songs for yet another new album. Instead, he was thinking about using his literary skills to pen a film script. Just then, however, he was distracted by a TV offer, when NBC TV invited him to make a one-hour special. After some debate with himself, Shelley Duvall and close friends, he agreed. Lorne Michaels would produce, Dave Wilson would direct, and friends Chevy Chase and actor Charles Grodin would join those taking part; Simon and Michaels pulled a script together.

The special took the inventive form of a dress rehearsal for a TV special and included comedy, comic skits and music. Garfunkel agreed to appear and with Simon he performed the oldie 'Old Friends'.

The Paul Simon Special aired on 7 December 1977 but did not go down well. One critic called it, 'About as funny as a case of fallen arches.' Poor ratings left NBC and Paul Simon disappointed. Disappointment became deep dismay when, throughout 1978, contract negotiations with Columbia Records became first mired, then broke down altogether. A maze of problems arose and in the end Simon wanted out. It wasn't quite so simple, however.

After much bargaining on both sides, Simon is said to have paid Columbia Records/CBS a substantial sum of money to be released from his remaining obligations. The situation darkened when the star instituted legal proceedings against the record company over a separate issue. Simon soon found himself another record company – Warner Brothers Records – but the whole messy business had left him with a bad taste in his mouth.

As the decade approached its final year, life again was not good. Amid all the wrangling with the record company, his personal life had reached another plateau. As a successful actress, Shelley Duvall often had to leave Paul for long spells to join film locations around the world. Consequently, their relationship had quietly wilted away. Simon later commented that his and Shelley's personalities had proved not to be a match.

Paul Simon was on his own again. But he had a demanding companion nonetheless in a film script idea. He threw himself headlong into the writing and was determined he would make it work.

CHAPTER 11

Love in the Park

IT WAS ALWAYS AN AMBITIOUS undertaking to write a screenplay for the first time, to star in that movie (also a first) and score the music. But Paul Simon needed the challenge. When deciding to deviate from the predictable path of producing another album, he had also considered writing a Broadway show. But he chose film because he felt it was closer to the recording process he was used to.

Simon had been quietly working on the project for months, even before he had signed to Warner Brothers Records. A bonus of this new liaison was that Warner Brothers was not only prepared to countenance Simon's experiment into film, they financed the $7 million dollar movie. A successful film with a tie-in soundtrack was potentially a big money-spinner, but it was a leap of faith, which the star appreciated.

It was no great surprise that Simon had been attracted by the prospect of creating a movie. A remarkable storyteller in his own field, he was also close to the film world. Some of his best friends were actors, directors and producers – and the new woman in his life was currently one of the most famous actresses in the world.

After his romance with Shelley Duvall, which suffered at least in part because of the profession's itinerant demands, Paul might have been wary of becoming involved again with an actress. But then he met Carrie Fisher through mutual acquaintances and before the end of 1978 they had become an item. Simon had never been romantically involved with anyone whose public profile was on a par with, or higher than, his own and who came from such a glamorous background.

Carrie Fisher's mother is Debbie Reynolds, one of Hollywood's favourite stars in the 1950s. Her father is singer Eddie Fisher. Fisher and Reynolds had been best friends with another celebrity couple, Elizabeth Taylor and her third husband Mike Todd. Some time after Todd was killed in an accident, Eddie Fisher and Liz Taylor ran off together, scandalising America.

Fisher went on to marry Taylor, only to be ousted himself by Richard Burton. But the scandal of ditching Debbie Reynolds took Fisher out of his children's orbit. Carrie and her brother Todd were brought up amid the glare of this publicity and it left its mark on Carrie. She once declared, 'My father was extremely unavailable and that has affected how I relate to men. I don't trust them.'

As a child she attended Beverly Hills High School before studying at the Central School of Speech and Drama in London. At 13 she had appeared with her mother in nightclub acts, and two years later she was in the chorus of a Broadway production of *Irene*. Then, in 1977, the petite, dark-haired actress catapulted to fame in *Star Wars*, the science-fiction blockbuster from George Lucas. Like her character in this movie, the beautiful intergalactic rebel Princess Leia, Carrie Fisher is feisty, smart, energetic and talented.

With this mammoth hit to her credit Carrie's public profile was massive by the time she and Paul Simon became romantically linked. She was attracted to his intelligence and they shared a dry sense of humour, but as both were independent and strong-willed it was clear that this was going to be a high-maintenance relationship. There was also a 15-year age gap between them. And while Paul had left his days of experimenting with drugs behind, Carrie, like some of her high-flying acquaintances for a while took a variety of substances. She later went public about the extent of that drug use.

It was inevitable that their individual egos would clash and it led to an invigorating but volatile stop-start kind of relationship, which on occasion left Simon at a loss as to what to do next. The actress's father, later commenting on the sometimes fractious nature of the couple's romance, revealed that he'd once been sent on a diplomatic mission by Carrie to check out the lie of the land with Paul, with whom she had again fallen out.

This was the first time Eddie Fisher had met Paul Simon. Fisher arrived at the Beverly Wilshire Hotel, where Simon had agreed to meet, with plenty of instructions from Carrie as to what to say but no clear idea of how to reconcile the warring couple. Paul Simon seems to have had little more clue. According to Eddie Fisher, Paul admitted to him that day, 'I don't know how to handle her.' Fisher's sympathy with his fellow singer centred on one fact – with having fallen in love with an actress.

Come spring 1979, Paul and Carrie went their separate ways in the course of their work. Joining the same core cast of Harrison Ford and Mark Hamill, she went to London to film the *Star Wars* sequel *The Empire Strikes Back*. Paul had to intensify work on his film project.

By now he had realised just how much he had taken on. His starring role meant that he had to take acting lessons, which he combined with a regime to shape up mentally and physically. In terms of the sound track, the onus was on him to come up with the score on time; there could be no elastic deadline. And he was without the cushion of being able to fall back on existing work if needed. All the songs had to be originals, and as with any successful musical production, each number had lyrically to advance the plot and enhance the development of the central character, Jonah Levin.

The rock drama, to be called *One Trick Pony*, focused on a once-popular recording star, now in decline, left behind by the shifting musical trends. Pressures abound from a broken marriage and clashes with a record company which is demanding he produce a hit record. Levin's one ray of light is his relationship with his son.

To clear up any misconceptions Simon clearly distanced himself from the idea that the plot was autobiographical. He especially made it known that the marriage depicted in the movie was *not* the story of his and Peggy's marriage. He did, however, see the film as a chance to reflect the experiences of some of his generation of music stars.

Injected into this was also a flavour of the plight that befell his idol Elvis Presley. With all his innovative youth and looks gone, Elvis became trapped in a depressing downward spiral with fatal consequences. Simon aimed to depict a cut-throat music industry where, once having slipped from a precarious pedestal, an ex-star fades as fast as he is trampled on by his younger successors. The prospect of taking on the lead role intrigued him. He was naturally wary about exposing himself to such scrutiny and criticism but he had decided that no one else could wear the skin of Jonah Levin.

His intensive involvement with the film did not prevent him from taking on the extra task of scouting out potential shooting locations. It was an ideal opportunity to start inhabiting Levin's world, so in summer 1979 Simon set off on his mission, first visiting Chicago where he had set *One Trick Pony*.

In this city he returned to the club scene that had once been so familiar, almost two decades before. He wanted to reacquaint himself with the vital nervous energy of the live club performer, to be reminded of the frustration of not being listened to, and to absorb the battered resolve of the musician on the road who, from somewhere, has to find the extra reserves to keep going.

He also wanted to capture the essence of the club owner who is reluctant to fork out the fee, the indifference of the pestered waitresses weaving around the tables, and the mixed bag of characters in the audiences. It was important to Simon to let the ambience of these forlorn, sometimes seedy, places filter into his consciousness so that he, now a cosseted millionaire and respected star, could realistically recreate the life of his fictitious screen character.

This effort was characteristic Paul Simon thoroughness. But would it pay off? Making the successful transfer from page to film of any screenplay is tough and many productions fall behind or drop away altogether.

Filming on *One Trick Pony* began in late autumn 1979, with Cleveland standing in for Chicago. Robert M. Young was at the helm. Young had been conscious that, in effect, this was Paul Simon's show, which could have hampered his direction. But after a brief teething period during which star and director got to know one another, a working relationship emerged. The film's producers were Michael Tannen and Michael Housman, and the cast included Blair Brown, Rip Torn, Joan Hackett and the singer Lou Reed. Other guest appearances saw an especially re-formed Lovin' Spoonful and the B52's.

The aspect of Jonah Levin's life that involved him fronting a rock bank was probably the most exciting to Paul Simon. He had assembled a group of familiar session musicians to portray the band on screen and he enjoyed filming the performance scenes. Otherwise, as the weeks rolled on in to 1980, it was hard going.

By the time *One Trick Pony* moved into post-production, which also required Simon's close collaboration with the music score, he had made his most substantial commitment to any project in terms of time, effort and artistic endeavour. He was also putting his professional standing in the firing line.

To get away from it all, in June 1980, Simon travelled to London to attend the UK premiere of *The Empire Strikes Back* with Carrie Fisher. But he soon left the hysteria behind to return to New York, since his soundtrack album was due out and plans were afoot for a tour. Paul also wanted to check in with Art Garfunkel.

His friend had been going through turbulent times. The previous year he had filmed a movie directed by Nicolas Roeg called *Bad Timing: A Sensual Obsession.* Location work with co-stars Theresa Russell, Harvey Keitel and Denholm Elliott had taken four months in London and Vienna and had been mentally fatiguing.

When Garfunkel had returned to New York in June 1979 it was to the shock discovery that his lover, actress Laurie Bird, had committed suicide in his luxury apartment by taking a drugs overdose. Shattered, Garfunkel had turned to Simon to help him get over the tragedy. Now a year on, a parallel thread ran through their separate lives once again – both were awaiting the release of their respective movies.

In August, the soundtrack album *One Trick Pony* was released. Its opening track 'Late In The Evening' also came out as a single, backed by the powerful ballad 'How The Heart Approaches What It Yearns', which in America reached number 6.

Not unnaturally, considering the film's downbeat tone, melancholy, fear of abandonment and dissatisfaction with life's lot permeated most of the ten tracks on the album. Paul Simon also illustrated what touring in shows inevitably does to family life.

The soundtrack chalked up a number 17 hit in Britain, and made 12 in America. But in November 1980 the second single, 'One Trick Pony'/'Long, Long Day' only creaked to number 40, and two months later 'Oh, Marion'/'God Bless The Absentee' failed to chart at all. The soundtrack's modest success and only the first single achieving a Top 10 chart placing was a commercial disappointment for both Paul Simon and Warner Brothers. But the movie's reception would hurt more.

At the beginning of October 1980 *One Trick Pony* had its New York premiere. It had to be by someone's design, rather than accident, that when Paul Simon's film opened at the Gemini One Theater, Art Garfunkel's *Bad Timing: A Sensual Obsession* opened on the same day at cinema number two in the same complex.

Prior to *One Trick Pony*'s release, Simon had made known his intention to take risks. He told journalists that not to try to expand one's range of talents was to become moribund, and he promoted a philosophy of go ahead and gamble, even if it ends with falling flat on your face. He insisted that when people continue to flow along successfully, it means the steps they are taking are too cautiously measured. *One Trick Pony* was one giant stride that did not pay off for Paul and it delivered him a serious blow.

With his circle of friends Simon ought to have been prewarned to steel himself against the possibility of bad notices. He knew some stars who blithely ignored poor reviews, but he was too curious to know what the critics thought of his work and most were painful reading.

Paul's friend Chevy Chase says of *One Trick Pony*, 'I wasn't crazy about it. It didn't stand out for me. I think some people stand out in film and others stand out in their own form. Paul just didn't hit me that well in that role. Anymore than if I went out on the road with an orchestra I would do well.'

Some film critics, though, were less diplomatic. *Time Out Film Guide* dubbed it a 'Shambling, self-obsessed and extremely irritating bleat of a film.' Another critic declared, 'You've got to admire Simon's guts because after amply demonstrating his profound lack of acting ability in *Annie Hall,* a lesser man than Simon would have gone back to what he is good at.'

Such adverse comment, and particularly the attacks on his acting ability, cut Simon deeply. He may have talked about risking failure, but he was hardly well prepared for it when it actually happened. He felt strongly that it was poor recompense for all that he had devoted to the project. *One Trick Pony* had taken a chunk out of his life, and now his foray into a possible new direction looked to have run aground.

It was in sombre mood then that he embarked on the planned *One Trick Pony* tour, which started in America, would take in European dates and end in Britain. He took with him the same session men from the Jonah Levin band in the movie.

To add to his burden, the fact that Art Garfunkel's movie *Bad Timing: A Sensual Obsession* had opened on the same day had prompted the press to start linking the two stars again. Garfunkel's film had also disappointed, so the inference was

'Wouldn't it make sense for the two to go back to square one where they had been massively successful?'

While on tour Simon found it wearing to beat off this kind of talk. He had hoped at least that the familiarity of performing live would expunge his feelings of failure, and certainly when he capped the tour in November at London's Hammersmith Odeon he was warmly welcomed. But his nerves could have done without the media constantly harking back to the past. His patience was wafer thin when he agreed to be interviewed on *The Old Grey Whistle Test*, a popular late-night television rock programme. The show's presenters included Bob Harris, famous for his softly whispering voice, and Annie Nightingale.

Simon was interviewed by Nightingale, who committed the memorable faux pas of asking Paul Simon if he missed collaborating on songwriting with Art Garfunkel. Simon made scant effort to conceal his utter disbelief at the question. His glacial expression conveyed his thoughts before he starkly corrected the presenter, '*I* wrote all the songs.'

For all his brave face and optimistic words to the press while on tour, by the time he saw in the new year in New York City he had slid back into depression. The *One Trick Pony* experience had undermined his confidence far more than he had realised and now sent him into an emotional tailspin that seriously affected his songwriting. Normally, even a major setback in life can provide material for a lyricist, but this time Simon hit writer's block.

Paul tried hard to work through it, but the block remained and he was sufficiently alarmed to seek professional help. Over time, he had steadily cut back his analyst sessions. Now he sought the counselling of a psychiatrist who had been recommended to him, California-based Rod Gorney.

Simon's sessions with Gorney began as soon as he flew to Los Angeles in spring 1981. There he confided in the psychiatrist his reaction to the recent failure of his film and uncovered, too, a stream of residual insecurities that had been gnawing away at him. His sense of self-worth was undoubtedly at an all-time low.

Paul Simon can be astonishingly frank and he later publicly revealed something of the advice the psychiatrist offered him. It seems that the crucial moment came when Rod Gorney handed Simon a guitar and suggested that he go back to his room and put down on paper just exactly what he had been unburdening in therapy.

There has to have been more to unlocking Paul Simon's problems than that. However, the moment certainly gave him the looked-for breakthrough. Within a couple of days he had tentatively begun to write a song.

Once back home in New York, Simon improved rapidly. He had left a lot of emotional baggage behind and felt liberated. He and Art Garfunkel had heart-to-heart talks, airing hitherto unspoken grievances between them. Their friendship had matured to the point where they could safely do this and each man emerged with a better appreciation of his own past actions and their effect on the other. Although on some issues both could remain stubborn, it was broadly speaking a healthy process.

Simon also intended to enjoy seeing as much of his son Harper as possible. Paul and Carrie Fisher were experiencing one of their positive spells, and they often teamed up socially with Art Garfunkel and his current companion, actress Penny Marshall.

It was at the height of this camaraderie that Paul Simon was approached by New York-based concert promoter Ron Delsener who, in conjunction with City Parks Commissioner Gordon Davis, was keen to stage a giant open-air free concert in Central Park, in aid of restoring the famous park's Great Lawn. Delsener wanted to know if Simon was interested in performing.

Originally it was envisaged as a solo Paul Simon gig, but Paul rang Art who was abroad on holiday and asked him to take part in it. They discussed different ways of managing this before they came to the conclusion that it should be a full-on Simon and Garfunkel concert. Art Garfunkel had followed up *Breakaway* with albums *Watermark* and *Fate For Breakfast. Scissors Cut* was due out in September 1981 and so he was keen to take part.

The concert was set for September but it was kept secret that it would feature the duo. A circus would erupt when it was known and they needed all their time to rehearse once Garfunkel sped back to New York.

These rehearsals quickly became fraught. Paul Simon called them downright miserable. There were only three weeks in which to prepare and they had much to do. Many changes had occurred since the two had last performed together publicly. Simon now played electric guitar far more often than acoustic and was used to performing with a backing band of musicians who were well in tune with his way of doing things – his songs now *needed* a fuller backing. In addition, Paul loved fronting a band.

Art Garfunkel's natural style, at least when performing with Paul Simon, was to rely on their voices and a trusty acoustic guitar. This was a no-go to Paul, and both knew it would be insufficient to cope with a sizeable outdoor crowd.

The burden, too, was heavy on Garfunkel to get up to speed with several solo Simon songs and ones sung at a much faster tempo than the sixties' material. Even the familiar Simon and Garfunkel numbers had over the years developed new, longer arrangements. If at times Art underestimated his own ability to handle all this in such a short time, Paul had great faith in his ex-partner. The tension produced, however, by the cocktail of anxiety and frustration made both men wish at times that they had never agreed to do the gig. But the date was drawing near.

It was also obvious to the few in the know that the event, now as a Simon and Garfunkel gig, had assumed a new, much greater significance. Although this increased the sense of pressure it also added to the excited anticipation.

When news was announced that it was not a solo Paul Simon concert after all the media, as predicted, erupted. Both performers stressed that it was a one-off gig, not a permanent re-teaming. Simon said that fun was the watchword. But he added that should it turn out to be a universally enjoyable experience, then who knew? Maybe more such gigs could be on the cards

There were very few reunions that popular music fans actively lusted after. On 8 December 1980, horrifically, John Lennon had been gunned down outside the Dakota building overlooking New York's Central Park where he had lived. Apart from being a tragic loss of life, Lennon's death had put the longed-for Beatles reunion beyond reach. As Paul Simon put it, there was now only one major music reunion possible – Simon and Garfunkel's.

In summer Simon had duetted with Garfunkel on 'A Heart In New York' from Art's forthcoming new solo album. In August this cut was released as a single, backed by Garfunkel's 'Is This Love'. It had lodged at a lowly 66 in the US charts, but this in no way reflected apathy towards the upcoming gig.

On Saturday, 19 September 1981 the crowds began streaming into Central Park, already in high spirits. They took with them blankets, deck chairs, food, drink and a bunch of great memories which they were looking forward to having reinforced, if only for one hypnotic night.

A dramatic backdrop designed to represent the famous New York skyline dominated the massive stage. The show was to be filmed to provide a future video release. Everyone already knew that it was an historic occasion and there to open proceedings was Ed Koch.

A lawyer, politician and author of several publications including *Citizen Koch*, Ed Koch was Mayor of New York at the time. He recalls, 'We had a practice in New York City of having free concerts in Central Park. And, of course, a concert by Simon and Garfunkel would be guaranteed to be one of the best attended because of their enormous reputation. The crowd that day was the biggest that we had ever had for a concert. Half a million people came. And yet it all went very orderly. Central Park, during the summer, is one of the most beautiful places you can be. Paul Simon was someone whom I had long admired. I loved his, and Art Garfunkel's singing. And 'Bridge Over Troubled

Water' is one of my all-time favourite melodies, which I still listen to when I'm at the gym.

'I opened the concert. But I knew, having learned it early on, that you never use a concert or any entertainment for the purpose of making a speech because the crowd resents it. They think you are abusing your position. Politicians who make speeches on these occasions ultimately rue the day. So all I did to open the concert was to say, "Ladies and gentlemen – Simon and Garfunkel!"'

Paul Simon and Art Garfunkel stepped through a cut-out doorway in the backdrop on to the stage. The sense of shared love for this duo already radiated strongly before the crowd cheered ecstatically when the two men smiled at each other and shook hands before standing side by side for a moment. They were soaking in the adulation and just trying to get their heads around the sight of the mass of people before their eyes.

When the deafening applause eventually subsided, the duo kicked off with 'Mrs Robinson', followed by 'Homeward Bound' and 'America'. It was the first time the pair had performed live in concert for 11 years, but the magic was as potent as ever. Sweet nostalgia hung in the air as Simon and Garfunkel classics mingled with Paul Simon solo songs, tonight sung by them both.

About midway through what was already a musical landmark event they had just completed Garfunkel's 'A Heart In New York' when Paul then strummed into 'The Late Great Johnny Ace'. A movement to the side caught Paul Simon's eye when a frantic young man leapt up on to the stage and started to rush towards him. Security guards pounced in seconds and grabbing the man, pinned his arms fast and dragged him back.

Paul had stopped playing his guitar. But apart from having instinctively stepped back a pace, he had stood his ground. Even as the clearly agitated man, who had urgently called to Simon, 'I've got to talk to you', was being led off the stage Paul resumed the song. But he had gone ashen white. Just nine months on from John Lennon's murder, it had been a heart-stopping moment for those watching. It did not hit Simon until later how lethal that split second could have been.

The show carried on and included the fabled 'Bridge Over Troubled Water' when Art Garfunkel was happy to be no match for the half-million fans who drowned him out. The show ostensibly ended with 'The Boxer'. But encores added 'Old Friends/ Bookends', 'The 59th Street Bridge Song (Feelin' Groovy)' and the show finished with 'The Sound of Silence'.

While performing, the sheer size of the crowd and the wave of emotion trading back and forth between the audience and himself and Garfunkel, had conspired to rob Paul of a proper sense of what was happening. Like being in the eye of a storm, it was impossible to get an overview of its impact.

He knew there had been an awesome sensation of warmth. But it was only later at home, watching the television news coverage of the gig that he began to grasp the immensity of the event. Next day the gig was also on the front page of every newspaper and he realised that something very special had happened.

The Central Park concert had certainly been the pick-me-up Paul had needed that summer. But perhaps, in some dark corner, it may have worried him momentarily that the really momentous high spot in his career since *Bridge Over Troubled Water* had come when he had teamed up yet again with Art Garfunkel.

The deluge of demand for the duo to re-form permanently began at once. In Britain a compilation album *The Simon and Garfunkel Collection* was rushed out and reached number 4 in December 1981. By the year's end there was an overwhelming approval for the pair that couldn't help but be alluring. Suddenly the prospect of turning back time didn't seem quite so unwelcome. At least it was worth some careful consideration.

CHAPTER 12

Classic Mistakes

IN MID-MARCH 1982 Paul Simon was inducted into the Songwriters Hall of Fame at the National Academy of Popular Music's annual award ceremony, held at New York's Hilton Hotel. The honour could not have come at a more apt time.

The Central Park concert was already legendary. The newly released live double album of the event would score a number 6 hit on both sides of the Atlantic, and the public appetite for Paul Simon and Art Garfunkel to make permanent their reunion was voracious.

Surrendering to the persuasion was easy. On 19 April it was announced that a series of reunion concerts would start in the summer. Moreover, they would be complemented by a new Simon and Garfunkel studio album, their first since *Bridge Over Troubled Water.* Because of the contrast between the cool reception given to his last solo venture and the intoxicating triumph of the Central Park gig, Simon had allowed himself to be swept along by nostalgia. But that was never going to satisfy him.

In all probability, by the time they kicked off the sold-out tour on 8 June at the Hippodrome d'Auteuil in Paris, both performers had doubts about the wisdom of their actions. On stage, professionally they presented a united, harmonious display, which the audience lapped up nightly, little knowing that the strain between the stars backstage was so great they were already scarcely speaking to one another. Why, neither man appears to know. Maybe it stemmed from the fact that there was insufficient foundation for being back on the road together again. When asked earlier by a journalist precisely what the decision had signified, Simon had replied, 'I'm not sure what the hell it means.'

Or perhaps it was no more complicated than the fact that, although they were able to be friends on a personal level and had successfully revisited their glory days for one night, too much had changed for them to be able to be a working duo again.

Each man cherished his own identity and felt choked by the other's perceived intrusion on to his patch. Simon's mindset was solidly solo and Garfunkel had an extra problem. He was still struggling to get over Laurie Bird's suicide and this inner turmoil made him more introspective, leading Simon, wrongly, to feel shut out.

As they travelled through Switzerland, Holland and Ireland, the tension between Simon and Garfunkel led them to deal with the media by giving separate interviews. Journalists spoke to one star, only to trot along to another suite to start all over again with the other. This led to conflicting remarks coming out of the same camp on the same day.

On 19 June Simon and Garfunkel performed a two-hour spectacular in a packed Wembley Stadium in London. The European tour had been intended to smooth out any wrinkles before taking the show to Australia, New Zealand and, of course, across the US. Now as they returned to New York the future of the tour looked to be in jeopardy.

The prospect of working on the studio album in summer 1982 was also unappealing, and there were problems from the start. The songs Simon had been writing since breaking his block were of a deeply personal nature. He felt very protective of them and ambivalent about their becoming Simon and Garfunkel property.

Once in the familiar studio setting old conflicts resurfaced. Simon saw himself as master of this domain. He had spent an entire decade in sole control – but so had Art Garfunkel when pursuing his own independent recording career. Neither took kindly to the other's need for autonomy.

The changes within them were too ingrained, as Paul demonstrated when he admitted that he had become unswervingly the guardian of his own music. Art knew that the songs were personal to Paul, but he believed that they could benefit from his 'outside' interpretation of them. Simon didn't agree.

Rather than this distinction creating explosive outbursts, with one or other of the pair storming off, their entrenched positions merely pushed them apart. They even argued about how Garfunkel should go about laying down his vocals for a song. Paul would record his vocals, then insisted on overseeing proceedings when it was Art's turn. This intensely irked Garfunkel, who felt that his freedom was being stifled.

When they had worked together in the 1960s, a younger, more malleable Simon had, for the sake of the team sometimes given way on issues in the recording studios. Now he was rigidity itself. He had a vision of how he wanted this album to go and would not deviate from it.

Art made his dislike of this stranglehold perfectly clear – he needed more artistic scope than he was being given. An uncomfortable inertia set in that put paid to plans for releasing the album any time that year.

As 1982 drew to an end, there were happier, more relaxed moments for Simon socially, some of which came when he attended dinner parties at the New York Mayor's mansion. Ed Koch recalls, 'The original owner of Gracie Mansion was Archibald Gracie – hence the name – and this is where the New York Mayor resides. It was built in 1799 in Manhattan. I held dinner parties there every week for groups of about 20 people and Paul came as one of my guests.

'He is a vegetarian so we had to prepare food especially for him. I know he is a Democrat but I never discussed his politics with him. The people at the Mayor's dinner parties are not invited on the basis of their politics. They are invited on the basis of having assisted the city of New York in different respects and Paul Simon was certainly qualified to be there. He is a very quiet, intelligent man. Obviously, he has a great reputation and at the dinners I could see that people clearly loved having the chance to talk to him.'

Communication between Paul and Art did not noticeably improve as 1983 got underway. To avoid a complete collapse in their relationship, they would probably have drifted apart again. But as spring came they were committed to the next phase of their planned tour, which took them to Australia and New Zealand, where their massive popularity surely brought each some much-needed pleasure.

Once back in the US, studio work had to resume as a priority. The expected album was now way behind schedule. They had managed to agree on a tentative title for the work, 'Think Too Much', but they were in an impossible situation.

Paul Simon later admitted to the *Los Angeles Times* that he had not wanted it to be a Simon and Garfunkel album. He conceded that Art undoubtedly added a more universally agreeable factor to his songs. But Simon stated bullishly, 'I don't care.' What Simon did care about was the ragged state of his relationship with Carrie Fisher which was currently teetering on a knife-edge. They had experienced long separations due to the demands of their careers. While Paul had had his problems in the studio and on the road, Carrie had gone off on location to film the third movie in the *Star Wars* trilogy, *The Return of The Jedi.* In the new blockbuster, a far sexier Princess Leia finally gets it together with her screen hero Han Solo, played by Harrison Ford. In real life, Fisher and Simon were about to split up.

Carrie's father believed that part of the problem stemmed from Paul's very competitive nature. Eddie Fisher has contended that Simon found it hard to handle Carrie's huge screen success. That, however, was a father's view, and may be well wide of the mark. Eddie Fisher also stated that his daughter had told him once that Paul would prefer it if she quit being an actress. Paul Simon has never at any time confirmed this.

Eddie Fisher also painted a picture of Paul finding it unacceptable when he once discovered Carrie, who had come to one of his lengthy recording sessions, quietly reading a book to pass the time. Matters between the couple had been coming to a head for a variety of reasons, and in June 1983 Carrie moved out of Paul's Manhattan apartment and headed for Hollywood.

The showbiz press, already hot on her trail because of her latest film role, tried hard to get the low-down on why she and Paul Simon had parted. But they got no joy. Neither would own up to harbouring any animosity towards the other; indeed, Simon's admiring comment to reporters was that Carrie was 'absolutely unique'.

Privately, Simon was in less than sparkling spirits when the following month he and Garfunkel again had to suspend work on the album to honour the US leg of the reunion tour. This would be Simon and Garfunkel's first live performance on home soil since the Central Park night, and the tour of open-air gigs in giant stadia around the country was much anticipated.

The first gig was to take place on 19 July in the sold-out Rubber Bowl in Akron, Ohio. Before that, the duo held a major press conference at which Simon's dampener to the flock of journalists was that they should not to be misled by the revival of Simon and Garfunkel appearing as a live-stage duo. This was clue enough for eagle-eyed reporters to realise that all was not well beneath the surface, especially when the songwriter also alluded to matters left unresolved.

Paul's brooding attitude matched the backstage atmosphere as the tour rolled out. In the Dodger Stadium in New York or Meadowlands in New Jersey the crowds cheered and clapped their way through the evening's entertainment. But the press, put on the lookout by that press conference, were searching for signs of trouble.

They began commenting in their reviews that there was a noticeable nip in the air between the two performers on stage. One Washington newspaper decided, 'The singers don't seem to like each other.' Some time later, Paul Simon told *Playboy* magazine that he believed that in one sense, not so very deep down, Garfunkel did not like him. As the press digested this, proof of the friction was apparent when the promised Simon and Garfunkel album failed to materialise.

When two independent minds are out of sync the relationship is bound to fail. Everyone had so wanted the fairytale reunion of Simon and Garfunkel to work. But the studio problems and the strain associated with touring were providing a fertile ground for niggling past hurts to flourish.

With one partnership on the rocks, Simon took a new look at his relationship with Carrie Fisher. They had been missing each other madly since parting. After one gig in August, Simon flew back to New York, where he and Carrie had agreed to meet to discuss their future.

One night during that weekend Paul went off to Yankee Stadium where among hordes of excited spectators he sat for once paying little attention to the baseball game. Instead, he was lost in his thoughts – thoughts that had become centred on marriage as the answer to his problems with Carrie. He was instantly nervous. Divorce had been emotionally painful. But regularly breaking up and making up with Carrie, whom he deeply loved, was hurting them both increasingly. He eventually came to a decision and returning to Fisher that night he proposed to her. She accepted and five days later, on 16 August 1983, they were married.

The private, traditional Jewish ceremony, during which the couple stood under a special canopy, was held in the elegant spacious lounge of Paul's New York apartment, with only relatives and close friends in attendance. It was a happy occasion when the long-estranged Debbie Reynolds and Eddie Fisher met for the first time in years and even managed to get along. Both bride and groom seemed more relieved than anything else. Their toasts spoke mainly of looking forward to what they hoped would be a quieter life.

There was abundant goodwill for the union to work and the marriage made headlines in America and Britain. There could be no immediate honeymoon as Paul had to return to the tour and Carrie had her own work commitments, but they caught up with each other in the coming weeks whenever they could.

The last of the American reunion gigs was at Folsom Stadium in Boulder, Colorado on 30 August. Extra European dates followed and the tour finished in late September with two very special charity gigs in Tel Aviv, Israel. They provided a moving climax to what had been an emotional, bittersweet experience.

Soon after his return to the States, Simon whisked his wife off on a belated honeymoon, taking her on a romantic luxury cruise. While Paul floated down the Nile in style, the public back home now heard what Garfunkel already privately knew – that the long-awaited and overdue Simon and Garfunkel album was now to be revamped as a Paul Simon solo album.

The switch had come as a shock to Garfunkel when Simon had told him. Paul had come to the conclusion that the album was not working out as a duo effort. It sounded too forced to his ears, so he had decided it should become a solo work. Whether artistically or creatively Paul Simon was correct to come to this decision, to say that Art Garfunkel had every entitlement to harbour hard feelings over it would be an understatement. A spokesperson for Paul Simon announced the change of status, stressing that it was Paul's view that the songs were of too personal a nature and so it had to be his own solo album. Art gave no clue to the press of his feelings.

The album, renamed *Hearts And Bones,* was released in November. Its tone was mellow, wistful and melancholy. Just as *Still Crazy After All These Years* had been the reaction to his divorce from his first wife, so now this collection of songs largely reflected Simon's relationship with Carrie Fisher.

The songs had all the depth and sophistication associated

with Paul's lyrics. They were clearly written by a man who, having moved into his 40s, is reflecting on this new phase in his life and how it affects his view of loves, old and new.

He articulates the experience of an intense, inspiring and volatile love as well as the contrasting emotions he had experienced. Musically, the album showcased Simon's already wide range of styles and highlighted his curiosity with some of the emerging new sounds. Interestingly there was one song, 'Citizen of the Planet', which dealt uncompromisingly with nuclear disarmament, that did not appear. Simon had written the song for the album but rejected it as being too direct.

Reaction to the album was mixed. Some critics felt that Paul Simon had fallen into a creative rut. Others liked the album and praised the lyricist's skill and intellect. But dismayed fans found *Hearts And Bones* an anticlimax. The single 'Allergies'/'Think Too Much' failed to chart in Britain and stalled at 44 in America. By December 1983 the album ran out of steam at number 35 in the States.

Warner Brothers were bound to be disappointed with *Hearts And Bones*'s performance after the success of the duo's live Central Park album. Paul Simon was devastated. Logically, he knew that in every career there will be failures but it didn't help. Anticipation had certainly been high for a Simon and Garfunkel album and it is possible that the lacklustre response to the solo effort was the backlash of the fans' disappointment at having their hopes dashed.

Looking back on this period, Paul Simon would see his and Art Garfunkel's decision to try to resuscitate their duo days as a classic mistake. The lack of interest in the new songs was further proved when 'Song About The Moon'/'Think Too Much' was released in February 1984 in America and vanished without trace. Matters then went from bad to worse. Paul's marriage, just months old, foundered and in April Carrie once again moved out. They had been quarrelling for some time and this time had decided to call it a day.

When Paul and Peggy's marriage had not worked out, Simon reflected that he had been too young. Now it seems that Carrie Fisher felt the same way. From her careful public comments after their official separation in July, it would seem that a difference in outlook on how to spend their time together had been a significant factor in the failure of their marriage. Fisher described the gap between them as being similar to her wanting to visit Disneyland while he preferred, say, Sothebys. She called Paul an artiste and herself an artiste's buddy.

Becoming a little more expansive on the subject, Carrie subsequently made it clear that, in her view, part of the problem had lain in the fact that both she and Simon had been used to being the one who is the centre of attention. With characteristic directness Fisher stated, 'I figured out what he needed was an intellectual geisha'. Whether this is a sentiment Paul would agree was true or not, their 11-month marriage was over.

Later on Simon realised that it had been another bad mistake to do something as important as getting married while coping with a tour and everything else that had been cluttering his mind. At the time though it was another personal blow.

By summer 1984 Simon was once again facing divorce. His friendship with Art Garfunkel was on the rack and *Hearts And Bones*, like *One Trick Pony*, was termed a flop. He was left not knowing which way to turn.

Once more music would be his comforter. He had worked through personal problems before by losing himself in exploring intriguing musical styles, and this time would be no exception. He was about to immerse himself in the most rewarding exploration of all – in the mesmerising rhythms of Africa.

CHAPTER 13

The Rhythm of Life

SUMMER 1984 SAW Paul Simon ready to stop and reassess his world after the disappointments of the previous months. Although his personal relationships had been important to him, music remained his lifeblood and he wasn't ready to be put out to grass. What he needed was a bigger canvas and he found it in South African sounds. This new direction would not only spark his commercial comeback, but it would also satisfyingly expand his creativity and result in, to his mind, his best work ever.

Simon was initially set upon this path by chance. He was having a new home built in Montauk, Long Island and he took a close interest in its development, often going out to the site. To fill the long drives to and from New York City he played cassette tapes in the car. One particular tape of upbeat music entitled *Gumboots,* given to him by a friend, intrigued and attracted him. So much so that he eventually asked Warner Brother Records to trace whose work it was.

The music was accordion and drum-driven South African township jive, a genre that Paul Simon had encountered in passing in his youth. Its attraction for him now, however, was to border on the obsessive. He started searching for more examples of this music, which he let saturate his senses for the remainder of the year.

By late 1984, Africa had become a world focus because of the devastating famine in Ethiopia. The harrowing television news reports of the desperate plight inspired Bob Geldof, singer with the Boomtown Rats, to rally the pampered music world to help the emaciated, dying multitudes. His efforts resulted in 36 rock stars, collectively calling themselves Band Aid, producing the charity single 'Do They Know It's Christmas' written by Geldof and ex-Ultravox singer Midge Ure. The humanitarian initiative was also to spawn the historic Live Aid concert the following July.

America's response to Band Aid was to form its own all-star band under the banner name, USA For Africa. Paul Simon joined Stevie Wonder, Diana Ross and Bob Dylan among others on 28 January 1985 in A&M Studios in Hollywood to record 'We Are The World', co-written by Michael Jackson and Lionel Richie.

This charity single topped the US and UK charts, shifting more than seven million copies, and the money raised went to benefit Africa and America's poor. Later, Simon applied for some of the proceeds to be directed towards providing child health care for the poor in New York City. But for now, soon after the LA recording session, he had a personal mission to embark upon.

For some time, the United Nations Anti-Apartheid Committee had imposed a cultural boycott, which prohibited artistes from performing in South Africa until apartheid had been eradicated. Nevertheless, greatly inspired by what he had been listening to for months, Paul Simon decided to go to South Africa to record with native musicians and singers. Accompanying Simon on this mission was his long-time friend, recording engineer Roy Halee.

In February they arrived in Johannesburg and immediately began work in Ovation Studios with three bands whose work Simon knew – Tao Ea Matsekha, General M.D. Shirinda and the Gaza Sisters, and the Boyoyo Boys Band. Altogether it was to be an out-of-this-world experience for the two Americans. Halee was accustomed to operating within a well-structured work system, but what transpired was a series of totally freehand, rambling and undisciplined jam sessions.

Paul was having a ball. The studio looked chaotic but it reverberated to a collection of natural, gifted musicians at work. Along with Simon, they played a wide range of instruments while surrounded by a troupe of singers dressed in all the colours of the rainbow, many of them mothers, who chanted rhythmically while carrying their babies on their out-thrust hips. Older children played games on any spare bit of studio floor space and an unspecified number of men seemed to be there purely to bob and weave to the music. The ambience was inspiring, playful and relaxed – almost therapeutic.

Simon later said, beaming, 'I'd finished with my disappointments and sorrows.' Indeed he had entered a world in which he felt completely at home. Reciprocally, he helped pave the way that led to South African music breaking into the larger commercial mainstream, and for that the South African musicians respected him. Joseph Shabalala, leader of the ten-strong a cappella band Ladysmith Black Mambazo, a powerful vocal group with whom Simon later worked in London at Abbey Road Studios on the track 'Homeless', subsequently bestowed on Paul the Zulu name *Vutlendela,* which means 'he who opened the door'.

The trade-off between the American superstar and the South African musicians was genuinely well balanced. Guitarist Chikapa 'Ray' Phiri reckoned that one side used the other in equal measure. 'There was no abuse,' he has categorically stated. That applied to financial as well as cultural aspects, which was important to Paul. Simon ensured at the outset that all those involved in the recording sessions were paid at the same scale as crack US studio session musicians. He also guaranteed that their collaborative work would be properly recognised on the album that would emerge from this long process.

Simon found the unhurried pace wholly absorbing. Musically he had the opportunity to become intimately acquainted with *mbaqanga* (township jive), as well as with *zydeco,* which is a hybrid of African dance music derived originally from traditional white Cajun mixed with blues.

For days on end he succumbed to a wash of guitar, saxophone, trombone and trumpet music, blended with percussion and even the humble washboard. All this was underscored by the strident rasp of accordion, the sound of which on record Simon later deepened with a synthesiser. The overall effect could sometimes become contemplative and poignant, but largely it was celebratory.

Simon didn't go to Johannesburg with his eyes shut. He was as aware as anyone of South Africa's oppressive and hated apartheid policy. But instead of exploiting the pervasive anger that existed, he wanted the music to illuminate the people's potent lust for life, to harness their indomitable spirit and their ability to laugh, sing and dance in the face of adversity.

He could scarcely have failed to be touched by the primitive squalor of Soweto, the notorious township on the outskirts of Johannesburg, which he visited soon after his arrival. But determined to be positive, he was receptive to the bustling eagerness among the younger generation on the black social scene to look beyond their own culture toward American music.

When Simon arrived in the region, hoping to enlist assistance from local musicians, he met with slight resistance at first. The breakthrough began with his being identified as the man who had written 'Bridge Over Troubled Water', but in addition to that, one musician can usually connect with another, no matter how wide the divide between them.

During the long jam and recording sessions in Ovation Studios, Simon gathered a great mass of material. And although he felt confident that it would allow him to frame, within an album, an accurate reflection of South African culture, he had no illusions that it could ever tell the whole story.

Paul was to call *Graceland* – the album this material would produce – a benign record, but the feelings he stirred up in some quarters by recording in South Africa were far from benevolent. By the time 1985 was well underway, he was embroiled in fierce controversy for having broken the international cultural boycott of South Africa. His name was added to the United Nations blacklist of musicians who had flouted the boycott, and the African National Congress took a similar stance.

Some music stars had broken the boycott by performing at the luxury Sun City complex, which was regarded as an insult to any right-thinking South African. Paul Simon was asked to play Sun City and refused. His 'crime' was restricted to recording in South Africa, but still feelings ran high.

Simon intensely disliked the furore and pointed out that the subsequent success of *Graceland* ploughed a rich furrow of pride back into the country's talented musicians. He has also cited the irrefutable fact that the worldwide profile bands such as Ladysmith Black Mambazo went on to enjoy came as a result of having worked on *Graceland*. There was little he could say, though, that could quell the row.

Simon returned to America with a wealth of material to examine. Several weeks later he brought some of the South African musicians over to New York for further recording sessions. He could see the pattern evolving and invited yet more guest artistes to contribute, including the Spanish-American band Los Lobos. In June 1985 they worked together at Los Angeles' Amigo Studios on Paul Simon's song, 'All Around The World Or The Myth Of Fingerprints'.

Good Rockin' Dopsie and The Twisters added their touch to 'That Was Your Mother', and the Everly Brothers and Linda Ronstadt were also pleased to be part of what was shaping up to be a groundbreaking album.

Simon once said that his lyrics are 'streams of consciousness, edited', and he can be tough on himself during this process. As a result, it added considerably to his task that on this album he started with the music. Of necessity, with *Graceland* songs the lyrics had to be suggested *by* the music and by Simon's acute analysis of the intricate mosaic of meaning and sounds that were entwined deep within the tracks.

It was long and arduous work. At first Simon did not realise that the pattern of sounds within a single piece of music played by the South African musicians could naturally alter, and do so sometimes so subtly that it would lyrically throw him clean off without him recognising why. A perfectionist, Simon found this frustrating but was always willing to try and conquer the problem. He described the whole concept of making this album as being like going back to school, and he thrived on the steep learning curve.

Many of the songs were written in his home in Montauk with simply his guitar, some paper and pen, and his home sound system – not forgetting a trusty old baseball that he bounced off a nearby wall while he was thinking. In the New York recording studio, deciphering sounds, analysing and adapting their uses required meticulous attention.

It had been vital in Johannesburg to ring-fence the collaborative spirit of camaraderie in the overcrowded Ovation Studios. And it was essential not to lose that now in the sterile environment of a modern recording studio. Simon's involvement with this album meant also that in addition to singing lead he handled some of the back-up vocals.

He sometimes just made up sounds that fitted in with what was going on instrumentally in the track. Small wonder that the album was not ready for release until late summer 1986 – more than two years on from his last album and an unusually long time for a record company to wait for a product.

Simon realised that he had slipped from the forefront of his record company's mind. Naturally Warner Brother Records would not have underestimated Paul Simon, despite his two disappointing albums with them to date, but neither was he top of their list at that time. According to the star himself, it was a positive advantage that he was deemed to be so cold professionally that no one from Warner was chasing him for constant progress reports. That way he was able to work privately and at his own pace.

Not that he dawdled. *Graceland* was a huge undertaking. And it was clearly only when it was ready to be played to the record company executives that it dawned on some of them just what a risk Simon was taking.

Roy Halee later stated his belief that there might well have been some at Warner Brother Records who had thought, when Simon headed out to South Africa to record in such an undisciplined way, that he had temporarily lost the plot. When it came to presenting the result of the past two years' work, Halee remembers how he enjoyed waiting to see the executives' reaction.

It must also have been an incredibly stressful moment. Paul Simon's friend, composer Philip Glass, put it best when he simply said, 'What if they had laughed?' Hindsight declares that *Graceland* was an instant classic, of course, but nobody knew that back then.

No one was laughing when the album's curtain-raising track, 'The Boy In The Bubble', began with the sawing sound of raw township accordion, punctuated by a quite astonishingly effective series of single drumbeats. Simon called the stark staccato strike of those belting beats an announcement to sit up and take notice. As such it was the natural opening track for an album that proudly proclaimed its African origins.

Written by Paul Simon, with music by Simon and Forere Motloheloa, 'The Boy In The Bubble' best captures the essence of the whole enterprise. Its unusual start is matched by startling lyrics that describe a cowardly terrorist bomb in a booby-trapped pram shattering more than the tranquillity of a hot, dry summer's day. As the melodic song unfolds, it brings an awareness of what disconnects, but should connect, us in an increasingly interdependent world. A familiar theme of pain turning to hope repeats itself via a refrain that urges an end to tears.

This optimism led straight on to the title track 'Graceland' about which Paul Simon has said, 'This is the best I ever wrote.' The song's construction had evolved over a long period and the early reference to visiting the famous home of the late Elvis Presley had never consciously been intended to remain in the song, despite Simon's life-long admiration for the legendary singer. Almost up to the last moment, Paul had assumed that he would replace the line, until he realised that by now the words had become branded on his brain.

Musically 'Graceland' takes its time before building up to an energetic tempo. Lyrically, having begun with a classically evocative Paul Simon description of the Mississippi Delta, the song trails the listener through aspects of America's past before moving on to express a poignant personal vulnerability. In almost vignette form, Simon gives a glimpse of private regret, yet queries whether any is justified.

By the end, the word 'Graceland' no longer refers to Presley's Memphis mansion, it hints more at a heaven into which all people hope to pass on death. Simon's subsequent pronouncement that this song was perfect to his ears is unusual enough to be remarkable.

The album comprises 11 tracks, probably the catchiest of which is 'You Can Call Me Al'. Paul described it as being 'South African funk'. Chris de Burgh says of this number, 'When you write lyrics, of course you want them to be to the fore because you want them to be heard. But if you filter out Paul's lyrics in this song and just focus on the music – what an incredible backing track it is. It's a dance record.'

It certainly had a great hook, a pennywhistle solo played by Morris Goldberg, and was backed up by an immensely popular video in which Chevy Chase appears with Paul Simon and lip-synchs the song. Chevy looks as upbeat and cheerful as Paul looks comically glum.

Chevy Chase recalls how his involvement with this video came about, 'Paul had a test pressing of the album and Lorne Michaels had a copy at his summer house. We all live out in Long Island in the East Hampton area and Lorne said, "Have you heard it?" I said, I hadn't yet. He said, "It's great." and Lorne played a couple of songs for me and then told me, "Paul's unhappy with this video." He said, "Why don't you do something with Paul?" I said, "I'd be happy to do something with him, if I knew what it was."

'We got Paul on the telephone and Lorne suggested that I sing. So I said, "Okay" and I memorised the lyrics over the car rides into New York City a couple of days after that. It was easy to memorise them although they are quite extraordinary. They tell three episodic portions of a story. They are metaphorical and beautiful lyrics. But, from my point of view, the idea was to take some of the thickness out of it and to make it into something lighter by my lip synching to Paul's voice.

'Paul then, on his own, decided it would be funny if he tried to carry these big instruments into the room during the song. So we put up three walls and a doorway and we shot it in an afternoon. At the time others were spending a million dollars to make a video. It took us hardly any money at all, one quick afternoon and a lot of laughter.

'I think *Graceland* is a great album. There are individual songs from all of Paul's work that I would pick out. But you know, Paul grows with each attempt at something new. And certainly up to that time there hadn't been anything as good or as interesting as that.

'There was the whole period when he was with Artie and they sang some beautiful songs. But that was a more ballad oriented time and music had a softer feel. Here, with *Graceland* there is more temper to it, more edge. Paul got the Ladysmith Black Mambazo group involved – that was such a good idea on Paul's part.

'He was really exploring new sounds and was somehow able to incorporate the beauty and poignancy of his lyrics with that sound. It was a remarkable album in that way. Art reaches across all ethnic and political boundaries. And music is certainly the purest of art forms.'

Asked if he felt that it had been the African rhythms themselves which had appealed to his friend, Chevy Chase replies, 'I don't know that it's the rhythms, so much as the syncopations and the harmonies. Because the 4/4 rhythms are still basically the same and the emphasis is relatively the same on the back beat. But the fact is there is incredible syncopation with some of the African players on that album. And some of the reed work which they did, which Paul and I were demonstrating on the 'You Can Call Me Al' video – some of the saxophone stuff for instance – it was all quite remarkable.

'The way of harmonising and the way of syncopating is really what gave the album a certain flavour that you could say was African. But it's not like we're listening to bongo drums or you can say that it's Cuban sounding or anything. It's the *flavour* of Africa. And that's due in no small part to the singers in Ladysmith Black Mambazo.'

Although pleased with the video he had filmed with Chevy Chase, Paul Simon would also note that, in a way, the success of its humour undermined those parts of the song which were intended to carry a serious important message. Some sections certainly made more than passing references to feelings of fear: fear of darkness, danger and death. Although, having said so, Simon later expressed a distinct impatience with the woeful self-pity exuded by the central character as the song progresses. It is unlikely that it was this part to which Simon referred when he declared of 'You Can Call Me Al' that he had been writing about himself.

Paul Simon's own fear is of his ever being considered an irrelevancy. If, by the mid-1980s, it was not already evident that that could never be the case, *Graceland* surely banished the thought from his mind forever. He considered the work to be an eloquent example of how an affinity can spontaneously occur between strangers. And although *Graceland* would take many commentators completely by surprise, it was not for everyone such an unusual development for the lyricist.

Iwan Morgan, Professor of American History, says, 'It seems to me a natural progression on Paul Simon's part to go back to the continent where it all began. And the fact that the album is called *Graceland*, Elvis Presley's home, suggests that Simon is making the connection between African music and American rock. There is often much focus placed on the Paul Simon of the 1960s. But I would argue that musically he grew even more significant in the 1970s and 1980s. *Graceland* is for me his best album – an album by someone who reflects the multicultural nation that America always was and has increasingly come to see itself as being in the last quarter of the last century.'

Graceland made many in the music world sit up and take notice. British singer songwriter Ralph McTell believes, '*Graceland* is the most perfect Paul Simon album, because it works from start to finish. It's wonderfully intoxicating. Paul always was a perfectionist in the studio. I know people who have worked for him and he has sometimes driven them crazy.

'I imagine Paul would make sure that every word is perfect, that every breath is in the right place and the result is extremely polished. He is a fine guitar player and a fine singer. But it wouldn't do if it wasn't perfect for Paul. There is a lightness to his touch that, if it was left with slips and rickets like you can get with Bob Dylan, it just wouldn't sound right. In his approach Bob is earthy, hard and strong. Whereas I think Paul has a lot more fragility in his work and that's deeply intriguing.

'Paul Simon is one of those rare human beings who goes into the studio knowing exactly what he wants something to sound like when it's finished. The only other person I've met like that is Gerry Rafferty. They've got the finished sound in their heads and they strive to achieve that.'

Paul Simon made his return to the public arena in September 1986, appearing as a guest on the television show *Late Night With David Letterman*. That same month 'You Can Call Me Al'/ 'Gumboots' was released and it peaked at number 4 in Britain. (It took the Chevy Chase accompanying video for the single to reach 23 later on in the States.) Then came *Graceland*. It zoomed to the top slot in Britain and was to remain in the UK charts for 99 weeks. In America it reached number 3.

Neither of the next two singles, 'The Boy In The Bubble' or 'Graceland'/'Hearts And Bones' would particularly glow in the charts, but the parent album's stellar performance eclipsed all, since it went multi platinum, selling in excess of 14 million copies worldwide. *Graceland* had award written all over it, but its success was still somewhat overshadowed by the continued furore surrounding Simon's blacklisting.

The cloud lifted on 30 January 1987 when Simon held an international press conference in London. He announced that the United Nations and the African National Congress had removed his name from their blacklists of artistes who had broken the cultural boycott on recording in South Africa. Paul's pleasure at this development was bolstered when days later he was named Best International Solo Artiste at the annual Brit Awards held at London's Grosvenor House Hotel.

Weeks later, at the 29th Grammy Awards ceremony held at the Shrine Auditorium in Los Angeles on 24 February 1987, *Graceland* won Album of the Year. As Paul, in formal dinner dress, went up to collect his 11th Grammy from actors Whoopi Goldberg and Don Johnson the audience gave the songwriter an enthusiastic standing ovation.

From the stage, on live television, Simon first thanked the South African artistes who had worked with him on the album before stating, 'South African artistes and their countrymen live under one of the most oppressive regimes on the planet today and still they are able to produce music of great power and nuance.' At the ceremony he performed 'Diamonds On The Soles of Her Shoes', a number that had been added to *Graceland* as an afterthought. The song, backed by 'All Around The World Or The Myth Of Fingerprints', was subsequently released as a single.

For some people, however, the recent honours did not take the heat out of Simon's past actions. Young irate black students at Howard University in Washington DC remained opposed to the star having recorded in South Africa under any circumstances at that time. And when Simon went to the university to address the students he became locked into an angry confrontation.

Throughout the clash Simon kept his cool and was prepared to meet any accusation hurled at him in a placid and honest manner, which he hoped would clarify the position and restrain the situation. For one particular student there was no calming down. He demanded Simon's explanation for, as he chose to see it, stealing South African music. He also accused the star of not understanding the music and yelled furiously at Paul that he had bought the musicians.

The talk ended without any particular resolution. Some critics, too, having already been quick to accuse Simon of having profited from black South African music, were in an uproar again when in spring 1987 Simon announced his intention to tour, taking with him, several of his *Graceland* collaborators.

The tour began in Europe and travelled to Zimbabwe where, before a mixed audience, Simon performed in Harare. The gig was filmed and became the best-selling video *The Graceland Concert*. On stage, Simon was the happiest he had been in a long time, and as the African musicians and dancers cavorted about him, the delirious crowd likewise bobbed and swayed to the music. It was hard to see anyone complaining.

In April the massively successful tour arrived in Britain where Paul was appearing at London's Royal Albert Hall. Anti-apartheid protesters had continued throughout to criticise him; now more turned up to picket outside this venue. It was obvious that certain minds were immovably set on the issue.

None of this, however, deterred Simon from furthering his interest in world music. His rebirth had been invigorating. And by August 1987 when, backed by 'I Know What I Know', 'Under African Skies' was released, Paul Simon was already looking towards another continent for inspiration.

CHAPTER 14

Phantom Philanthropist

THE NEW YEAR SAW Paul Simon showered with yet more trophies at the annual American Music Awards ceremony, an event thronged with celebrities and held amid the splendour of Los Angeles's famous Shrine Auditorium.

But infinitely more rewarding to him by then was the progress in an ambitious initiative – of which he had been one of the prime instigators – to bring free health care to the undernourished, homeless children of New York City.

This philanthropic scheme is the Children's Health Fund and its seeds were sown during the time Simon had spent in New York shaping *Graceland* in the recording studio. It is, of course, impossible to live in a big city and not be aware of the poor and homeless. Paul had not been blinkered all these years, but he had lately become particularly sensitive to the problem.

Simon's co-founder of the Children's Health Fund is Dr Irwin Redlener, a top paediatrician who, in addition to being president of the Children's Hospital at Montefiore in New York, is lecturer in paediatrics at Harvard Medical School. From 1992 to 1999 Dr Redlener was also to serve as a physician special consultant to the White House.

In 1986 the responsibility for controlling the dispersal of the millions raised by USA For Africa (whose single 'We Are The World' had been in response to the Ethiopian famine) lay with Dr Redlener as the charity's Director of Grants, and he recalls how he and Paul first became acquainted:

'When he was working on the *Graceland* album, Paul would walk every day from his home on the Upper West Side of Manhattan to the studio, and over time he met a woman who was living on the street. Because of his personality and his sensitivity to these kinds of problems he came to know this woman, named Maria. He spoke with her every day and gave her money periodically. Then one day she disappeared and Paul was very distressed. He had his office spend time trying to figure out where she was and what had happened to her, but they were never able to do that.

'Meantime, homelessness was becoming a very serious social problem in New York City – indeed across the US – and there was a dramatic rise in homeless families. There was an article one day in the *New York Times*, which Paul read, about some programmes being set up to work with the homeless and he contacted the organisers.

'But he also contacted USA For Africa and said that he was concerned about this situation in New York. Ten per cent of the money raised by 'We Are The World' was designated to remain in the US to help deal with the problems that we had in our own country and Paul wanted to tap into that ten per cent. He wanted to see what we could do to help out. So he called the charity headquarters. Although I was based in New York, running the foundation, its headquarters is in Los Angeles. I happened to be there for a meeting when Paul rang and they put him on to me.

'I spoke with him and we met when I came back to New York. At Paul's request, I arranged for he and I to go on a tour of some of the shelters called welfare hotels in New York City where homeless families live. There were 100 shelters like this around the city and all of them were in pretty bad shape. They were basically warehouses for very impoverished people. We were accompanied by a mutual friend, Dan Klores, who was Paul's publicist. Dan turned out to be very helpful when it came to establishing the organisation that Paul and I formed.'

What Simon and Dr Redlener found shocked them to the core. Simon later described it like being back in the Third World he had so recently visited. Dr Redlener recalls, 'We had the chance to go and see first-hand some of the conditions and the dire problems that people were experiencing and it was unbelievable.

'We went to a place called the Martinique Hotel which was in midtown Manhattan on Broadway and 32nd Street. There were a thousand homeless children and their families living in that place, amid conditions of very serious squalor, deprivation and danger. We went round various places and afterwards I made inquiries to get an understanding of what their needs were. It was clear that these children were not getting health care and I got back to Paul and told him so.'

The immediate dream, they discovered, of the people working with the homeless centred on having a mobile medical unit that could bring health-care out on to the streets, directly reaching those who needed it. Simon was instantly excited. He later revealed, 'I asked how much one unit cost.' The answer was over $100,000 and Simon promptly said, 'Okay, I'll buy it.'

Dr Irwin Redlener was the head of outpatient paediatrics at New York Hospital and was able to arrange for this state-of-the-art mobile unit to be based there. From the hospital, fully staffed by a professional medical team, it could head out to various sites in Manhattan to offer help. A computerised patient record system would help them keep track of people with no fixed address.

Paul Simon recalled that within weeks they were completely inundated by people seeking help. Clearly more than one unit would be needed. Dr Redlener continues, 'We got a program up that we eventually called the New York Children's Health Project. We developed a mobile-based paediatric service for homeless children and we did that under the umbrella of the Children's Health Fund that Paul and I started. He and I have been working very closely together since that project started back in 1986 and have become very connected over it.'

The Children's Health Fund is now a national network. Sixteen different medical units are treating hundreds of thousands of patients in more than ten states throughout America.

In 1988 – content that his plan to help those far less fortunate than himself was being successfully implemented – Paul Simon turned his thoughts to his own future and where he wanted his recording career to go next. Later in the year a 16-track compilation album *Negotiations And Love Songs 1971–1986* was released . It performed far better in Britain than in America, where accusations of exploitation over *Graceland* still occasionally reverberated.

Proof that Simon had no intention of allowing such opinions to hamstring him musically came when, in spring, he took what he deemed to be the next logical step and turned to South American music. He was particularly interested in Brazilian percussive sounds, having been nudged in that direction during a chance meeting with singer Milton Nascimento.

This attraction was not new, for Latin music had long drawn Simon. As during the genesis of *Graceland*, Paul began listening to endless tapes of Brazilian music. Before long he headed to Rio de Janeiro to record with the cream of the local musicians.

At one point, his travels took him to Salvador, where he recorded in the city square one day. The raw, elemental sound was complemented by the ebullient atmosphere among the approving crowds, gathered to watch this extraordinary open-air jam session.

Simon's experience of making *Graceland* allowed him to hone the way in which he worked and soon he was back in the confines of a New York recording studio, sifting through his haul. He was well pleased, as he had known he would be, with the rich texture of his taped material – essentially a blend of Brazilian sounds and West African rhythms.

Once again, Paul set himself the lengthy task of writing lyrics that were shaped by his singing aloud whatever words were subliminally suggested by repeatedly playing the music. Determined to seek a new language in rock music, he later explained that what he derives from working in this seemingly back to front way is an invitation to rely lyrically more on the abstract, because music itself is abstract.

If that made it sound a tough task, it was sometimes made harder still, because Simon would craft a lyrical structure to overlay the musical structure that he had meticulously interpreted and fashioned from the tapes, only to discover that, sometimes these structures refused to gel, leading to a frustrating, jarring effect.

The work spread over two years – his fame and wealth accorded him the luxury of being able to devote long periods to projects. He was also living alone and quite happy that way, with no pressure arising from personal demands on his time and no emotional turmoil to distract him.

Working on an album can be a claustrophobic existence, however. In summer 1989, he prised himself out of the studio and returned to live performing with a short tour of Europe. He also took part in September in a special anniversary edition of *Saturday Night Live*. And, as the decade drew to a close, his professional past was about to notch up a proudly memorable statistic.

In December 1989, 32 years after Paul released his first record, UK music pundits compiled a table of those popular music stars who had spent the highest number of weeks in the British album charts from the first chart in November 1958 to the end of 1989. Simon and Garfunkel's 1,034 weeks placed them second only to the Beatles, who had notched up 48 more weeks. Elvis Presley came a close third, and a long way ahead of Queen, David Bowie, U2 and the Rolling Stones.

Given such statistics, it was no wonder that in January 1990, at the Waldorf Astoria Hotel in New York, Simon and Garfunkel were inducted into the Rock and Roll Hall of Fame. Simon didn't intend to look backwards, however, and for the coming months he put most of his energies into the new album.

In October 1990, the single 'The Obvious Child'/'The Rhythm of The Saints' was released. In Britain it reached number 15 but it took months to stall in the US at number 92. Its disappointing performance in America did not, however, spell commercial obscurity for *The Rhythm of The Saints* album, which quickly followed. The ten-track, self-produced work, engineered by Roy Halee, incorporated the talents of collaborators such as singer Milton Nascimento and Vincent Nguini, as well as Ladysmith Black Mambazo and guitarist Ray Phiri.

The presence of some of the key *Graceland* musicians and singers was in a way an open acknowledgement that *The Rhythm of The Saints* was a conscious extension of the earlier ground-breaking album. But it seemed the new arrival was less palatable. *The Rhythm of The Saints* was not a flop. The album made number 1 in the UK in its week of release there and number 4 in America, but it fell well short of achieving the sales attained by *Graceland*. Some observers felt that, although tasteful and innovative, the plaiting together of many, vastly different, musical strands hadn't always worked this time. Predictably, too, some accused Simon of again poaching on the preserves of Third World musical culture. Two further singles from the album – 'Proof'/'The Obvious Child' and 'Born At The Right Time'/ 'Further To Fly' – failed to chart in the coming months.

Simon set out to bolster the album with a worldwide tour dubbed 'Born At The Right Time' which began in America in early January 1991 at the Dome in Tacoma, Washington. His backing band included musicians who had worked on the last two albums, and he looked forward to the challenge of taking this new show on the road.

There was no detectable apathy among Simon's fans as he packed out prestigious venues such as Madison Square Garden. He made some personal points along the way, too. After his concert at the Desert Sky Pavilion in Phoenix, Paul donated a sizeable chunk of his share of the proceeds to assist those in Arizona who were endeavouring to establish a State holiday in honour of the murdered civil rights icon, the Reverend Dr Martin Luther King.

In late spring, the tour landed in Britain for a 16-date leg, ending in June. When playing at Manchester's G-Mex venue in May, Simon also appeared by satellite that same night during a benefit gig that was going on at London's Wembley Arena in aid of Kurdish refugees.

Unlike some of his contemporaries, Paul Simon does not advertise his charity work, but over the years he had been steadily active. He regularly appears at concerts in aid of nature conservation, and in 1990 he played at a benefit gig to preserve the Montauk Point Lighthouse. He has appeared as a guest artiste at fundraising events in support of the Rainforest Foundation, and has done his bit for AmFar (The American Foundation for Aids Research). He has commented regarding philanthropy, 'It doesn't really matter what you choose, as long as you get involved.' And he stressed the importance in life of giving, as opposed to taking.

For years, Paul Simon had given his support to the Democrat Party and he had recently maintained that tradition by performing at a gala benefit at Meadowlands in East Rutherford, New Jersey in aid of re-electing Bill Bradley to the US Senate.

After many years of having a Republican President in the White House, with ex-actor Ronald Reagan followed in the late 1980s by George Bush, the return of the Democrats was not too distant. After Bill Clinton's victory in 1992, Simon was one of the guest performers at the Inaugural Ball in Washington DC the following January.

Meanwhile, for a spell in summer 1991, Simon managed to freewheel, spending time mainly at his fabulous seafront property on Long Island. Having spent so many years as an itinerant performer, he remarked, 'All of this is about finding peace and sooner or later I'll have to say this is home.'

Yet he saw less of home throughout the year as he continued his Born At The Right Time world tour. And there were other memorable occasions in store. On 15 August 1991, almost exactly ten years since the historic and still talked-about Simon and Garfunkel reunion concert in New York's Central Park, Simon returned to the famous Great Lawn for a one-night-only, solo, free concert to be broadcast live on the HBO television channel.

This time a mind-boggling 750,000 people turned out. The great mass of humanity stretched out in a wide avenue, flanked on either side by trees, from the front of the stage back as far as the eye could see. Simon performed material from his solo 20-year career to date. He also made room that night for a handful of Simon and Garfunkel classics, including 'Bridge Over Troubled Water', 'The Boxer', 'America' and 'The Sound of Silence'. The gig spawned a 23-track double album.

The Born At The Right Time tour left America for the Far East at the end of September, kicking off at the Dome in Tokyo. During his spell in Asia, Paul Simon became the first western artiste to perform a concert in China since the pro-democracy mass demonstrations of June 1989.

While Simon continued to roll on his way, another Simon and Garfunkel compilation album, *The Definitive Simon and Garfunkel* was released; it rose to number 8 in the British charts. Simon wound up his travels in mid-December 1991 with two sold-out gigs at the National Auditorium in Mexico City. Financially the almost year-long tour was extremely rewarding, with the US leg alone said to have grossed in excess of $20 million.

But by the time Simon walked away from the microphone for the last time that year he was tired. He needed time off to recuperate both physically and emotionally. Although he had found it wearing at times, he felt that he had weathered well the resurgence of controversy and accusations of exploitation over *The Rhythm of The Saints*. He had no idea, however, what was in store for him in the near future.

CHAPTER 15

Bridging the Gap

THE MOST FRIGHTENING EXPERIENCE a performer can surely face is becoming the object of serious death threats. This befell Paul Simon when, in early 1992, he took his Born At The Right Time tour to South Africa. He planned to play five gigs there, starting at Ellis Park Stadium in Johannesburg. Paul had been invited to perform in the country by the South African Musicians Alliance. The African National Congress sanctioned the tour, as did ANC president Nelson Mandela.

Radical anti-apartheid groups, however, protested vociferously at Simon's plans. The star had been the brunt of anti-apartheid protest before. But this opposition took on an altogether more sinister aspect when threats of violence began to be levelled against Paul Simon personally and any venue at which he planned to appear.

Death threats made against performers and against the public coming to see a concert have always to be taken seriously, even if they turn out to be no more than hot air. But no one was left in any doubt as to the fanaticism of certain of these South African radical groups when, within hours of Paul Simon flying into Johannesburg, the local offices of the company providing support services for the tour were bombed. It was reported that the Azanian National Liberation Army claimed responsibility for the action.

The planned gigs became headline news and it was a tense and worrying time. But Paul Simon announced his intention not to be intimidated by a group of extremists. He was not chest-beating. He genuinely believed that, although it had been controversial, by recording and performing in South Africa he had helped to promote greater acceptance of black music. And he wanted that to continue.

Naturally, he ensured that for his own safety and that of the people coming to see him, that security was significantly tightened. Sniffer dogs scrambled all over the venue. Police set up security checkpoints in the surrounding streets to vet people arriving. With extra stadium guards in place, his own personal protection arrangements were strengthened too. Yet, as a man whose stock-in-trade is communication, what he wanted to do was to open dialogue with the very people who had threatened him.

It was reported that a member of the volatile black nationalist group, the Azanian Youth Organisation (AZAYO) had been arrested as a terrorist suspect. Yet in a move that few other stars would have even contemplated, Paul Simon managed to arrange a series of meetings between himself and prominent members of AZAYO. He spent almost an entire day locked in discussion with them in an effort to establish a way of working through their differences. He wanted to reach an understanding that would mitigate the violent attitude towards him and his concerts, scheduled to start in two days' time, on 11 January 1992.

Whether this courageous meeting had been successful could only be proved by going ahead with the gigs. Nelson Mandela, South Africa's future President, publicly welcomed Paul Simon, maintaining that the American star's arrival to play in his country was a very happy occasion, and he urged Simon to feel that he was among friends.

With a warm welcome on one side and, with luck, a defused and diminished threat of violence on the other, what Simon now needed was for a crowd to turn out for the concerts. But, undoubtedly put off by the much publicised bomb blast and the subsequent threats, people stayed away in droves. At Ellis Park Stadium the 70,000-seater venue was not even a third full. Simon also later admitted that while on stage he had second thoughts about allowing himself to be carried away with the passion of some of his lyrics and to close his eyes as he sometimes did, in case he never got to open them again.

It was not what he had wanted, but by the time Paul returned to America he must have been relieved, if disappointed, at the outcome of what he had hoped would be a memorable finale to his tour.

Performance got back to normal when, in February, Simon sang at the Grammy Awards ceremony at New York's Radio City Music Hall. *The Rhythm of The Saints* had earned two nominations, one for Album of the Year, and Roy Halee was up for Producer of the Year.

When Simon had returned to play Central Park the previous August there had been the inevitable rumour that Art Garfunkel, now remarried and with a baby son, would make a surprise guest appearance on stage. That hadn't happened. But now, in May 1992, Paul did partner Art when, for the first time in ten years, they teamed up at New York's Brooks Atkinson Theater. The gig was to help raise money for a foundation that concentrates on helping Aids sufferers. The reunion was a one-off; the pair had long gone their irrevocably separate ways, but yet again there were parallels. For just as Art had acquired a new wife and family, so too did Paul.

In the late 1980s Simon had been seen often enough in the company of Carrie Fisher for the gossip columnists to speculate that the pair were renewing their love, for clearly they were still close. However, that was mere bridge-mending for the sake of a lasting friendship. But new love had come Paul Simon's way – and from a most unexpected direction.

It's not that falling in love for the first time with a fellow recording artiste should be so strange. If anything it made sense, after his failed relationships with women who were not directly involved in the music business. It was also no surprise that the woman was a songwriter and so someone who could understand the demanding creative process.

The shock came in the fact that she was a mere six and a half years older than Simon's son, Harper, who at 19 years old, was a budding musician, interested in following in his famous father's footsteps. Edie Brickell, at 26, was half Paul Simon's age, yet having met on the music circuit they had fallen in love.

Born in March 1966 in Oak Cliff in Dallas, Texas, Edie Brickell had joined a band called the New Bohemians while studying at the Southern Methodist University. As a singer-songwriter with a taste for mellow, intuitive lyrics, she ended up fronting the four-piece outfit. In 1988 Edie Brickell and the New Bohemians recorded their debut album, *Shooting Rubberbands at the Stars,* which found instant success and became a million-seller, producing the single, 'What I Am'.

The follow-up album *Ghost Of A Day,* though, was a commercial disappointment and, dispirited, the band broke up just before Brickell met Paul Simon. On 30 May 1992 they married in a secret civil ceremony held at Simon's Long Island home.

Paul's happiness with his third wife was increased by the fact that she was pregnant; a son, Adrian, was born before the year's end. In the future, Paul and Edie would have two more children. Always prepared to learn from the past and at a different point in his career, Paul Simon stayed more at home during summer 1992. When they wanted to work in the recording studio, he and Edie would travel into New York City and return home afterwards to Long Island.

In late September Paul performed at the 'Hurricane Relief' concert held in Miami, Florida, to help victims of the recent devastating Hurricane Andrew. Paul Simon's charity, the Children's Health Fund, had mobilised the necessary medical units into the area as soon as possible, to help cope with the emergencies the disaster had left in its wake.

The Children's Health Fund was making a significant difference to the lives of a colossal number of children right across the

US, but required a constant high level of funding. To help keep the expanding organisation afloat, therefore, on 1 March 1993 a benefit gig was arranged at the Dorothy Chandler Pavilion in Los Angeles.

The appearance Paul Simon had made ten months earlier with Art Garfunkel in New York had been successful enough for them to feel able to repeat the experience. The whole evening, which also featured Hollywood comic actor Steve Martin and stalwart singer-songwriter Neil Young, was an unqualified success, raising over $1 million.

By autumn Paul and Art were back communicating on a level that encouraged them once again – as if it were an eternal itch that they had periodically to scratch – to mount a short reunion tour. The shows, which would include an appearance at Madison Square Garden, started early October in New York.

Around this time Paul Simon had been profiled by Britain's arts programme *The South Bank Show*, during which the subject of his recent difficulties in South Africa made for a dark contrast with his sunny contentment with life at the time. The perception of Paul's personal happiness with married life was strengthened when the 52-year-old told the press in his deadpan manner that never having been a sex symbol, he was spared the problem of trying to act like a young thing. With typical style he commented, 'I'm in my life now, not in my imagination.'

True to his protestations, Paul Simon deliberately slowed down throughout 1994, concerning himself with his young wife and son and with Edie's solo recording career. When Edie released her first solo album, *Picture Perfect Morning*, that year, Paul produced the record and guested on guitar. And he continued to lend his services to charitable endeavours.

He didn't hop on every one of the many charity bandwagons around. He preferred instead to stick to particular causes, most of all the Children's Health Fund. Simon's commitment to the organisation strengthened with every year. Dr Irwin Redlener reflects, 'A lot of celebrities who get involved with causes or issues are kind of brought in, and they have a fairly superficial connection. The Children's Health Fund has become the largest health care program for homeless children in the world. And from the start Paul was connected in a much deeper, much more important way than most of the artiste/charity connections that I am aware of. Paul is in a rather small subset of artistes who have really been able to make a difference, in a sustained way, over time.

'My original impression had been – here was a superstar, a creative genius with international recognition who was expressing compassion about homeless people in his neighbourhood. And I mean, really saying, "This is wrong. Let's do something tangible about it."

'The other thing about Paul is that he is completely disinterested in his personal publicity. He doesn't mind attention for his creative accomplishments. But he has never sought – in fact, I would say he shuns – any focus being placed on his charity work and the compassion he has in abundance.

'He just doesn't see value for anybody in him making a big deal publicly about the fact that he is trying to do something for people who need help. I think in his heart that Paul expects or hopes that everybody would be charitable and giving. I don't think he is comfortable with calling attention to himself for doing what he thinks is an appropriate human response to a tragedy like that.'

Reflecting on his own life at the time, Simon had certainly benefited from taking time to step back from recording and only sporadically performing live since the end of the Born At The Right Time tour. In the last couple of years, however, he had not been idle.

In the early 1990s he had become acquainted with the West Indian-born poet and playwright Derek Walcott. Although Simon had deliberately kept it under wraps, for some time he had been working with Walcott on a project that would prove that his determination to explore new creative boundaries had in no way diminished, nor had his capacity to attract controversy. This time he was thinking about a Broadway show.

CHAPTER 16

Crossed Wires

PAUL SIMON IS A BELIEVER in learning from one's mistakes and it could be argued he ought to have known better than to think that he could suddenly break into the world of the Broadway stage musical. After all, his attempt to enter the movie world with *One Trick Pony* had been a painful experience.

But then again, why should an artiste not wish to spread his wings? Paul still had the guts to experiment, and perhaps creating a stage musical was not in itself an unattainable achievement for such a skilled lyricist. The problem, however, lay primarily in that the subject matter he chose to put on for public entertainment was dense enough to sink a battleship. It was also a real-life story, over which feelings still ran very high.

It concerned *the* sensational news story of late summer 1959 in America about a 16-year-old Puerto Rican named Salvador Agron, from New York City's Spanish Harlem district. Agron was convicted of killing two young students.

Agron, from a seriously disadvantaged background, had come out of reform school only to run wild as a member of an Upper West Side Latin street gang called the Vampires. The gang members careered around the city dressed in dramatic black capes with blood-red lining.

The Vampires' traditional foe was another New York gang called the Norsemen. Out one night, looking for a fight, Salvador Agron mistakenly attacked two innocent students. They were not affiliated to any gang but had the misfortune to be in the wrong place at the wrong time. In the melee, Agron fatally stabbed both boys with a Mexican dagger and fled. Witnesses to his flight described him as a tall Puerto Rican in a flowing cape, so the press dubbed him 'The Capeman'.

His trial was a cause célèbre in which Salvador Agron was portrayed as a heartless killer. He stoked this evil image himself when, on becoming the youngest person to be sentenced to the electric chair in New York State, he defiantly declared, 'I don't care if I burn. My mother could watch me!'

Pleas for clemency on the grounds of his youth and the fact that he had grown up in terrible poverty and was a victim of his deprived circumstances, were made from people as influential as Eleanor Roosevelt. Governor Nelson Rockefeller subsequently commuted the death sentence to 20 years imprisonment.

While incarcerated, Agron renounced violence completely and embraced a programme of rehabilitation. He was released in 1979 and died of natural causes in the Bronx seven years later, two days before his 43rd birthday.

Paul Simon recalled the whole case, which had happened at a time when doo-wop Latin music had predominated, in vivid detail. Recollections of the Capeman killings, Agron's capture and trial, had thrust themselves to the forefront of Simon's mind in the late 1980s, a time when he had started to immerse himself in the South American sounds that would culminate in *The Rhythm of The Saints.* An interest in Latin street culture had lain dormant within Simon for more than 30 years; he admitted that in his youth it had seemed to be an alluringly exotic, if edgy, subculture in New York City.

He liked the idea of taking his memories further and telling this true tale to a wider audience in the form of a stage musical.

The chance to write original songs that were unashamedly Latin in style also held a strong appeal.

Work had begun in earnest in 1993, the starting point of his collaboration on the project with St Lucia-born, 63-year-old poet/dramatist Derek Walcott. He scooped the Nobel Prize for Literature in 1988 and his poetry is frequently either autobiographical or concentrates on thorny social issues. The stage musical which Simon and Walcott finally came up with was to provoke much heated criticism. But no one could fault Paul Simon's sincere commitment to thoroughly researching his subject.

He started by delving back into New York newspaper archives, reading the passionate articles inspired by this media story and told in the language of an age that predated political correctness.

Enlisting the valuable assistance of an old friend, Carlos Ortiz, Simon turned investigator and successfully scouted out people who had been around that Spanish Harlem scene in the late 1950s. Some had known Salvador Agron personally. Paul took time to travel to Puerto Rico and, once back in America, went to see for himself the forbidding confines of Sing Sing prison where Agron had served his time.

These attempts to get close to his central figure were boosted when Salvador Agron's mother and sister agreed to talk with Paul. He was also able to read some of Agron's prison writings, giving him crucial insight into the man's changing state of mind during his prison term.

Researching in a more general sense, Simon went to the theatre to catch the current Broadway shows. Apart from old favourites, such as the rock musical *Tommy* and *Guys And Dolls*, he found nothing much to interest him. Theatreland, he must have felt, was screaming out for something fresh and more meaty.

The root of the controversy Simon was to spark over *The Capeman* lay in the fact that having analysed his intensive research, he came out with a desire to present Agron in a sympathetic light and to show how his tough life was reflected in his deeds.

Already concerned with the state of poverty in various parts of the world, Paul Simon could well understand that constant and desperate social, financial and emotional deprivation can unite to create in someone an innate callousness. This in turn can breed an absence of respect for the sanctity of human life: a chillingly detached state abhorrent to most of society. The unpalatable truth of this would become apparent later.

At the time, convinced of his direction, Simon sought to write a musical that set out to examine issues such as the importance of genuine atonement being more valuable than a natural thirst for vengeance. Salvador Agron had made dramatic differences to his life and his thinking during his years behind bars and Simon wanted to take the story beyond the brutal darkness of the gory murders and the sensational glare of his trial.

Simon said later at a press conference that he hoped he had written a story 'that would sweep you up and that examines the moral questions of forgiveness and the possibility of redemption.'

The time-consuming project trundled on over the years. Simon wrote the original songs for the musical, since every word in the show would be sung. In spring 1995 he had held a contest to discover an a cappella group which would be suitable for the stage. Now, 18 months on, in late summer 1996, auditions began at New York's Musical Theater Works for the show, still more than a year away from opening on Broadway.

The core cast for the two-act play featured Ednita Nazario, Renoly Santiago, Philip Hernandez and Sophia Salguero. Portraying Salvador Agron as the teenage killer would be the responsibility of singer Marc Anthony. Born of Puerto Rican parents in New York, the future hot star of salsa music had met and was already friends with Panamanian-born salsa star Ruben Blades, who would take over the role of the older, imprisoned Agron.

The cast in place, work on the musical moved on to its next

phase. In addition to Derek Walcott, Paul Simon also involved Jerry Zaks and Joey McKneely, both experienced in Broadway productions. Stage directors during *The Capeman*'s development, came and went: Simon was used to being in control and did not always appreciate warning voices trying to steer him down conventional paths.

In November 1997 Paul Simon's first album in six years *Songs From The Capeman* was released. It was not a cast album, but Ruben Blades and Marc Anthony vocals did feature on it. Roy Halee was producer/engineer and the 13-track record boasted the skills of a mass of session musicians. Notably, Paul's son Harper Simon is credited as having contributed guitar and harmonica. The album stopped in the US charts at number 42, but served nonetheless as the precursor to preview performances of the show, which began in December at the Marquis Theater on Broadway in Manhattan. Opening night was supposed to be 8 January 1998.

Problems, however, cropped up straight away when *The Capeman*'s first preview performance drew fire from the protesting relatives of Salvador Agron's two young victims. These family members were naturally outraged at any sympathetic spin being attached to the killer and controversy mounted. The first knock-on effect was that opening night was put back. Paul Simon's publicist Dan Klores, who was also one of the musical's producers, categorically refuted the notion that the production could be in any way construed as exploiting anyone. To add to Simon's woes, tepid reactions from sample preview audiences meant that more time was needed to add new material to the show and to allow the cast and all involved to refine their delivery.

The Capeman opened three weeks late on Thursday, 29 January 1998 to uniformly poor reviews. One of the critics' more persistent complaints was that it seemed to be a choppy, disjointed production. In the opinion of the *New York Times* theatre critic, 'Everything in the musical melts together. Practically nothing that's said, done and shown on the stage seems to connect with anything else.' *USA Today* maintained,

'The performers seemed lost.' And the *Daily News* remarked that those sections of the play that did work, unfortunately seemed only to illuminate other parts that did not.

The ambitious production, which had already assumed an air of siege, was now in trouble. The circling sharks in the press homed in on almost everything, from the outrage of the victims' families to the fact that not enough seasoned Broadway campaigners had been involved in the musical's development. To some, this indicated arrogance on Paul Simon's part.

Paul Simon, in turn, saw the critics' reaction from a different angle. He was later to point to reviewers' intrinsic inability to distinguish between a safe bet, and a risky project which might sink, but may have planted the first seeds of something big. He was also frank about the disappointing habit of those who prefer to pigeon-hole performers in their own individual fields and give no encouragement to attempts at artistic cross-pollination.

Paul's personal hopes for *The Capeman* had been to revel in success for a certain, not necessarily long time, and to be content with that. The thought of his musical going on to take legs around the world, indeed, did not hold the expected appeal for him.

As he saw it, a musical would probably in those circumstances mutate in ways in which he wasn't involved and would not necessarily approve of. He considered too that it would feel odd if something live like a stage production – say ten years down the line – had *not* changed dramatically. As he would not be the same person in every respect in that space of time, so he anticipated that he would find himself frustrated at the framework of his musical remaining unmoved.

In the event all of this thinking was made obselete when, after a heavy bombardment of criticism, *The Capeman* was withdrawn on 28 March 1998, just one day short of two months into its run. In addition to being a creative blow, the premature close of *The Capeman* cost Paul Simon and fellow investors a staggering $11 million. Yet for some experienced observers the spectacular flop was not a great surprise.

Sir Tim Rice is one of the world's most renowned lyricists whose stage musicals, in collaboration with Andrew Lloyd Webber alone, include the colossal hits *Joseph And The Amazing Technicolor Dreamcoat, Jesus Christ Superstar* and *Evita.* He says, 'I've heard *The Capeman* album, which is nice. I wouldn't say it was Paul Simon's strongest work but I certainly enjoyed it. But the stage musical – it struck me from a distance that the subject matter was just a bit too depressing.

'The number one rule for any musical is get a good story. I think the subject matter of *The Capeman* was an almost insuperable handicap. I was hoping to see the show but it didn't run for very long and when it was on, I wasn't in America and so I couldn't get to it. But such a depressing story meant that it was an obvious risk. You can get muggings and the murders on the street outside for real. Why bring it into the theatre?'

Asked whether New York newspaper theatre critics can single-handedly sink a Broadway production, Sir Tim is categoric: 'No. I've had terrible reviews for a number of my shows and they've been hits. I mean, it doesn't help. If a show is teetering on the edge already, then I think a really bad review from the *New York Times* can be the last straw.

'But it's absolutely not true that the *New York Times'* critics can kill a show. In my own experience, over the years, they have got nearly everything wrong. *Evita* got bad reviews, *Phantom of the Opera* got bad reviews. *Les Misérables* on the other hand got some good reviews. But I really don't care too much what the critics say. I want to be fair about what I say about *The Capeman* as I didn't see it. But the only reason people go to see shows is because a friend or someone says, "You must go!" *The Capeman* never got the chance to get word-of-mouth trade.'

Paul Simon's skill as a lyricist was clearly no guarantee of success in writing for the stage. Sir Tim Rice says, 'There *is* a difference although I'm not sure what it is at times. I think the difficulty comes usually in the construction of the piece. You can have a great score. For example, the songs of *Sgt. Pepper* have often been put into musicals that have never really worked. But they've not worked because there's no story line and a rather strained one has had to be concocted.

'Actually when writing a song, it doesn't really matter if you are writing it for the charts or whether you are writing it for a stage musical. It's getting the context right that is much harder for people. A lot of people in the pop world can write a decent lyric or a great tune. But whether they can construct them together around something that really makes sense is another thing entirely.' In whichever medium, a songwriter generally will have the last laugh though. Sir Tim adds, 'Songwriting is a good insurance policy for your old age.'

Paul Simon's friends meantime had their own views of how *The Capeman* project turned out. Chevy Chase declares, 'Paul was given a lot of crap for no reason. People just didn't get what he was trying to do and that was a shame. The music, I thought, was rather remarkable. But it was the story that everyone made such a fuss over and that ruined it. I don't think when Paul took it on that he foresaw any of that happening. I don't think that he thought that suddenly the yellow press would come after him and start endlessly talking about him. It was just a musical at the end of the day. But he got screwed.'

And Simon has a supporter, too, in former New York Mayor Ed Koch. Says Ed, 'I very much admired Paul's musical which regrettably failed. It was a wonderful show, with great music. Paul though lost $11 million when it failed. It didn't take because people didn't like the story. There was public feeling against the musical. People thought that it extolled the virtues of a killer. Paul Simon would take the position that it did not do that at all. That it simply showed all of the influences upon the killer that had brought him to the point it did. And I come down on the side of Paul Simon.

'Marc Anthony wasn't very well known at that time – certainly not as well known as he is today, and he had a glorious voice. I recently saw Marc and when I told him how wonderful the show had been and how sad I was that it had closed so early, he told me that he had heard that it might be revived.'

Away from his supporters and his detractors, the bottom line was that Paul Simon had once again invested a great deal of time, emotion, ability and endeavour in an ambitious project only for it to fail to live up to his expectations. His sense of dismay that not enough people could see what he had been trying to achieve with *The Capeman* was deep and must have been made worse by his huge financial loss.

He had tried to step outside the circle of his accepted genre and been attacked for it. It might have come as some consolation that in that same circle he had continued to receive recognition.

Back in 1986 Simon had been given an Honorary Doctorate of Music by America's Berkeley College. This had been repeated in 1997 by Queens College in New York City where he had once been a student. In between, in 1996, the prestigious Yale University in New Haven, Connecticut had bestowed on the star the degree of Doctor of Music.

At the Yale graduation ceremony the citation had begun, 'Troubadour to the world, you have taken the rhythms of life as they pulse along from the bridges of Manhattan to the banks of the Amazon and given them back to us transformed into poetry.'

As Dr Robert L. Blocker, Dean of Music at Yale University explains, 'Nominations for honorary degrees at Yale occur several years before they are actually awarded. These degrees acknowledge the international influence of individuals who have distinguished themselves in their respective fields. Paul Simon is considered one of the great songwriters of the present generation. His creative work speaks to both the heart and mind, and the underlying message is one of justice, peace and understanding among all peoples.'

By August 1998 Simon had another problem to grapple with in the shape of a stalker who would not be dissuaded. For much of the past seven years a 25-year-old college student had been trying to gatecrash gatherings held by Paul at his New York home or elsewhere.

Finally, with Simon's patience at an end, she was arrested for having approached him closely enough to talk to him. She was charged with first-degree harassment – in US law, a misdemeanour charge – and was released on bail. Simon could only hope that this charge would convey his wishes that she curb her interest in him, but it was a sour note to add to another personal disappointment in his life.

The public didn't know it, but yet again something had gone wrong with the bumpy friendship Simon had had with his oldest friend Art Garfunkel. Their worlds had regularly spun away from one another for spells but would periodically converge, at which times they usually managed to develop a new understanding.

That all seemed to be at an end when Paul Simon candidly stated in February 1998 that he felt very little affection now towards his one-time professional other half. 'The friendship,' he categorically declared, 'is probably irreparably strained now.'

It wasn't perhaps his biggest blow. Taking everything into account that dubious distinction had to rest with the debacle of *The Capeman*. And Paul Simon had been a show business trouper too long to give in to self-pity. But to eradicate his immense disappointment he needed a mission, so he immersed himself once more in familiar ground.

CHAPTER 17

Timeless Troubadour

IN THE LIGHT OF recent events it made sense for Paul Simon to return to the familiar surroundings of home and the recording studio and concentrate on starting work on a new album. It took time to assemble the band of musicians he wanted to work with, those who would do justice to the material that would come together over an unhurried period of time.

Paul worked at his latest songs in a systematic manner, which meant putting in long hours every day. But two events were to interrupt his work, the second of which would come as quite a surprise to his fans and to the music world.

Simon's first step back into the limelight happened in early May 1999, when he sang part of his 1968 hit 'Mrs Robinson' at a tribute held at New York's Yankee Stadium in memory of Joe DiMaggio, who had recently died.

By this time, news had leaked out that Paul Simon was going on the road in the summer for the first time in years, playing big arena venues. The big surprise was that it was to be in conjunction with Bob Dylan. Their initial plan was to tour together through June and July, but that was extended and by now the intended gigs spread into September.

The shock felt by many at this proposed double-header was

entirely understandable. Each star had once covered the other's work, but the pair had never performed together and had never been what might be described as bosom buddies.

After appearing at Joe DiMaggio's tribute, Simon went straight into rehearsal for the tour, while speculation in the press centred on why these giants had decided to team up. New York's *Daily News* wondered if money was the motive, while pointing out the obvious – that both stars were loaded. But then Simon's major financial loss over *The Capeman* was still being talked about.

Bob Dylan had been touring regularly for so many years it was felt that perhaps he had become jaded with the old routine. And certainly the fascination of having the opportunity to catch these two legends on the same bill was why ticket sales rocketed and the tour had to be lengthened. Asked if there hadn't once been some needling rivalry between them, Paul Simon responded, 'If there ever was, it ended years ago.'

Rehearsed and ready to go, the stars, accompanying musicians and others took to the road in two large luxury coaches; one of which was reserved for the non-smoking, quieter types among them.

On 1 June 1999, Paul Simon played a solo gig at Philadelphia's Theater For The Living Arts. Four nights later Bob Dylan played with his band at the Fillmore Auditorium in Denver, Colorado. And it was the next night, on 6 June, that the double-bill tour officially kicked off at the World Arena in Colorado Springs.

Both adopted a casual dress style. Simon favoured jeans, T-shirt and a baseball cap. Each night they would do a separate 75-minute set, and in between these they performed together for half an hour. It was enough, in places, to have audiences on their feet and dancing in the aisles.

Hopping from state to state, they took in Oregon, Washington, California, Nevada, Missouri, Utah and Connecticut. Early on, they headed to Vancouver in British Columbia, Canada. And throughout, the tour was punctuated by single nights when only Simon or Dylan appeared – on 23 June Paul played the House of Blues in Los Angeles solo. The night before that, Simon and Dylan had packed out the Hollywood Bowl. In early July they showed up for a memorable night at Bayside Park in Dylan's birthplace Duluth, Minnesota.

With a combined age of 115, the seasoned stars were not expected to make headlines for breaking any laws. But in mid-August, when they played at the Tweeter Center in Mansfield, Massachusetts the town's city fathers imposed fines, totalling just over $5,300, when the show ran a few minutes beyond the strictly observed 11 pm town curfew on events.

The tour had worked so well that by its end on 18 September 1999 at the Starplex Amphitheater in Dallas, Texas, there were even rumblings that the two might do this again in Europe and Japan.

Paul Simon was content enough with the success of the US gigs. In fact, when he returned to New York City directly afterwards he felt invigorated, eager to return to work on his new album, which gratifyingly began to take shape. Even with the five-month gap because of the tour, the album had already been over a year in the making and would occupy most of 2000 before he judged it ready for release.

It had been recorded at The Hit Factory in New York. And the material, perhaps appropriately for Simon's first release of the new millennium, was a melding of all the musical styles he had embraced in the 43 years since his first record. Tracks such as 'Darling Lorraine' showed that Simon had lost none of his sensitivity, his ability to touch the listener with his words. And his knack for storytelling still provided a quick, usually illicit, glimpse into someone's private pain.

'Darling Lorraine' had had the power to move Simon emotionally while writing it, and since it had been the first song he'd penned for the new album it had made a lasting impression on him. It also paved the way for the rest to follow.

Unlike his 1970s and 1980s solo albums he was not concerned this time with dealing with aspects of his own personal relationships, although the opening track 'That's Where I Belong' was definitely, at least in spirit, inspired by Simon's lively young wife Edie. Nor were there on this new album any throwbacks to past marriages. In *Hearts And Bones* (whose songs largely spoke of his life with and love for Carrie Fisher) the track 'Train In The Distance' had been about Paul's first wife Peggy. On the new album there was no reference to his romance and short marriage to Fisher.

The new songs had all suggested themselves lyrically in a relatively short time. It was the music that had taken longer. He had indulged himself by allowing the process of development to be almost organic, his preferred way of working these days. Of course, the depth of the music and the complexity of marrying so many of the styles that had attracted him over the years meant that he had had to make progress in a series of carefully crafted layers, with particular guitar pieces proving troublesome to write. He had been determined , though, that success would not elude him.

The album, titled *You're The One,* was released in early October 2000 and was subsequently nominated for the Grammy Award for Album of The Year. A tour to back it had previously been announced and, 12 months on from the end of his tour with Dylan, Paul was set to hit the road again.

He had had the chance to perform live already that year when in September he had been one of the guests at 'The Concert', an all-star fundraiser for the Democratic party held at Radio City Music Hall in New York. Compered by Hollywood star Michael Douglas, it had raked in $6.5 million for the Al Gore/Joseph Lieberman presidential campaign.

That night, referring to the outcome of the upcoming election Paul Simon had said, 'I hope things work out the way we want them to.' They didn't. Republican George W. Bush, son of former President Bush, made it into the White House by the skin of his teeth after a highly unusual ending to a tight election battle.

Simon's 'You're The One' tour set off in Sweden on 16 October 2000 with two sold-out nights at Stockholm's Globe

Annex. He had with him an 11-man band. All their rehearsing in Manhattan paid off handsomely and, following the three gigs at London's Hammersmith Apollo at the end of the month, their polished nightly performances also went down a treat in Germany, Italy and France.

Performing live, even after all these years, was still important to Simon, as was the reception it elicited. Singer Ralph McTell believes, 'When I look at Paul there's still an evident need in his presentation to be loved. We all go into it in a way, wanting that. It's not adoration. You just want to be liked at first. Then, I think, you kind of want a bit more. And I can still see that in Paul.

'I saw one of his performances recently in America and I looked at him and thought – he doesn't need to keep pushing himself to perform as he does. But he still needs, I believe, that affection that you can only get from live performance. Paul is still discovering music. He continues to educate himself and continues to push the boundaries of his own musical ability. I admire him tremendously for that.'

On a roll, from France Simon had headed home to America where he launched the US leg of the tour on 10 November at the Paramount in Seattle, Washington. In keeping with the style of the album his two-hour and 15-minute stage set mirrored the span of his career to date, and Simon displayed an almost bewildering array of musical styles.

He delivered the show with a panache that prompted Charles Bermont reporting on the gig for *Rolling Stone* to remark, 'Were he a pitcher, Simon would be a master of the change-up.' Simon now nearly always wore a baseball cap on stage, so the sporting metaphor was apt.

In December, after criss-crossing the country, Simon performed at the Beacon Theater in New York City where, in a touching moment, Harper joined his father on stage to duet on the classic 'The Boxer'.

This far happier end to the year spilled over into 2001. In February Paul had the pleasure of seeing *You're The One* nominated for the Grammy, even though Steely Dan picked up the trophy for their new album, *Two Against Nature*.

The next month Paul Simon was, in his own right, inducted into the Rock and Roll Hall of Fame at a ceremony held at New York's Waldorf Astoria Hotel. Other artistes honoured that night were Michael Jackson, Steely Dan, Aerosmith and Queen. Simon's induction meant that he joined a small number of artistes in the category of multiple inductees. This exclusive club includes John Lennon, Eric Clapton, Neil Young and Paul McCartney.

Simon performed 'Still Crazy After All These Years' and 'Graceland' and was inducted by Latin star Marc Anthony, who announced that he was particularly delighted to see Paul there that night. He added, 'Because after we did *The Capeman* we were put into separate witness protections programs.' The quip raised much laughter from the audience, and presumably enough time had elapsed since the musical's costly demise for Simon to appreciate the joke.

Simon was waiting to make his own surprising remarks. Accepting the honour, he spent ten minutes reading a list of his musical inspirations down the years, which included Johnny Ace and his own father. Paul then announced with reference to Art Garfunkel, 'I regret the ending of our friendship. But I hope one day, before I die, that we will make peace with each other.' The crowd showed its approval with ringing applause.

Leaving awards, but not applause, behind Simon picked up his tour again in late April at the Smirnoff Music Centre in Dallas, Texas. Within days he was performing at the New Orleans Jazz and Heritage Festival in May, before gigging through June and July, ending at Jones Beach on Long Island.

Had he been seeking to purge the memory of failure from his mind he would certainly have succeeded by summer 2001, when he was able to relax contentedly with his family, which had by now expanded. In addition to Adrian, Edie had produced a daughter they named Loulou. And another son, Gabriel, made three children for the couple, and a family of four in all for Paul.

His close friend Dr Irwin Redlener says, 'Paul's a wonderful father. He gets up very early in the morning with Edie and together they take care of their kids. They are a great family. I don't think people have a true sense of that.'

That summer practically every person on the planet was suddenly forced to examine the true sense of what was precious in their lives and in the world when on that September day the burning World Trade Center twin towers collapsed and terrified people ran for their lives against the flow of the immensely courageous rescue service personnel rushing to the scene.

Before the Federal authorities could have time to organise their full emergency response, the Children's Health Fund sent in two of their mobile medical units immediately to the scene. They set up at the Chelsea Pier Emergency Medical Community Center, and several members of the staff also went directly to ground zero.

Dr Redlener adds, 'Since then we have also put together a special mobile unit that does crisis mental health support. The children throughout the city have been very affected by what went on that day.'

The terrorist atrocity had countless consequences, down to the rescheduling of many events. The Children's Health Fund had entered its fifteenth year and to mark this a special gala was to have taken place before end of 2001. This was now held on 5 February 2002 at the Marriott Marquis Hotel in New York City. After cocktails at 6.30pm and dinner commencing an hour later, the evening was capped by a special musical performance. Paul was asked to close the event, as Dr Redlener recalls, 'Our original plan to hold the gala in the fall was pre-empted by 9/11 and when we did hold it we didn't know what to expect because since the terrorist attack the economy has been shaky. We asked Paul if he would perform, which he does gratis, and he agreed of course.

'In the event we were happily surprised at the response to the gala. There's a lot of personal connection and an intimate relationship between our donors and the organisation. We had 730 people there and yet everyone felt that it was a very intimate event.

'The new Mayor of New York, Michael Bloomberg came. And Jane Pauley who co-hosts *Dateline* was our host for the evening. The actor Michael Keaton joined us. My wife works with me on this whole program and she and I were kind of the moderators. Paul's performance, which came at the end, was actually spectacular. We were all very moved by it. It was a wonderfully connecting evening.'

Taking centre stage was not something Paul Simon always did, however. Over the years, with respect to his commitment to the Children's Health Fund, he took pains to cloak the full extent of his generosity, which was not only of the financial kind. The person best placed to illustrate this is Dr Redlener.

He reveals, 'Starting about four years ago I got involved in the development of the building of a new children's' hospital in the Bronx, which medically is a very underserved and economically disadvantaged urban area. This is, in fact, the first children's hospital ever in the area.

'Paul gave a very substantial gift to this hospital because I was involved in it – he gave a million dollars, in fact. Now, most of the other people who gave large gifts were having a floor or a ward named after them. Paul refused to do that. And to my surprise he named the hospital after my family. I am very moved by that. And I think it's indicative of what he is about.

'I lost a son in an accident a few years ago. Paul and I had been close before that. But I would say that the bonding since between Paul and his family and me and mine has been rather extraordinary.'

In a wider sense an extraordinary bond has, over the years, been forged between Paul Simon and countless people around the world. Professor Iwan Morgan observes, 'I don't think Paul Simon has Bob Dylan's grittiness. He was not influenced in the same way by the folk traditions of the American Depression of the 1930s. Nor does he have John Lennon's ability to integrate a single issue into his music.

'But Simon's songs, and what he voiced in the 1960s, reflected the ideas and disillusion of college-educated youth. And I think that distinction is important. He remains primarily a singer about the emotions and feelings of the individual, rather than the collective.'

It is that individual connection which is timeless and therefore, special. There have, of course, been some enormously successful songwriters in popular music history. But few have been able to touch individual hearts for a lifetime. Once the man who provided the soundtrack for an entire generation, Paul Simon has grown and developed, explored and experimented in the decades since, unafraid to take risks and exhibiting a rare candour when something hasn't worked out.

Dogged determination is the hallmark of his character, which is itself a mosaic of intriguing contrasts. The same man who would write a four-page letter to a north of England folk club owner justifying his intention to raise his nightly fee by £3, will – under the cloak of anonymity – donate $1 million to the building of a children's hospital in one of America's most neglected areas.

It is by the worth of his craft that he rightly wants to be acknowledged. His deep passion for music has come at a heavy personal cost. Three times married, he has also been plunged into periods of depression and self-doubt, from which he has always emerged.

Sturdy confidence in his ability is offset by an inner vulnerability. Deeply complex, he is a private man who has led a roller coaster life during which he has been largely able to apply and let go of the brake at his own discretion.

He has eloquently identified man's frailest fears while, typically, he carries one of his own. 'Probably all artistes fear that their lives will outrun their gift,' he has said. 'And that's a moment you don't want to face.' For four complete decades already Paul Simon has been an important star in music's firmament. One of life's few certainties is that he will eternally remain so.

Index